Yours Till The End

Yours Till The End

Jackie and Sunnie Mann

with Tess Stimson

HEINEMANN : LONDON

William Heinemann Ltd
Michelin House, 81 Fulham Road, London SW3 6RB
LONDON MELBOURNE AUCKLAND

First published 1992
Copyright © Jackie and Sunnie Mann 1992

A CIP catalogue record for this book
is held by the British Library
ISBN 0 434 44844 3

Phototypeset by Falcon Graphic Art Ltd

Printed in Great Britain
by Clays Ltd, St Ives plc

To Val Tatham
for all her love and help to us,
particularly during the dark days
in Beirut before Jackie's release.

Contents

Picture Credits

Acknowledgements

So many people have helped us both during the terrible times of Jackie's captivity and the joyful days of our reunion that it would be impossible to thank them all. But it is with especial gratitude we thank all the RAF officers at Lyneham and Headley Court for their tremendous co-operation and support. Squadron Leaders David Stevens and Keith Lane were wonderful to both of us throughout our time with them; so too were the officers of RAF Akrotiri in Cyprus, with their outstanding medical care and patience during Jackie's stay there.

We would also like to thank all our friends in Cyprus for their help in making us feel at home in Nicosia. In particular we thank High Commissioner David Dain, Air Vice-Marshal Sandy Hunter and Doctor Cecelia Stephanou for their joint efforts in getting Jackie to Akrotiri when he developed pneumonia. We have no doubt that their prompt actions saved his life.

So many friends and relatives in England unstintingly gave their help during Jackie's captivity and afterwards. It would be impossible to mention them all, but we would like to thank especially David and Val Tatham, who never failed to give their help and support through the years of Jackie's absence. We also thank Brent Sadler for his lasting support, and unfailing love and friendship; and Tess Stimson, for her excellent research and efforts in the writing of this book.

Lastly we thank Missy, whose gaiety and enjoyment of television has made her more of a star than either of us, and helped me to recover from the loss of my beloved Tara, who kept me sane during the horror of Beirut – kidnapped, but never forgotten.

Sunnie and Jackie Mann, *February 1992*

ONE

The Return

'The VC10 touched down at RAF Lyneham and, as Jackie and I started to go down the steps, we heard the drone of an aircraft. We looked up, and there she was – a small speck against the blue sky, getting larger by the second. It was a Spitfire.

'We gazed enthralled as this little miracle of World War II came round again and did the victory roll, right over Jackie's head. It was the moment when I knew, after eight hundred and sixty-five days of utter horror, that Jackie was finally free.'

At this moment, as the elderly couple gazed up into the bright blue skies over Lyneham, the diplomatic success the release signified faded into the background. There were few dry eyes amongst the thousands who had turned up to watch the return of the Battle of Britain hero. As Jackie and Sunnie Mann prepared to descend the steps from the VC10 to the tarmac, it was their personal triumph which shone through. Despite everything, they had survived an ordeal which would have shattered the hearts and minds of a lesser couple.

'Two or three minutes before we landed, Sunnie and I were peering through the windows, through the tufts of white cloud,' Jackie recalls. 'I couldn't believe the sheer greenness of the land, after so much brownness in the Middle East. September is England's most lovely month, when she is decked in her richest, brightest colours, and I was

1

deeply moved as I glimpsed the land beneath me for the first time.

'It had never occurred to me that I'd be so renowned in England, despite warnings by the British Ambassador in Damascus. It never crossed my mind that I would be such a celebrity, even though I knew I would never be able to go straight back into my old life. But as we landed I saw what seemed to be thousands of people, all craning their necks to see my aeroplane land. I was deeply touched.

'Sunnie and I could see the waiting Press, in a giant bank behind iron railings, trying to prevent their tripods from being blown over as they took pictures of us landing. It was almost frightening.

'We landed, and Sunnie and I started to go down the steps, as I tried to take it all in. She immediately spotted an old friend of hers, Val Tatham, the wife of the British Ambassador to Lebanon, and clutched my arm, pointing and screaming towards her. It was the picture all the newspapers had on their front pages the next day, with various captions – most of them inaccurate – beneath.

'Sunnie had told me there was a big surprise for me waiting at Lyneham, but she wouldn't give me the slightest idea what it was, no matter how hard I pressed her. She refused to give me the slightest indication. I love surprises – who doesn't, if they're pleasant, and I wasn't expecting any unpleasant surprises from Sunnie, in the circumstances.

'As we reached the foot of the aircraft steps, I suddenly heard the throb of an engine, an engine I hadn't heard for fifty years, the old familiar roar of a Merlin engine. We all looked up, and the Spitfire came over and did a slow roll over the top. I have never been more thrilled and amazed all at once. It was so wonderful to see that Spitfire rolling. I was catapulted back half a century – the last time I saw a Spitfire was in 1944, towards the end of the Second World War. A tear came to my eyes, very definitely. The Spitfire is such a wonderful aircraft – I've always considered it to be the best aeroplane of its type and from now on it'll be the best in the world for me. I thought about that Spitfire for hours afterwards. I think it's the moment that will stay in my mind for the rest of my life.'

Only twelve hours before, on 24 September 1991, Jackie Mann, the oldest Western hostage held captive in Lebanon's city of terror, Beirut, had been handed over into the hands of the Syrians.

It was the culmination of months of negotiation, part of a complex formula that had been worked out by the then Secretary General of the United Nations, Javier Perez de Cuellar, designed to satisfy everyone who had a stake in the hostage drama. The apparent stalemate over the Western hostages was broken with the release of the captive journalist, John McCarthy, only six weeks earlier.

Alight with hope and expectation, Sunnie had then dashed to Beirut along with most of the world's media to await what she believed to be the longed-for release of her husband. Despite statements from the kidnappers that Jackie's freedom was imminent, once again – as so many times before – the release mechanism had broken down. This time, so did Sunnie.

'I was so sure it was going to happen this time. Everything had been ready – the VC10 with its own medical team waiting at Cyprus, the escort cars sitting outside the British Embassy in Beirut, where I was staying, waiting to rush us to Jackie.

'I was with my dearest friend, the television news reporter Brent Sadler, who worked for the British network, Independent Television News. We met as colleagues on different sides of the same fence – he wanted a news story and I was providing one. But we became terribly close – I couldn't have survived this nightmare without him.

'When we heard there'd been a short delay over Jackie's

3

release, Brent took me out for a meal, since we didn't know when we'd next get a chance to eat. I was so full of hope, yet so afraid something would go wrong.

'As we walked back into the Embassy that evening, I knew my worst fears had been realised. John Tucknott, the acting Ambassador to Beirut, greeted me at the door, and one look at his face was enough. He turned to me and said, "I don't know how to tell you this, Sunnie, but it's been cancelled again."

'For a moment the horror was too great, and I couldn't take it in. Then Brent put his arm around me and said "Hold on", and I knew it was for real. For the first time in almost three years I broke down and sobbed on his chest.

'The next morning, I was so depressed I felt I couldn't just pick myself up and start again, as I'd done so many times before. I could still see the cars that had been waiting to escort me to Jackie outside the Embassy, a hollow mockery of my hopes. I was desperate to leave Beirut, that city which had been my dearest friend, now turned my most implacable enemy. Brent suggested that I return to his home in Cyprus with him, to give me a change of scenery whilst I waited for the next slim ray of hope.

'I tried to settle in Brent's home, whilst all the time I was awash with nerves and anxiety. I had all but given up, after so many disappointments and false alarms. I felt numb; it was as if my last hopes had been shattered forever, and I was broken with them. My only consolation was seeing my beloved poodle, Missy, once more – she'd been staying with a friend in Cyprus whilst I'd been in Beirut.

'It was impossible even to go back to the daily routine of misery which I'd accustomed myself to over the years. Everyone around me was so sure things were coming to a head that I couldn't shut it out and pretend it wasn't happening. The VC10 was still at Akrotiri base in Cyprus, waiting. I sat on my bed, by the telephone, waiting. Journalists thronged Beirut, waiting. All of us waiting, as we had been for so long. We packed our suitcases again in readiness, and as I folded Jackie's clothes I couldn't help but remember the times I'd folded them before, and I dreaded the times I might have to fold them again. At one point, Brent had carried them with him for a whole year, in the hope that Jackie would be freed, until we finally mothballed everything.

'My feelings as I went to bed, two days after moving to Cyprus, were entirely negative. I refused to allow myself to hope, and then go through the misery of disappointment – my health was beginning to fail and I was feeling every one of my seventy-eight years. I fell asleep in despair.

'Suddenly my door was flung open, and a voice started shouting "Sunnie! Sunnie!" I sat up in bed screaming with fright, thinking I was back in Beirut, and someone had got into my flat to kill me.

'Then I recognised Brent's voice, and I was hearing him say "It's all right, it's happened, we're on our way. Jackie's free, darling, it's happened."

'I could hear him but I couldn't understand. I groped for some clothes which were lying by the bed, and dressed, fumbling in the dark, not even thinking to turn on the lights. I half ran, half fell down the stairs, even now thinking how much I needed a coffee, and that I hated the shirt I was wearing – deliberately blocking out my thoughts of Jackie.

'Brent handed me a coffee, which I drank so quickly it scalded my throat. We waited for the High Commission car to arrive to take us to the VC10 at Akrotiri. The half-light of dawn gave everything a surreal glow, and it seemed to me I was moving through a dream. Brent looked at me and smiled. I clutched his hand and whispered, "I'll only believe it when I'm actually on the 'plane and we're on our way to Damascus."

'Two doctors whom I'd already met at the RAF club in

Piccadilly, in London, were waiting at the airport when we arrived, squealing tyres, and dived out of the car before it had even come to a halt. Squadron Leader David Stevens and Wing Commander Gordon Turnbull were part of the medical team which had helped John McCarthy to recuperate, and would give the same attention to Jackie. We were all given more cups of coffee – tepid this time – and taken straight out to the 'plane. As we boarded Brent turned to me and grinned, "Now do you believe it's real?"

'As we settled on the 'plane for the hour-long flight to Damascus, where Jackie was being taken after being handed to the Syrians in Beirut, David and Gordon started preparing me for my reunion with my husband. It was a scene I'd played so many times in my mind before, it was like a worn photograph, torn and battered through so much handling. They tried to warn me how he might look, saying they'd heard he'd lost three stone in weight, and was very frail. I didn't care about any of that. The thing was he was alive. After nearly three years of not knowing if he was living or dead, I didn't care what he weighed or how he looked, if I could just see him and know that at last he was free from his terrible ordeal.

'During the interminable wait for Jackie's release and the many false alarms over the years, Brent and I had often discussed how and where Jackie and I would live when he was finally freed. We had very little money, and couldn't afford to live anywhere more expensive than Beirut – which meant practically everywhere these days – and of course Beirut was now out of the question. We were in a financial dilemma.

'I had never accepted a penny for any of the interviews I did whilst Jackie was being held captive. I did them to bring Jackie to the world's attention, to try to help free him if anything could. But now I had to think of Jackie and our future together which we planned to have in Cyprus. I had no choice. I needed Brent to be with me every step of the

6

way, primarily as my dearest friend and support but also as a journalist. It was our livelihood he was building and protecting.

'The British Government seemed almost paranoid about their determination to protect the ex-hostages by keeping their post-release recuperation secret, and stifling the media's voracious interest. I knew I couldn't afford to let that happen, and arranged for Brent to be part of the official party travelling with Jackie and myself to the RAF base at Lyneham, where all the hostages began their entry into the real world.

'We arrived in Damascus where we were met by a member of the Embassy staff who drove with us in convoy to the residence of the British Ambassador, Andrew Green. I held tightly to Brent's hand as we dashed across Syria's capital, as I had done in British armoured Land Rovers in Beirut, during all the false alarms I'd endured, and now, at last, the same for the real thing.

'It was pitch black when we arrived. There seemed to be hundreds of Press thronging the street outside the Residence, pressed against the railings. As we stepped from the car, the light from a hundred flashbulbs seemed to make the whole street shimmer. Television camera lights arced overhead, and reporters surged forwards, thrusting microphones towards me and screaming questions, each desperate to outshout their nearest rivals. Camera cables snaked across the street, and dazedly I gazed into the crowd, trying to focus on faces, but seeing only a blur of cameras.

'Embassy staff and Syrian security guards held the mass of journalists back, and Brent squeezed my arm as we slipped through the iron gates. Suddenly I realised that I was about to see my husband, for the first time in twenty-eight months. My mind went completely blank. I walked up the steps to the door, and was met by Andrew Green and his wife, who told me Jackie was waiting in a small study off the main salon.

'I looked at Brent and he whispered, "It's real darling. Go on."

'I walked slowly into the room, and there he was, looking as the doctors had said, frail and tired, but alive. Neither of us had many words to say. It was too emotional, and it had been too long. We just put our arms round each other and kissed, and said, "Yours till the stars lose their glory."

'Moments later I rushed to the study door, and flung it open wide, calling for Brent. I wanted him to share my joy, since he had shared so much of my pain. He'd never met Jackie, and suddenly I wanted the two people dearest to me to be with me. Brent walked in, his small television camera – a Video Eight – on his shoulder, shook hands with Jackie and sat down. The moment was terribly charged with the raw emotion of a hostage release and Brent was uncharacteristically silent. I think we all cried with happiness then.

'Suddenly I noticed the camera, still zipped up in its bag at Brent's feet. I wiped the tears from my eyes roughly, and gestured towards it.

'"Come on, Brent, this isn't a holiday," I said, "You've got work to do! Get filming!" I'll never forget those first pictures of Jackie and myself together, after so long apart. We talked a little, and I told Jackie that we'd no idea he was alive until he was released, which stunned him – he thought we'd had various messages.

'As Brent finished filming, Andrew Green came in and gave Brent a very grey look as he zipped up the camera bag. He asked me if I felt up to making a statement to the Press as they were all waiting whilst Jackie was examined by a doctor to determine if he was fit enough to fly straight to Lyneham or whether he should stay awhile in either Damascus or Cyprus. I agreed to talk to the Press, and went into the salon to meet them. As always they all started shouting questions at the same time and, laughing, I tried to answer as many as possible. Over all the preceding years the media had always been very kind to me and I've made many friends amongst them. I needed them now more than ever if Jackie and I were to survive.

'When I'd finished I went and found Brent to ask him if the pictures he'd shot had come out OK. I found him unhappily sitting in a corner of the salon, and he explained that whilst I'd been talking to the Press he'd slipped into the garden, and handed the tape over to the ITN producer, Mike Nolan, who was still stuck on the other side of the iron fence. On his return he'd been cornered by the British officials, who'd had their feathers severely ruffled by this breach of protocol, despite his explanation that he'd been acting on my instructions.

'I was furious. Where had all these do-gooders been when I needed them? Nowhere to be seen. Brent was the only one who had ever helped me, and was protecting my interests. I rounded on the Government News Department head, Peter Willis.

'"Brent Sadler is a very close and dear friend," I shouted. "He is doing what I ask him to do. I trust him, and you should do the same."

'They nodded, looking peeved, and we left the Residence, Brent in the front of our car with the Syrian driver, and Jackie and myself in the back, holding hands and feeling as if the intervening months had never existed.'

The decision was made for Jackie and Sunnie to fly straight to RAF Lyneham that night, since Jackie seemed to be relatively fit, given his incarceration. A short time into the flight, the VC10 developed problems. Jackie's recollection of his reunion with Sunnie was blurred by the incredible media attention – he remembers little of Damascus but the flashbulbs – but like the true Battle of Britain pilot that he was, his memory of the aeroplane problems was clear.

'Apparently the VC10 developed an hydraulic leak on one of

the main undercarriage legs, and they lost all the hydraulic oil from that leg, which spread itself over the countryside,' Jackie remembers. 'The pilot was unable to retract it, and because of that the increased drag from the undercarriage being down meant that we didn't have enough fuel to fly from Damascus to Lyneham as had been originally planned. We had to divert to the RAF base at Akrotiri in Cyprus so see whether it could be fixed. For several hours mechanics tried to repair the fault, and finally it was decided that we'd have to stay overnight.

'Frankly I was glad of the rest. I'd been up since seven o'clock that morning, when I'd been awakened by my kid-nappers, unaware that today would be any different from any other. I'd been eating my lunch – the usual sandwich – when two of them came in to me and told me to shave and shower, and gave me a razor. They said I was going to be released, but they'd said that so many times before I didn't really believe them.

'I wasn't normally given a razor, although my beard had been cut a few days before, so it wasn't too long. It still took me three-quarters of an hour to shave, and halfway through they had to change the razor because it had grown blunt. They told me to get dressed, and gave me some clothes they'd bought a week previously. They'd been sitting in a corner of my room, a few feet away from my mattress – a pair of shoes, a pair of socks, some slacks, a vest, pants and a shirt. I dressed in all these things and sat down and waited.

'They told me when I was released I'd be handed over to a Mr Picco – in their ignorance they called him Dicco – and then I'd be free.

'Just after dark, they brought in a big cardboard carton in which I'd been carried before, and put me in that. It was about a metre and a half long, and around three-quarters of a metre wide, and a metre high. I had to lie crouched in it, half sideways. If I'd been asked to do that three years before,

I would have said it would have crippled me. Now, I did it without arguing. It's amazing what the human body can endure if it has to.

'They folded over the top of the box, so that I couldn't see, and carried me out, two or three of them. They stumbled, and I was shaken around – they weren't used to carrying a box down some steps with a person inside. It was uncomfortable, but I'd put up with it before. They'd told me I was going to be freed, and that was all I could think about. I began to believe it, after the shower and the shave, the clothes. I'd been told I was going to be freed before, and pushed into this same box, and then nothing but a new jail. But they'd never bothered to prepare me like this before, and a tiny spark of hope stirred inside me.

'The box was loaded with me in it. I could just see the broken rear window of a van through the top of the box, but that was all. No one spoke to me. We drove for about five or ten minutes, whilst I wondered what would happen next. I hoped and prayed it would be my release, yet dared not think the thought too loudly in my head in case I jinxed myself.

'After ten minutes the van stopped and I heard the faint thunk of the doors being opened. Two men roughly pulled the cardboard box from the van and dumped it on the ground, gesturing for me to climb out. I tried, but I was so stiff I kept falling back into the box, and eventually one of them came forward to help me from sheer exasperation with my attempts.

'I noticed a car parked near the van, and I was led to it, and told to climb in the back. Two of them got into the front, and shouted at me to keep my eyes closed. After two and a half years shut in a room that was the last thing I was going to do, and I narrowed my eyes and peered as best I could through the windows. The first thing I saw that I recognised was the sports stadium in Beirut, where Sunnie used to race

11

her horses in the days before the terrible wars that tore the land apart. For a moment it seemed more real than the past years of despair, hopelessness and desperate loneliness.

'Suddenly the car stopped, somewhere on the outskirts of West Beirut. Through my half-closed eyes I could see people passing on the pavements, unaware of the drama being played out right beside them.

'The car door opened, and a tall, good-looking man climbed into the back of the car with me. He grasped my shoulder and said, "I'm Mr Picco, of the United Nations. You're free."

'It was my first moment of freedom, and I have never had a sweeter one. Suddenly the light seemed brighter, the air fresher, and unafraid now I opened my eyes fully and looked around me. I gazed at the people bustling by, their arms loaded with shopping, children tugging on their mothers' skirts. I saw the taxi-drivers careering madly past me, honking and gesturing to boys dashing haphazardly across the street. Every battered fender seemed to glow with the brightness of freedom.

'For several moments I didn't take in what Giandominico Picco was saying, and he paused and looked at me. Then he smiled, and held out his hand, looking suddenly very British.

'Mr Mann,' he said, 'how are you?' We could have been two old acquaintances meeting by chance in a theatre foyer. My world tilted, and fell back into its right orbit. He was businesslike, friendly but unemotional, and it was exactly the right note. Had he been anything else, I think I would have fallen apart.

'Mr Picco outlined what was going to happen – that I'd be taken to Syrian headquarters where I'd be handed over to the Syrian army and they'd take me to Damascus. As I listened to him I felt anew the undiluted joy of hearing a voice not raised in anger, not giving me instructions or threatening to kill me.

'Minutes later, the car stopped again. Mr Picco leant towards me, and smiled again, shaking my hand reassuringly. "I'm leaving you now," he said, "and you'll be taken to the Beau Rivage hotel." Then he got out of the car, and into one that had been following us since he joined me, behind us. Two of my kidnappers were still in the front, one driving, one sitting silently in the passenger seat. They didn't turn round once the whole time Giandominico Picco was in the car. As he left, they told me again to keep my eyes closed. I ignored them, glaring defiantly out of the window.

'It was the moment that I climbed out of the car, as we arrived at the Beau Rivage hotel, that I realised it wasn't a dream. Guards in jeans and shirts lounged around the foyer entrance, and guests milled about unconcernedly. I stood on the steps for a moment, unsure what to do next. I wasn't used to making my own decisions any more.

'I couldn't believe how quiet it was, how little excitement there seemed to be. I wanted to shout, "I'm free! I'm Jackie Mann and I've been held hostage for eight hundred and sixty-five days and now I'm free!" But the world didn't stop spinning, and people passed by me as if I were just another guest – an elderly British gentleman unsure where to go.

'At last a couple of the guards came over and escorted me into the hotel where a senior officer, who seemed to be expecting me, asked me to sit down. He looked at me somewhat perplexedly and spoke to one of his fellows in Arabic. Then he turned to me and smiled at me in a rather bemused fashion.

'"Mr Mann," he said, rolling the words as if he'd never heard them before, "Would you like some tea?"

'The officer sat down behind a desk, facing me, whilst I perched on the settee, balancing my cup of tea on my knee. We looked at each other, neither of us quite sure what to say next. After about five minutes an interpreter came in, in an

13

attempt to help break the conversational impasse, but as his English was as non-existent as my Arabic, we didn't get very far. We struggled for a while, until we came to a full stop. The officer exchanged more Arabic with his fellows, looking even more confused, and finally a young man of around eighteen came in. He spoke quite good English and told me they were taking me by road to Damascus.

'"But first General Ghazi Kenaan would very much like to meet you," he added, "so you'll stop on the way to meet him."

'Ghazi Kenaan was the head of Syrian Army Intelligence. It was very much a courtesy call that I should visit him after my release – publicly, the Syrians were to be given some of the credit for the freedom of Western hostages, whatever the manoeuvring behind the scenes. The message delivered, events again moved very quickly. I wasn't even given time to finish my tea before being escorted to what seemed to me to be a taxi of some kind, with an armed soldier on either side of me. One of them smoked, and gave me a cigarette. I inhaled deeply, relishing every moment, as we drove off.

'The visit to Ghazi Kenaan's house in Lebanon's Bekaa Valley was both more friendly and more organised. The General himself came to his front door to meet me and we shook hands before he escorted me to his office, where he asked me to sit down. The shoes the kidnappers had bought for me were too small for me – I later learned they made the same mistake with all the hostages they freed, misunderstanding the system of shoe sizes in the different countries – and I asked if I could take them off, as they were beginning to pinch my feet. Just the freedom to take off my shoes meant so much – only someone who has been deprived of the right to make any decision can truly understand what liberty is.

'Immediately the General called to one of his men, who came back moments later with a much larger pair of sandals.

14

They were too big for me, but a vast improvement on the shoes. I wanted to leave them behind, but for some reason – I never found out why – he insisted I brought them with me to Damascus. Heaven knows what happened to them in the end.

'Again I was invited to have some tea, which this time I was able to finish before I was escorted on to Damascus. Ghazi Kenaan's name was familiar to me, but it wasn't until I met up with Sunnie again and discussed it with her that I realised why. He used to be one of her riding friends when she ran her equestrian school in Beirut.

'The two soldiers who had escorted me to the General's house had left and presumably returned to Beirut. I was joined for the final drive to Damascus by a Syrian who spoke quite good English, and he and I sat in the back of the car, with the driver and another man in the front. We chatted together and the Syrian with me told me that he'd done this before – he claimed to have been involved in the release of an eighty-two-year-old Englishman who had been captured. I immediately disbelieved his story – there was no such man whom I knew of who'd been taken – but he was convinced he was correct. I was used to such claims that seemed to have no basis in reality after nearly three years with my abductors, and I focused on the landscape racing past as I fought to adjust to my freedom. Even as I sped towards Damascus I still found it hard to believe that the nightmare was ended. I kept grasping solid objects, like the seat in front of me, to prove it wasn't a dream, that I wouldn't suddenly wake up chained once more in my cell. As we entered the Syrian capital – not the most lovely city in the world – it seemed to me more beautiful than any place I'd ever been to.

'I was taken to the Syrian Foreign Ministry, through the back door – hundreds of journalists thronged the front entrance, kept at bay only by iron gates guarded by armed soldiers.

15

Whilst I waited in a small ante-room with the British Ambassador and various Syrian officials, the journalists were led into an entrance hall, complete with marbled floors and gilt chandeliers, where they set up their cameras and microphones. I didn't realise it at the time, but representatives from all over the world were there. The American twenty-four-hour news service, Cable News Network, was pumping out live coverage of my arrival, and Syrian television cameras darted about everywhere, trailing thick black cables behind them, tripping up other journalists who cursed loudly at them in a variety of languages.

'I walked into this room, escorted by the British Ambassador Andrew Green and the Syrians, and we took up our positions behind a small wooden desk, puny compared to the numbers of journalists desperate to reach us. What seemed like thousands of flashbulbs went off as I walked in – the room seemed to shimmer and glitter with them – and I gazed at a sea of camera lenses. A Syrian official spoke briefly in Arabic and I was officially handed over to Andrew Green, who thanked the Syrians for their help and made the usual plea for all those detained in the area without "due judicial process" to be freed.

'Then the journalists were given free rein and bombarded me with questions. As I gave them a few brief replies, photographers fought with one another to get the one picture that would put them ahead of their fellows. One zealous cameraman climbed on top of his soundman's shoulders to get a better shot, and clouted his head on the gilt chandelier, which shook dangerously. Another Syrian woman punched a rival network's cameraman in the eye when he blocked her camera. Nearly a hundred people were crammed into a hall that could comfortably hold twenty and I was relieved when I was escorted out. I couldn't believe the attention I seemed to be causing – all these people doing all of this for a picture

16

or a few words from me. I was stunned. It was the one thing I had never envisaged.

'Finally I was taken to the British Embassy, and greeted by Andrew Green's wife, who took me inside. She was calm and efficient, and I was grateful for her cool competence after the mayhem I'd just witnessed. As she took me inside she offered me a drink and I asked for a beer. She left to get it and I called after her that she'd better get one ready for Sunnie, who hadn't yet reached the Embassy. Moments later she produced two cans of Carlsberg, one for each of us, and told me Sunnie was still on her way from Cyprus but would be with me within the hour. I sat placidly, waiting. Strangely I wasn't impatient – it was as if after so long, half an hour was nothing.

'I'm not an emotional man. I was brought up in an era where one didn't show one's feelings – men didn't cry in those days. One just got on with things, however bad they were and however painful it was to endure. It was that which helped me survive my incarceration. But when Sunnie came in, and I kissed my wife for the first time in two and half years, I was more moved than I had ever been in my life.'

Jackie and Sunnie spent their first night together at the RAF hospital at Akrotiri, exhausted by the journey, the attention and simple joy of being together again after so long. Neither slept a great deal, but lay on their beds, holding hands and staring up into the darkness. There was so much they wanted to say to each other, yet none of it seemed important then. They had both survived their own private battles, and been changed by them, but they were together again, and that was all that mattered.

The following morning, the mechanics reported that the problem with the undercarriage was not serious but could not be repaired at Akrotiri. It was decided that the VC10 would fly to RAF Lyneham in Wiltshire with the faulty leg locked down, since it still would not retract. The drag would put an extra hour on the flight, but the Manns were not going to complain. They were going home.

Sunnie was secretly pleased that the aircraft wheel had jammed. The official party of doctors and Foreign Office officials were again pressurising Brent Sadler not to film anything on board the aircraft and, had the VC10 not been grounded in Akrotiri, she was quite sure they would have had no record of their freedom flight.

'I asked Brent how much he'd been able to film on the way from Damascus to Akrotiri and when he told me nothing I was furious. It was all very well them going on about protocol – but protocol wasn't going to feed Jackie and me, nor give us a house or any means to live. I couldn't believe it – everyone seemed to understand that we needed the money, and for once we had the chance to make the media work for us, but they still put their hostage policy before our practical needs.

'After a few hours' rest at Akrotiri, the doctors decided to give Jackie a quick medical check. He was put in a wheelchair and as I saw him being taken down the corridor, flowers covering him from head to toe, and hospital staff hurrying out from wherever they were working to wave to him, I called to Brent to get his Video Eight camera out and film it. I wanted Jackie to be able to see his face, alight with joy and hope and freedom – I wanted the whole world to see it. They'd shared our suffering and now they could be a part of our joy. Thankfully the stopover had meant we were now travelling in daylight, which of course made Brent's job so much easier. He asked the hospital chief if they minded him filming and, smiling, he agreed.

'We boarded the VC10 again for the final flight home. Jackie was physically exhausted and I was anxious to get him to Lyneham. He couldn't get to sleep again – people kept coming up to him and saying hello or welcome back and I could see that Jackie was getting tired. It was extremely nice, of course, but still rather exhausting. I kept thinking how much I wanted to get him on his own, away from all this kerfuffle, but it was impossible at this stage.

'I was still appalled at Jackie's appearance. When they weighed him at Akrotiri he was only eight stone and three pounds. He was haggard and unkempt, his hair long enough to almost touch his shoulders. We didn't talk much about his captivity during those first few hours, although every so often he'd suddenly say something about those missing three years: how he'd filled his time, what he felt towards his abductors. Mainly we discussed everyday things, his family, my family. He seemed so normal, despite everything. I'd been prepared for such horrors, and had almost expected to face a stranger, but he was still Jackie, my Jackie. He was so tired though; every word was difficult for him because he hadn't been allowed to talk much during the whole of his captivity, and his few remaining teeth were in a ghastly state, impairing his speech. We were trying to get to know each other again, and I was beginning to tire of the constant questioning by doctors and Foreign Office officials. I didn't want Jackie to have to think back – I wanted him to look towards the future.

'I asked Brent to get out his camera again on the aircraft, and once more the wrath of Whitehall came tumbling down on his shoulders. This time I was very angry and demanded that Brent be allowed to continue to do what was his job and my wish. I had already explained to Jackie what we were doing, and why it was financially necessary, and he understood. I thundered again at the little Jobsworths who were making our life difficult, and eventually the penny seemed to drop. The Government News Department man, Peter Willis, even co-operated at the end and held the camera and filmed Brent talking to Jackie, so that he could include that in his piece for ITN.'

Later that day, in a draughty minibus at RAF Lyneham, Brent Sadler put together a seven-minute piece for *News At Ten*.

Jackie delightedly watched it later, thrilled to have a permanent record of what had seemed to him to pass by in a blur.

'I don't really remember a great deal about the flight home,' he recalled, 'so I was doubly glad Brent had filmed it for Sunnie and me. I felt quite a star with all the pictures of me talking to various people and drinking some champagne and a couple of beers. I believe there was a "No drinking" policy on board, but they waived that for me. They also dropped the "No smoking" ban and I felt quite spoilt.

'The crew were extremely nice to me. There were two nurses, one holding the rank of Squadron Leader, who was there for my benefit, and another who appeared to be in a naval uniform, although she was RAF, a stewardess on the aircraft. One of them actually accompanied me when I flew back from England to Cyprus a couple of months later. The Wing Commander who was flying the aeroplane came back several times and actually took me up to the front of the aircraft, so that I could see what the cockpit of a VC10 looked like. I even volunteered to fly the aeroplane – jokingly of course!

'I can't begin to describe what it felt like to be free. I had stopped feeling apprehensive about the future – I was so relieved to be out. Not to feel afraid of what is to come is a great gift in life, one it's taken me a lifetime and two-and-a-half years' imprisonment to learn. I had never tried to plan for the future, since I had no idea what it might be. I had no idea what life would be like once I was freed. I had simply longed for the moment of freedom and never thought beyond it.

'I had my first taste of chocolate on that flight. Ten days before my release, Sunnie and Brent had been shopping in

Smith's, and Brent had asked what my favourite treat was. Sunnie knows I adore chocolate and so they bought some for me, little Cadbury's bars, those small blocks of chocolate. I can remember clearly sitting next to Sunnie on the aeroplane, tucking in to those chocolates. I hadn't had any the whole time I'd been imprisoned. Once or twice one of my nicer kidnappers had brought me something special – wafer biscuits with chocolate on them. Never any real chocolates, and the bliss of tasting those first ones aboard the VC10!

'I know I was incredibly excited about travelling back to England, but I'm a controlled sort of person, except for losing my temper on occasion. I suppose that's my flying experience – after all, you can't afford to be excitable and unstable when you're flying an aeroplane. So it's my natural temperament to be calm. Yet I had this inward excitement bubbling inside me, which I kept firmly under control.

'The aircraft seemed to be full of doctors and psychiatrists, who spent a good deal of time telling me what would happen to me once I reached RAF Lyneham. The representative of the Archbishop of Canterbury was also on board, a strange fellow called Francis Witts. I can't think why he was on board, but still, there he was.

'The doctors explained all the tests I would undergo and the process of rehabilitation which had been tried out on John McCarthy before me. I expected I'd go into hospital for one or two weeks to recover some sort of physical stability, but I never expected it to take the time it did.

'Sunnie and I never talked about the things that really mattered, in those early days. She updated me on the current affairs I'd missed – I knew very little but the headlines, such as John McCarthy's release, and John Major's election as Prime Minister. That surprised me; I was astounded to learn that Major was a Conservative. I'd never heard of the man before and I'd only been away two and a half years. I naturally thought there'd been a General Election and that Labour had been voted in to power and he was their Prime Minister. I'd never have guessed that Margaret Thatcher had been unseated and he was her replacement.

'Sunnie also told me she'd given away my cat, Sasha, to the wife of the British Ambassador in Lebanon, Val Tatham, a close friend of Sunnie's. I'd never liked cats before Sasha, and Sunnie had never liked them full stop. But Val took to Sasha, who was given to her when I moved to Cyprus to avoid six months' quarantine. All those trivial things we talked about, the way one does in times of stress.

'The very fact of having so much contact with other human beings was overwhelming. They wanted to shake my hand, to be nice to me, to help me and do things for me. It was totally astounding to have so much happening in such a short time. I'd had nothing of the kind for two and a half years. I was forbidden to talk to my abductors, and they to me. One or two risked a few words, but it was never a conversation, and always in whispers so that we wouldn't be overheard. I thought of the people who had held me for so long, but dismissed them from my mind. At this stage I could feel nothing, not even hatred.

'As we crossed the English Channel and came over the English coast – the sight with which I'd been so familiar in my Battle of Britain days – and I saw the green countryside, half aloud I repeated part of a Sir Walter Scott poem to myself, dimly remembered, which flowed into my mind as I saw England spread out beneath me:

> *Breathes there the man, with soul so dead,*
> *Who never to himself hath said,*
> *This is my own, my native land!*
> *Whose heart hath ne'er within him burn'd,*
> *As home his footsteps he hath turn'd*
> *From wandering on a foreign strand.*

TWO

The Kidnap

Friday, 12 May 1989. A day that, for Sunnie and Jackie Mann, started like any other.

The situation in Beirut had been gradually worsening, but the last few weeks had been so difficult that even the Manns, grown used to life deteriorating, had noticed the change. The water supply had long since been cut off and electricity to their fifth-floor flat in the Raouche district of West Beirut was now rationed to one hour a day. It was erratically distributed on a rota system, which meant that frequently the chosen hour of electricity fell in the middle of the night. Shopping trips had to be synchronised with the 'Power Hour' so that they had the benefit of the lift to haul heavy bags to their apartment. Often it was impossible and Jackie and Sunnie, both in their mid-seventies, had to carry shopping, water, gas bottles – everything they needed – up five flights of stairs: ninety-nine steps. It was a very different place from the Lebanon they had chosen as their home forty-five years before.

In 1975 a civil war, which had been simmering below the surface for many years, erupted in a storm of violence. On one side were the Christians, the dominant force in Lebanese politics, and on the whole the middle-class, educated stratum of society. They had ruled since the sixth century, and until recently had been the single largest community in Lebanon. On the other were the Muslims, the Shia and the smaller group of Sunni Muslims; from the mid-sixties they outnumbered the Christians yet were vastly under-represented politically. They were poorer, ill-educated, and determined to readjust the balance. The Christians, on the other hand, were desperate to retain their advantage.

It was a situation exacerbated by the Palestinian 'state-within-a-state' which had been formed by Palestinian exiles from the occupied lands in Israel. Conditions in the refugee camps set up to receive them were appalling and they became breeding grounds for discontent, manifesting itself in various gangs which eventually became organised militias. By the late sixties there were already armed clashes between the militias and government forces. The Palestinian numbers were significantly added to by the diaspora who were finally thrown from their refuge in Jordan in 1970. They were headed by Yasser Arafat, the chairman of the Palestinian Liberation Organisation, who waged his war against Israel from the centre of Beirut.

In 1982, the Israelis invaded Lebanon, determined to drive the Palestinians out, and to destroy the PLO infrastructure. They swiftly established themselves in the south of the country, and began their northward advance towards Beirut. The battles were bloody and fierce, and many Lebanese as well as Palestinians fled their advance. The Israelis then laid siege to Beirut, beginning a brutal bombardment with the intention of forcing the Lebanese to put pressure on the Palestinians to leave.

Throughout the horrific shelling and air raids conducted by the Israelis, Jackie and Sunnie refused to leave Beirut. Literally driven out of their home by the bombing on occasions, they returned, undaunted, every time the shelling ceased. The battle for survival was constant; obtaining enough food and drink became the focus of every day. In the midst of all this, Sunnie still ran her riding club, although the bombing drove many of the horsemen and women away. As often as possible, she battled across the war-torn city to check on the horses and feed them. It meant waiting until the shelling stopped – usually at six in the morning – then dashing out to the club, praying the soldiers would be busy making themselves coffee until she was safely back home.

One day Sunnie made the mad dash to the riding club to find an Israeli battery had razed it to the ground. Twenty-two horses lay dying in their own blood, their backs broken and, with no means to put them down, Sunnie had to stand weeping and watch them die.

The siege of the city finally ended with a truce; the PLO agreed to withdraw from Beirut and, for a short while, there was a lull in the fighting.

It was not to last. In September of 1982, the Christians turned on two Palestinian refugee camps, Sabra and Chatila, and massacred hundreds of people whilst the Israelis stood by. Less than a month later, a Hezbollah suicide lorry driver blew up the American Marine Base, killing 241 marines; as the dust settled, another explosion killed fifty-eight French paratroopers at their base.

The British First Secretary to Lebanon contacted Sunnie and Jackie and said he was arranging a convoy of cars to leave for the Syrian capital, Damascus. Everyone had to provide their own cars and fuel; the only possessions they could take were those that would fit into their car. If they broke down, they were on their own. A convoy of twenty or thirty cars left two hours later, led by the British Consul wielding his loudhailer. Sunnie and Jackie stayed on. Sunnie even began searching for new horses and started rebuilding the shattered riding club.

Eventually the Israelis withdrew from all except the south

of Lebanon, where they continued to maintain an occupied zone to protect their northern border. The vacuum was filled by warring militias – Christian against Muslim, Syrian-backed Amal against Iranian-backed Hezbollah. Gradually the Palestinians began to return and, by 1989, had again established themselves. The Syrian army moved in, ostensibly to keep the peace, and the city fell under their control.

Remnants of the Lebanese army – largely Christian – now banded together under the leadership of General Michel Aoun, who set himself up in the presidential palace in East Beirut when the outgoing President's term of office ended. Aoun wanted to end Syria's dominance of affairs in Lebanon, and launched an unwinnable war of liberation, pitting his forces against the vastly superior Syrian army. Syria's Muslim supporters in West Beirut – the Amal and Druze militias – retaliated, Hezbollah joined in the bloodletting, and East and West Beirut began shelling each other night and day. It had been possible to cross from one side of the city to another, via a number of checkpoints. Now, one risked one's life to do so.

Over the years, it had been suggested to the Manns that they leave Beirut a number of times, and each time they refused. Now the plea was renewed. Jackie visited the British Consulate – the Embassy had been closed some time before – where officials again tried to persuade them to go. The dangers of the war in Beirut were replaced by a sinister new peril; already, a number of Westerners had been kidnapped by guerrilla militias. Adamantly, Jackie refused to leave. The couple were warned that the Consulate simply did not have the facilities to look after them if they stayed, but Jackie was dogmatic.

'I thought I had enough friends in Beirut,' he says now. 'I was sure that I was sufficiently well known, that I wouldn't be kidnapped. I never dreamed they'd want me.

'I told Sunnie why I'd been to the Consulate, and what

they'd said. We talked over whether I should stay, but really there wasn't much choice. It had always been the same, every time we were warned. We'd get a letter from the Embassy, delivered by hand by a messenger, advising us to go. We'd talk about it and every time for one reason or another we'd stay. The first time was when I was still flying for Middle East Airlines, back in 1955. MEA moved all their aircraft out of Beirut and although they still operated there, they kept their aircraft elsewhere. I ended up in Bahrain on the Bahrain–Karachi–Bombay flight and Sunnie was by herself in Beirut for weeks at a time.

'It was impractical for us to leave, what with the animals, the horses, all our things – and besides, we had precious little capital, so how would we live?

'If there had been an alternative we would have taken it, but the difficulties of going vastly outweighed the possible problems if we stayed. We were always fairly confident we could survive virtually whatever happened. Sunnie wasn't happy about it, but she did concede that in most ways we were better off staying where we were and taking a chance. Our rent was fixed by law at a ridiculously low amount and even if we'd managed to overcome the difficulties of moving we couldn't have afforded to live anywhere else.

'Life wasn't easy in Beirut. Aoun's war had cut off the water and made our electricity unreliable – the times it would be available on any given day were published in the newspaper, but they didn't stick to it. I can't remember the number of times you'd carefully plan your shopping trip to coincide with the lift working, only to have it fail when you were in it. That meant an undignified and difficult scramble out of the lift, which invariably stuck between floors, and your shopping would sit in it all day until the electricity came on again. The problems with the electricity were caused mainly by lack of oil, since it was difficult to get it to the power stations, but it was made

27

worse by the fact that the militias were deliberately shooting down each other's power cables. We cooked by butane gas, although even that was in short supply.

'Most of the time we didn't think about the conditions we were living in. We weren't happy about them, but in general we were reasonably content. Sunnie still managed to get to her riding club almost every day, whilst I'd sit terrified until she got home safely. No one could be sure what might happen on the roads, with the shells and the various militias and so on. Yet she'd go out there religiously, and often when she did the shelling would start whilst she was out, and she'd take a chance and come home in the middle of it. On numerous occasions she was late back and I'd get rather worried by it, but she'd come up with some plausible explanation that she'd gone to see a friend or whatever – she always had some reason – and in time I got used to even that.

'After General Aoun declared war on the Syrians, putting the Christian East side at war with Muslim West Beirut where we lived, many of our supplies, which came through the port on the East side, were cut off. It became almost impossible to get fresh fruit and vegetables, and even fresh bread was unobtainable. The beer depot – always close to my heart – closed because no new crates had been delivered, and our usual staple supplies seemed to vanish from the shops.

'But it was the stairs that nearly killed me. It was hard for Sunnie, who exercised and ate and drank very little, but it was a torment for me. I had to rest after every ten stairs or so, and there were ninety-nine of them: I counted.

'We got used to going to bed very early, when the light faded. In the winter we'd light the candles, and play a word game called "Boggle". I always won, much to Sunnie's annoyance. The light wasn't bright enough to read by and of course there was no television, so we had few enough options.

'I don't think we realised how the quality of our lives

had deteriorated. It was so gradual – the civil war broke out fifteen years earlier – that we hadn't noticed the slow slipping away of comforts and luxuries, and later necessities and essentials, that one would usually take for granted. We'd come to Lebanon just after the Second World War, and were used to hardship. It was like someone who hears a buzzing noise for so long that gradually he doesn't hear it any more. It's only when it stops he notices.

'The day I was kidnapped was unremarkable. Usually Sunnie would go out, to check on the horses and take her toy poodle Tara for a walk. I'd do things about the house or maybe plan a meal – I did all the cooking – and wait for the French paper which Sunnie would always bring back, *L'Orient du Jour*. It was the only foreign newspaper we could get. I couldn't read it completely, but I managed to teach myself enough French to get by. They had a word puzzle which I used to do every day, which took about half an hour, or three quarters if the shelling was too noisy. There was little else to do, other than drink a couple of litres of my favourite beer, Amalza beer, which was usually lukewarm because the refrigerator was off due to the lack of power.

'We needed some money, so I had decided to go to the bank. I also loaded up the boot of the car with two or three cases of empty beer bottles and a couple of empty gas bottles. I had my chequebook and the savings account book from which I was taking the money. I had to present that in person to withdraw money; it was in my name only, not Sunnie's, since she can be a little bit of a spendthrift. The bank was my first call and then I was going to call in at the Duke of Wellington, my local public house, for a few drinks on the way back with a friend of mine, Adib.

'Sunnie was going on again about the danger of kidnapping. It was very much on our minds – already a number of Americans had been taken, and the British journalist John

McCarthy, and of course Terry Waite. We were by now the last English couple living in West Beirut.

'"Be careful," she warned. "I don't want you getting kidnapped. Just watch what you're doing and where you go."

'I tutted. "Who'd want to kidnap me? I'll see you later – I'll be back around three, as usual." I always made a point of returning in time to hear the afternoon news.

'I drove my Simca to the British Bank of the Middle East in the centre of town. There was a slight disturbance in the bank, which I thought a little odd, because in this bank they had a guard standing inside the door and I'd never seen any trouble before. But on this occasion a strange character was jumping up at the counter, shouting through the little hole at the bank clerk behind. I couldn't understand what he was saying. I wasn't alarmed by it, but it occurred to me afterwards that he might have been just keeping an eye on me. They were fully prepared when I started to walk back to the car, having cashed my cheque.

'I got into the Simca, and pulled away from the kerb, unperturbed. Not far from the bank the road narrows into a bottleneck, and it's not unusual for there to be a traffic blockage there. As I drove to this point, a big American cream-coloured car pulled out from the car-park on the side of the road which narrowed, preventing me from going forwards. I thought he intended to come out in front of me, but he didn't. I backed up to allow him to go past me into the entrance to the street through which I'd just come. He then backed up, I presumed to allow me to go forward, which I did.

'The American car then pulled forward again, and stopped me once more. I thought everyone was getting thoroughly confused, so I decided to reverse and go back the way I'd come. I was having a few problems with the car, which was relatively new to me – it had power steering and automatic gear shift, to which I wasn't really accustomed, and I dislike automatic gears anyway. So I struggled with the reverse and finally managed to get it to work, a little out of breath by now. I backed up so that I could turn and ran into a pile of rubble, which stopped me going back far enough to turn. Instead I pulled straight forward across the road into a little recess, intending to drive in there and reverse out.

'Suddenly the American car pulled out and parked itself immediately behind me. I couldn't move. Four or five men piled out of the car, at least three of them holding handguns and waving them at me. Several started rattling the door handle. I thought it was one of these little street quarrels which frequently happened in Beirut when someone obstructed another person's car – people have been shot or killed for doing no more than that.

'I sat completely still. I wasn't thinking of anything other than stopping myself being killed for no reason. My heart pounding, I opened the door of the car and immediately two hands came in to try to pull me out.

'"*Schwei, schwei*", I called – slow, slow – climbing out of the car, their hands grabbing and starting to pull me. I saw the lid of the boot of their car already lifted and felt myself being dragged across the street. As much as I dared I dug my heels into the ground and stumbled on the rubble. The dust was rising, choking me, and my chest tightened. They forced me to the car boot and gestured me to get into it. I couldn't have climbed in if I'd wanted to, for I was terribly stiff. Suddenly one lurched towards me and took me by the shoulders, and another took me by the legs and lifted me up bodily and dumped me roughly in the boot. A young man, no more than twenty, climbed into the boot with me, holding an automatic gun which he had pointing at me. The boot was slammed down and the others climbed into the front of the car and drove off.

'It was dark and stifling. A chink of light let me see the revolver pointing at me. The young man holding it tightly to his chest gestured at me. He just said, "Be quiet." I had never felt more alone.

'We drove first of all to the outer suburbs of Beirut. The car came to a stop and I asked the man with me if I could be let out for some air for a few minutes. The young man called to the others and they opened the boot and helped me out of the car. I staggered against the side, and one of them put out his hand to stop me falling. I leant against the side of the car, and another of them yelled at me to stay still. I froze. They told me to keep my eyes on the ground, and I didn't dare look around me, although I did see one building which I feel sure I'd recognise again, if I had the chance. We were right in the countryside. I could see the undergrowth, several feet high – it prevented me from seeing far along the ground.

'I couldn't take in what was happening. I had no idea that I'd been kidnapped, despite Sunnie's last words to me ringing in my ears. I thought it was robbery. I spoke sternly to myself, saying, "It's only for a little while. They'll get what they want and then it'll be over. You probably won't even be late home. Just stay calm."

'The men held a few minutes of conversation between themselves and to my surprise I heard a woman's voice reply once or twice. From their conversation – which was mainly in English – I gathered that we'd stopped at someone's house, but the man who owned it wasn't there. It seemed they'd been planning to stay there awhile but, without the man of the house there, they decided against it.

'Finally they turned to me again and thrust me back into the boot of the car. We drove some distance, my spirits sinking as we travelled further from the centre of the city. If I was being robbed, why were we going so far out of town?

'We stopped twice, maybe three times. Beirut is a network

of checkpoints – official Syrian ones and those unofficial roadblocks set up by the various militias. Each time I heard the slam of a car door as the driver got out of the car and walked a few paces from it to chat to the soldiers, luring them from the immediate vicinity of the car. I heard them talking, although I could not make out the words. My heart pounded so loudly I felt sure it must be audible feet away. I offered up silent pleas for them just to open the boot. How many times had I been stopped and my car checked? I wondered. They always wanted the boot opened, usually when one was already late for an appointment. Was it too much to ask that they'd check this one, now, before I vanished for good?

'But my abductors were plausible liars, it seemed, and the soldiers manning the checkpoints were obviously convinced they were not guilty of anything untoward. They were allowed to proceed unchecked, and unhindered.

'After a time we arrived at our apparent destination. I was helped from the car and managed a quick look about me before I was told to keep my eyes on the ground. I concentrated on observing as much as possible, so that when I was released – I refused to countenance the word "if" – I could give the police as many details as possible. We seemed to be at a villa, which was partly furnished. I was taken to what I presumed was the kitchen, although it had only a built-in sideboard, with no other furniture. I was forced to empty my pockets, which I did without reluctance, since I believed it to be a precursor to my release.

'I wasn't terrified or even frightened. I just thought that I'd lost the hundred and thirty-five thousand Lebanese pounds – about a hundred and fifty pounds sterling – that I'd withdrawn from the bank that morning. I thought, "Well, I've lost a hundred and thirty-five thousand Lebanese pounds, but so what?" It didn't matter in a sense. They'd have that and then they'd let me go. I didn't realise I'd lost my freedom as well.

'The money was swiftly taken from me, along with various other bits and pieces I had, and placed on the sideboard. One of them dug me in the back and gestured for me to follow his colleague, which I did, and found myself in a bedroom.

'I sat down on one of two queensize beds in the room and gazed for a moment at the lady's dressing table opposite me. It was still equipped with all the accoutrements one would expect to find. The whole situation seemed unreal, like a dream or a cheap Hollywood film.

'The men again talked amongst themselves, as if I didn't exist. Annoyed, I demanded of the nearest one who their head man was and said I wanted to speak to him. Unperturbed, he turned and faced me.

'"He's not here yet," he said, and turned back to his fellows and carried on chatting.

'"Then when will he be back?" I demanded testily.

'"Maybe an hour. Maybe more."

'I sat back on the bed and regarded my fingernails. I felt frustrated and impotent, but realised the futility of my anger. After forty years living amongst Arabs, I understood their enormous capacity for waiting. They lacked Western impatience, and were not about to make allowances for it now. I was forced to adopt their stance and wait. I little realised for how long.

'Eventually, another man entered the room and I asked if he was their chief, but was told no. A while later another came in and the answer to my question was again negative. Darkness fell and still I was sitting alone on the bed. I asked if I could stand by the window for some fresh air and they allowed me to do so. I leant my head against the pane, and peered into the darkness, although I could see little. There were houses near-by, and I heard children calling and shouting to one another, and the light scatter of their feet. I stood there for ten or fifteen minutes, listening to the sounds of a normal suburb at dusk.

The children, the doors banging shut, dogs barking and the occasional sound of a car. I couldn't believe the world was continuing just the same, whilst I sat in this bedroom, only feet away. It might just have well been a thousand miles.

'Finally a man entered the room and those already there jumped up. One said, "This is the boss," and we looked at each other a long moment. Then I said, "Good evening," and waited.

'"Good evening," he said, and walked past my bed, and out of the room.

'Too tired even to be angry at the way I'd just been dismissed, I fell back on the bed. I must have fallen asleep, for it was two or three o'clock in the morning before I was awakened again. I later came to learn that they always moved in the small hours of the morning, when other movements would be limited and they'd have more chance of not being seen.

'They didn't bother to tie me up. After all, there were four, five, six of them there, mostly with handguns. What could I do, alone and unarmed?

'Before I had a chance to think too deeply, I was hustled from the room and back into the car. I was too dazed and exhausted to observe much or even think. Eventually we came to a built-up area, and I was escorted to the first floor of a somewhat ramshackle building. We passed through the front door, and down a long, badly lit corridor. I was taken into a small room, tastefully furnished with furniture in the French style. I registered a large table in the middle and two windows, one on the left-hand wall as one entered the room and one facing it.

'I sat down tiredly. It was four o'clock in the morning, and this strange dream was still going on. I'd started the day with a fresh pack of cigarettes, and I fumbled about in my pocket to find them. They were still there, if somewhat broken down. It didn't matter. I managed to get one or two of them out, and

I looked at them earnestly. They seemed smokeable to me. I lit one and inhaled deeply.

'One of the men entered the room, dragging something clumsily behind him. With an Arabic curse, he flung it down in the corner of the room. It was a stained, yellowing foam mattress. Grunting to one of his colleagues for help, the man began pulling the settee away from the wall. The mattress was thrown down behind it, between the wall and the settee. He gestured for me to lie down on it, and I did. The settee was moved back into place tightly against the mattress, effectively blocking me in.

'I lay back, my eyes fixed on the ceiling, and for the first time I thought of Sunnie. I glanced at my watch, which I still had at that stage. I'd been missing hours – what on earth would she be thinking? Tired, worried, confused, I fell asleep.'

For Sunnie, the terror – and the waiting – had begun.

She had spent the day as usual, finishing various household chores whilst Jackie was out. Her daily trip to the riding club was ruled out, as there had been particularly bad shelling in that area during the afternoon. Sunnie took her usual siesta, expecting to be woken by Jackie's return as she frequently was.

Instead, she was awakened by her pet poodle Tara pulling at the bedspread. Startled, she sat up, surprised that she had slept until it was dark. The flat was silent. Sunnie swung her legs over the side of the bed, absently patting Tara's head. There was an unnatural stillness to the silence, and a faint flicker of alarm twisted her stomach. She quickly dressed and picked up Tara's lead, which lay on a chair by the bed. Calling affectionately to the dog, Sunnie walked briskly into the drawing room. Jackie was not there.

Sunnie glanced at the clock. It was six o'clock. A knot of fear grew and settled like lead inside her. She dampened it down, telling herself that he had stayed late for an extra drink.

36

Perhaps the shelling had been particularly heavy in their area and he had delayed his return until it ceased. She ignored the fact that there had been little bombardment of their section of West Beirut that afternoon, and resolutely headed for the front door.

'I told myself he'd be back when Tara and I got home from our evening walk,' Sunnie recalls. 'I spent the entire forty-five minutes walking the broken pavements, imagining him sitting in his favourite chair when we returned. I rehearsed what I'd say to him, how I'd scold him for making me worry. It was always him telling me off for making him fret whilst I was away at the riding club. Now I knew how he felt, and I didn't like it.

'I dragged out that walk, wanting to prolong the moment of return as long as I could, to give him plenty of time to get back. The knot of fear in my stomach curled and tightened every time I thought of it. Jackie was never late. I refused to allow myself to think anything really drastic had happened. Determinedly, I stamped on my fears. He'd be there when I got back. He had to be.

'I slowly climbed the stairs to our apartment. I counted each of the ninety-nine steps, promising myself Jackie was at the top. My mind was spinning. I thought, there can only be two explanations for this. Either he's had an accident and he's in hospital or the worst has happened and he's been kidnapped. Tara bounded on ahead, turning to look at me as if to hurry me up. She seemed to sense something was wrong and came back to nuzzle my ankles. At each landing I paused, telling myself I needed to catch my breath. I dreaded entering our flat. I knew what I would find.

'I put the key in the lock, and opened the door. The silence was deafening.

'I panicked, and rushed to the telephone and rang my friend Amine Daouk. Hysterically I told him what had happened and begged him to check the hospitals for me. I was in too much of a state to do it myself.

'"Don't worry," Amine said reassuringly. "I'll call the hospitals for you, and one or two places he might have gone. Now you are sure he was coming straight home?"

'"Yes, of course," I sobbed. "As soon as he'd been to the bank and got money to buy the beer and gas bottles, he said he was coming back. He's never late." My voice rose as I struggled to get my emotions under control.

'"Just hold on, darling, and wait for me to call you back," Amine promised, and I sank into a chair, hugging Tara to me. An hour later, Amine rang, and my last hope was extinguished. Jackie wasn't registered at any hospital and Amine hadn't been able to locate him anywhere else.

'"Darling, I'm so sorry. But I think you're going to have to take a deep breath and face the truth. He must have been kidnapped." My nightmare had begun.

'I'm not religious in any way at the best of times, and at that moment I knew I couldn't even believe in God anymore. I thought, if he could do this to me, then there couldn't be a God – certainly not one I was interested in knowing. But my link with animals is unbreakable and it was Tara who kept me going that first night. I talked to her like a human being and she seemed to understand, better than many people I know. Somehow the fact that I had to take her for walks and find food for her somehow, in between the shelling, gave me a purpose in life and pulled me through. It might sound odd to someone who is not an animal lover, but my life has been associated with animals from a very early age. Jackie is always saying that horses and dogs come way ahead of him on my list of priorities! Later, when my relatives begged me to return to England, I couldn't do it because of Tara; I would have had to put her into quarantine for six months, and that I couldn't do. I loved her far too much.

'I awoke stiff and aching in the armchair where I'd sunk when I grew weary of pacing the apartment. I must have fallen asleep at some stage during that endless night. Dawn was sending fingers of cold light along the windowsill, and I sat up, cradling Tara. My first dawn alone. I made a vow then, not to leave Lebanon, as long as there was hope that Jackie could be released. If he could survive there, then so could I.'

THREE

The First Week: Sidon

Jackie awoke to find bright daylight pouring into the room. He sat up, the events of the preceding day flooding his mind immediately. He glanced at his watch: quarter past eight. Anxious to explore his surroundings as much as he was allowed to, he asked for the toilet.

'They conferred for a few moments, then one of them came forward and pulled back the settee, so that I could get out. I was taken to a typical Arabic toilet – just a hole in the ground, with two footprints on either side. They left the door open, and one of them stood outside, with his gun in his hand, whilst I urinated. Then I was taken back to my room, and given a cup of tea and some unappetising food. I was beginning to think the money they'd found on me wasn't enough, and they wanted some ransom as well. I wondered who they'd expect to pay it. Sunnie and I didn't have anything to speak of, and I knew the British Government's policy on ransom demands.

'I managed to snatch a glimpse out of the windows, when I had the chance, and recognised one or two landmarks. During the course of the morning, one of them told me I was being held inside a town about thirty miles south of Beirut, between two Palestinian refugee camps which had been established there: Mieh Mieh and Ain El Hilweh. I could roughly recognise where I was, and later learned I was in a town called Sidon. Mountains rose up sharply behind the house where I was, towards the south-east, and I recognised the town of Jenin, which is situated on top of the hill. I also remember seeing a rather distinctive chimney, or air vent, around two or three hundred yards from the villa where I was. It was about three metres in diameter and around five or six metres high, with white and red bands painted around it. It looked to me like some sort of air raid warning device. About halfway up it had a walkway around it, and a ladder going up to it, presumably for painting purposes. It seemed around the height of the building in which I was being held, judging by the eyeline I had. I spent many fruitless hours contemplating it, wondering what it might be. I never found out.

'Two or three times during that day – and each of those that followed – I was allowed to walk around inside the room and exercise a little. I persuaded them after a time to allow me to walk down the corridor which led to the front door by which I had first entered, just for exercise. One member of the group would always stand keeping watch on me, a gun in his hand, to make sure I didn't escape, and the front door was carefully guarded. If the front doorbell rang, one of them would rush to the door, brandishing his gun – with the safety catch off, I'm sure – and demand angrily who it was, before they ever opened that door. They were very security conscious, even of me, a seventy-five-year-old man too stiff to move quickly and too tired to run far even if I did manage to escape. Whilst I walked there was someone holding a gun towards me. If I woke up during the night, and poked my head over the settee to ask to go to the toilet, there were two men sitting there holding their guns towards me, one on the settee itself and one opposite. If I asked to go to the bathroom – and they always co-operated and allowed me – they would come to the entrance to the toilet and stand there, guns drawn and aimed at me, ready to use, until I had finished. Physically I

41

was never alone, yet I had never felt so isolated and lonely in my life.

'All my clothes were taken away from me and I was given a tracksuit to wear. I never saw my own things again. Roughly once every week to ten days during the two and a half years I was held, my abductors would replace the tracksuit I was wearing with a fresh one. I welcomed any changes in my stagnant life, even if it was just the colour of the tracksuit I was wearing.

'I had no shoes, no sandals, no socks, except in that first week. I never saw a comb, a hairbrush or a toothbrush in the whole time I was held. I wasn't allowed to shave for months at a time, after Sidon, where I was given a razor on two occasions, although each time it was reclaimed.

'My possessions were taken from me – my watch, my Colibri cigarette lighter, a Parker pen, my wallet, my bankbook. Everything was later restored to me, presumably after they had thoroughly examined each item, and then taken from me again a few days later. I was left with my watch, but that was all. I remember in those early days, there was one of my abductors who could not speak English. Rather earnestly, he confided to me that to learn how to was his greatest wish and asked me to teach him as much as I could whilst I was there. He went out of his way to be friendly; every time I asked for a cup of tea he would go out and make it for me. Tea was the one thing they always did make for me, including milk and sugar. A sop to my Englishness, perhaps. The second day there he even went into the centre of the town, and came back with a roasted chicken, presumably from one of these places which sold chicken whole, and gave me a large portion of it. I wasn't there long enough to get the chance to improve his English vocabulary.

'At lunchtime, perhaps rather foolishly, I said I didn't need any lunch because I wasn't hungry. I rather expected them to provide me with a solid evening meal, but they had their main meal around three or four in the afternoon. When it came to the evening they had nothing and I went hungry. I soon learned to eat whenever I was provided with food, however little I liked it.

'I had slept fitfully the previous night, as much from discomfort as because of the situation I was in. The foam mattress was very thin and felt to me like sleeping on a piece of wood. The second night I was there, I was brought a second layer of foam, which was placed on top of the first and served a little to alleviate the discomfort of my body, if not the anguish in my mind.

'Two days after I was abducted – Sunday, 14 May – they held a meeting of nearly all of the kidnappers, excepting one whom they left to guard me. I managed to get a glimpse of the room where they were meeting on one of my journeys to the toilet one day. It was simply furnished; all I could see were two beds. There they counted all the money they'd taken from me and my hopes rose. Perhaps now they'd be satisfied and take that and let me go.

'When they finished, one came back into my room. "It's not enough," he said. They obviously weren't happy with what I'd had on me and the man indicated they wanted to get more, from somewhere else. Where, he didn't say, and I had no idea.

'I was convinced now I was going to be held to ransom and a riot of new worries broke out in my head. Discounting the small amount Sunnie and I had amassed over the years, there were few alternatives. Mrs Thatcher had stated often enough that the British Government would not pay ransoms when John McCarthy and Terry Waite were kidnapped. I still didn't bracket myself with them, however. I saw it in monetary, rather than political, terms. I knew there had been many occasions recently when Lebanese were kidnapped and released on payment of a ransom. The son of a great riding friend of Sunnie's, a young man called Omar Dhabbari, had been abducted in 1986 and only returned when his parents paid the half million Lebanese pounds demanded. He returned a very different, subdued person, and I worried anew at the anxiety Sunnie must be feeling on my behalf. I had been away two days now.

'A guard rota was organised by one of the men holding me. Each of them seemed to have a particular role, be it organising the duty roster or arranging food. Every evening two guards would come into my room, armed with their automatic weapons. Throughout the night they stayed near me, silent and watchful. Each pair would be on duty for two nights, before being changed for two more.

'One day the man who organised the roster came to see me, with an air of not wanting to be seen. His eyes darted around the room and he came close to me, so as not to have to talk too loudly. He told me he would take me home for five thousand sterling pounds – a great deal of money to the average Lebanese. I was puzzled. How could he spirit me away without being detected by his fellow abductors? He seemed serious: he told me he was getting married and needed the money and seemed convinced he would be able to accomplish it without being caught.

'I found it difficult to believe, but after three days imprisoned in that room, I was prepared to put my faith in anyone. This fellow was also in charge of transport, as far as I could make out, and eventually I was persuaded that he could take me back to Beirut if I chose to accept this five-thousand-pound deal. But nothing came of it. I was offered a number of similar deals in those early days – whether they were made by individuals who saw a chance of making some money or whether it was designed by the kidnappers to torment me in the hopes of breaking my spirit, I don't know. Once another man offered to take me home for eight thousand sterling pounds and when I asked how he'd get me to Beirut, he said, "In your car", as if I had it parked outside.

'On another occasion, one character told me boastfully that he could get a million dollars' ransom for me. I said, "You won't get it from the British Government," and he laughed.

'"We will get it," he said easily. "Maybe even two million dollars."

'Whether he had the Americans in mind or was just idly boasting, I don't know. Again, nothing happened.

'On the Monday morning, three days after I was taken, several of them came to me in a deputation and informed me exactly how much money I had in the bank. There was only one way they could know that: they had to have a contact in the bank itself. It was a fraction over eleven thousand pounds sterling in my savings account. I pointed out to them that I couldn't get the money out of the bank unless I presented myself in person, and that no one else could get the money out, not even my wife, because she wasn't a signatory on the account. It was information they had to have received from an insider.

'It made me think anew about my capture. I had been walking from the bank to the place where I'd parked my car, a walk of no more than seven or eight minutes, perhaps less. They simply wouldn't have had the time to get their men and car in position if they'd been acting on a telephone call from someone who saw me in the bank. It had to have been prepared in advance.

'I mused over the weeks leading up to my abduction. The men holding me said they'd been watching me for some time and cited an Englishman who, they claimed, came to my apartment every day. That itself was hopelessly untrue. There was no such Englishman who came to our flat at all, let alone every day. We did have one friend, a Pakistani, who had a very pale skin and could have been mistaken for an Englishman from across the road, but even he came only once every two or three weeks. I didn't know it then, but the story was part of a pattern of misinformation and half-truths which they fed me throughout my captivity, until by the end I was unable to distinguish truth from fiction. I learnt to disbelieve everything they said on principle.

'I thought some more. I remembered a group of four or five youths who used to hang around outside the entrance to our apartment, sitting on the low walls there, doing nothing except sitting, talking amongst themselves and smoking. I had thought nothing of it; as far as I could see, they were typical young people who had nothing else to do but loiter. Now I considered it afresh. I decided they could well have been giving information as to when I came and went, establishing my routine for my abductors.

'The kidnappers told me they'd seen me on the television. I wondered what they could mean, until I remembered a free-lance photojournalist who had done a story on Sunnie and myself. He'd been out to the riding club and photographed Sunnie and her friend and colleague, Amine Daouk, along with a number of other riders. He'd then come to our apartment where he'd interviewed and photographed me following my daily routine. He followed me with a video camera when I went on my usual errand to the bank, filming me the entire time I was walking, from where I parked the car along to the bank. I recalled him asking me to stop once or twice and look at some posters on the wall, to add colour to the story, as all such journalists do, and then I walked into the bank, at which point he stopped and left.

'The broadcast aired on Lebanese television a short while before I was taken, although no one I knew had seen it. I knew it could have played no part in my abduction; I was a prominent figure in Beirut and if they wanted to take me they could do so easily – it required no detective work to identify me and track me down. When the abductors told me they had seen me on television, I assumed they meant this incident. It might have made me more easy to identify positively but, as far as I'm aware, Sunnie and I were the only married British couple our ages living in West Beirut. There were a few English women married to Lebanese men, but we were the only couple. We weren't difficult to find.

'I always thought I was too old and not wealthy or any-thing of that kind. I thought I was safe from kidnapping. But all they wanted was an Englishman and I was the only one available. They told me frequently, in those early days, that if they could get another Englishman, they would take him and let me go. I remember defiantly pointing out that there were no more Englishmen they could take, and they said they could always go to the East side of Beirut and take one. I didn't see how they could abduct someone from the Christian East side and said so.

'One evening, four or five of them gathered in my room, chatting casually. I recognised one of them as the character who had ridden in the boot when I was first kidnapped. He was waving his gun around casually, gesticulating with it. Suddenly he seemed more familiar and I blurted out that I recognised him stupid of me, but I was startled by the sudden rush of memory. He looked just like the eldest son of the concierge at our building, who had more or less deserted his family and taken to the hills, which meant he'd probably joined a Palestinian group. Fortunately the moment passed, the kidnappers evidently not recognising my *faux pas* for the blunder it was and I took care not to repeat it.

'Amongst the men was a Pakistani fellow and one evening I spoke to him for five or ten minutes undisturbed. His English was excellent and we talked about Middle East Airlines, for whom I'd worked for many years when I first came to Beirut. He knew Salim Salaam, the chairman and managing director of MEA and also chairman of the Golf Club in Beirut. The Pakistani said he was a member of the Golf Club, which puzzled me. I couldn't imagine any member of such a group of kidnappers mixing in the same circles as members of Beirut's élite Golf Club. He waved his Kalashnikov at me as he talked, enjoying the moment of conversation to while away the dull hours of his guard duty. His girlfriend's father was a member, he explained, which was how he came to join. He told me her name was Hilda and I filed the information away. I always intended to contact Salim Salaam one day and ask him which of his members had a daughter named Hilda, to try to find out more about this character. I haven't done it yet, and now I shouldn't think I ever will.

'I wasn't ill-treated at Sidon. At one stage I had some sort of infection or discolouration in my ear, and one of my abductors noticed it. He asked me what it was.

'"I've no idea," I replied, somewhat testily. "I can't see it. You're the one who can see it."

'Ignoring my sarcasm, he called a doctor along to examine me. There was a freelance journalist, a young man in his mid-twenties, who used to come to Beirut fairly frequently. He used to visit me at the pub I ran, the Pickwick Pub, and I knew him by sight, if not intimately. His sister was a professional nurse who'd married a Lebanese doctor, now living in Sidon. When the doctor came to examine my ear, I asked him if he knew of a doctor married to an English nurse living there and he said he did. He must have been local himself to know the couple.

'I'm sure he knew who I was. But he was Palestinian, and clearly on the kidnappers' side. There was little point asking him for help or to pass on a message for me. I met him once more, months later, when I had been moved to another part of Lebanon. He was one of two doctors who performed a heart scan on me.

'When I'd been there five or six days, they began using their walkie-talkie radios a good deal. They never seemed to have much success with it. They would call frequently during the course of the day: "Arabia, Arabia," – probably a general call sign for their station. I never once heard a reply, just static.

'That first week at Sidon, the kidnappers were relatively courteous and considerate. I smoked Players in those days and for the first few days I was brought several packets from the shop in Sidon, until it actually ran out of them. The cigarettes stopped then too; they didn't think of getting another brand. I wasn't pushed around too much and I had enough food and drink. I managed to get some sleep; at around nine or ten in the evening they'd tell me it was sleeping time and I'd go to my double layer of foam mattresses and lie down and sleep. They used no chains or handcuffs at that stage. If I woke up, as I usually did, at around three or four in the morning to go to the toilet, they always let me. My only problem was the fact that the light was always on – often only candlelight, but always some illumination.

'I was even brought a package of clean underclothes, with the name and telephone number of a shop printed on the outside. I came to think of those days, later on, as luxurious. Looking back, the conditions came to seem tolerable, although I chafed desperately at them at the time. But then I also had that essential ingredient – hope. I still believed my incarceration was to be temporary. Had I any idea what was in store for me, I would have given up there and then. The only thought that kept me battling on was what Sunnie must be going through, alone in that flat, not knowing if I was alive or dead.'

For Sunnie, the days were beginning to melt into one endless nightmare. Every night she staggered to bed, exhausted, hugging Tara to her, telling herself that tomorrow there would be news, if only she could hold on. With Amine she visited various Syrian officials, who promised to do their best to help, then shrugged and went back to their work. Nothing had been heard of Jackie. No informers carried tales of his capture, no ransom demands were made, no statements were issued. Each return to the flat became harder. Sunnie climbed the stairs, feeling her age for the first time, dreading the emptiness of their apartment.

It was a horror that seemed to have been going on forever. The days when she and Jackie sat together in the evening playing 'Boggle' seemed remote, set in the distant past. Sunnie felt she was in a tunnel, which was getting tighter and dimmer by the day. She found it hard to believe that someone could simply disappear without trace.

On the Monday morning, the third day after Jackie had disappeared, there was news.

'I was sitting in the drawing room, trying to encourage Tara, when a Syrian soldier arrived at our apartment and came in bursting with importance at having some concrete information. Jackie's car had been found, abandoned in a street near Al-Hamra, Beirut's main shopping thoroughfare.

'It seemed this was a surprising development. Usually with a kidnapping – and I had no doubts that that was what had happened to Jackie – the car was taken with the hostage. The Syrians seemed a little confused by this change in tactics, but said I could keep the car as long as I didn't use it.

'When I went to get something from the boot of Jackie's car, I discovered the reason the kidnappers had abandoned it so unexpectedly. Jackie used to keep the keys for my Honda as well as his own car on his keyring and jammed in the boot lock was the Honda key. It was obvious that the kidnappers had

50

tried to carry out their usual policy of throwing their victim into the boot of his own car and driving off with it, only to use the wrong key. They must have panicked and driven off in their own car.

'I thanked God that Jackie hadn't been forced into the boot of his tiny car. With his stiffness I didn't see how he could have survived.

'I took the car around to a garage, owned by a good friend of mine, Mahmoud Khashfi, who got out a magnet and managed to draw the broken key from the lock. When we opened the boot, we saw that the two gas bottles which Jackie had meant to exchange were missing, but the crates of empty beer bottles were still there. It was the only clue I had as to what had happened to my husband.

'Three witnesses to Jackie's kidnapping came forward. Each reported seeing four or five men bundling Jackie into a large car, but neither the car nor any of the men were traced. It was like throwing a rock into a pool – after a few faint ripples, the water subsided and it was as if the rock had never existed. Jackie lay submerged somewhere in Beirut, I was sure, yet I had no way of knowing where.

'I seemed to spend the whole of that first week talking to the Press or wandering round my flat in a daze. I'd pick up something, then look at it in my hand and wonder what I was doing with it. Nothing seemed real, only this nightmare I was having to live through. I kept trying to wake up, but the terrible dream went on.

'The morning after Jackie vanished, Amine came round to the flat. He warned me not to go out and, whatever happened, not to open the door and to put the chain lock on. It was good advice. By lunchtime I was besieged by reporters. They hammered on the door, screaming and calling for me to come out and make some sort of statement. From the balcony of the apartment I could see television cameras set up, ready to leap on me the minute I appeared outside the front door. When I did open the door to tell them to leave, the flat filled up with reporters, trying to tear pictures of Jackie from my few photograph albums that had survived the shelling, thrusting microphones under my nose to get my reaction to his disappearance. I collapsed and sobbed that I couldn't cope with any more that day. I promised to give them a statement the following day, when I'd had time to think a little, and eventually they left.

'I'd had very little experience with the Press at that stage. I hated being in the public eye; all I wanted was my old peaceful, quiet life, looking after my horses and dogs and husband. I was happy in old jeans and a shirt; I loathed the occasions when I had to dress up. I'd had to do one or two interviews before, about how Jackie and I were coping in Beirut as it was destroyed around us and why we didn't leave along with the other nationals, but nothing like this. I didn't know then that the Press would prove to be my shadow for the next two and a half years. I would learn to use them to get publicity for Jackie as much as they used me for a news story. Many would become close friends. But along the way there would be many times when I cursed their very existence and sympathised with Royalty and film stars, who have to endure this sort of hounding constantly.

'No one came to visit me from the British Embassy. I felt I was alone and that when I needed my country's support, they failed me. I had a couple of calls from a woman called Sylvia at the Consulate, who asked if there was anything I needed, such as water or something like that, and I spoke to the Ambassador, Alan Ramsey, once or twice. One of the main problems was the fact that I was living on the Muslim West side of the city, and the Embassy was on the Christian East side. It was virtually impossible to get from one side to the other because of all the fighting and shelling. Indeed, the

Ambassador wasn't permitted by the Foreign Office to cross to the West side, because of the high likelihood of his being kidnapped.

'Everything was against them managing to get to me, yet I still felt that much of my neglect was pure indifference. It became much better when there was a change of ambassadors and the Tathams came to Beirut. The British Ambassador's wife, Val, became a mainstay of my life. We formed a very strong friendship and Val helped me a great deal. She'd always manage to get something to me, a bunch of flowers or a card or sometimes a telephone call when the telephones were working, which wasn't often. David, the new Ambassador, was himself very kind to me, helping me enormously over financial problems, and arranging a resident's card for me – previously I had to leave Lebanon every three months, which was the length of my visa, and come back again. They even helped me get to Cyprus for short breaks or a holiday. But their valued help and friendship was personal, not Government policy. It wasn't until Mrs Thatcher was ousted, and John Major made a point of introducing a more human and caring note to Government attitudes, that I noticed a thawing on the part of the Foreign Office.

'Amine suggested that I make an appeal on behalf of Jackie, in case we were dealing with an ordinary kidnap group who simply wanted money. He told me to play up the fact that we didn't have any money and to make myself look as poor and distressed as possible. Accordingly I wore my oldest clothes, and, my face unmade up and my hair unbrushed, I pleaded for his release or at least news that he was alive. The distress I didn't have to fake for the cameras. A week later, I made a second appeal, this time to the Syrians, who, it was believed, might have more influence on the kidnap groups. Still no news.

'I woke up in the middle of the night, a week after Jackie's capture. I lay there for an endless time, staring at the ceiling, my eyes focusing blankly without seeing anything. He had been missing for seven days, seven days of questions and no answers, seven nights of sleeplessness and desperate loneliness. Where was he? Was he in pain? Was he even alive?'

At that moment, thirty miles away, Jackie was very much alive and determined to stay that way.

His captors had wakened him as he lay on the foam mattress in the corner of the room and told him to get dressed. He was told to hurry – he was being taken to a hotel.

'It was a story I scarcely believed,' Jackie said later. 'I pulled on my shirt and trousers, which I usually took off when I slept, and stood up not knowing what to expect.

'As I was escorted out of my cell, which had held me prisoner for the last week, there was a whole crowd of Palestinians outside, waiting for me, trying to grab me and pull me. All their hands were coming out, reaching over each other to try to get a hold of me. It was mob rule, and I was their prize.

'There were so many people and so much noise. Desperate to urinate, I asked one of the guards to intercede for me, which he did. I was jostled along the corridor, tugged at in a way that was not so much unfriendly as frantic. It was just their way of doing things and I didn't feel afraid or angry.

'I forced them to drag me down the stairs, making life as difficult as possible for them without bringing their anger down on my head. We reached the foot of the stairs and I saw the same American car as the one in which I'd been abducted parked outside. As we drew near, I saw that the boot lid was up. I tensed, looking into its blackness with apprehension. I wasn't sure how many journeys I'd survive using that particular mode of transport. "Not in there," I said and willed my feet not to move forward.

'One of the men came forward out of the shadows. I recognised him as the man who had come to me the first night I was captured, and identified himself as the boss of the group. He again seemed to be in charge of the men around him, and had just finished his tour of guard duty that night. I later learned he was known as Abu George.

'"No, not in there," said Abu George, his eyes never leaving mine. "In the back of the car."

'I was put into the back of the car, much to my relief. The car boot was slammed down and two men climbed in with me, one on either side, armed with Kalashnikovs and handguns. I was still dizzy with the result of my small defiance. I did not want to go in the boot of that car; I decided it was not my favourite pastime. It had been extremely uncomfortable before, and during my previous ride I had had something hard protruding into my back. For weeks afterwards I had a pain in the back where I'd been resting against it. The victory was slight, but to me it was everything. For seven days I hadn't been able to make a decision or exercise my own free will and the constriction was stifling, especially to someone like me, used to having his own way.

'After driving for a while, the car suddenly felt as if it were going down a steep slope, and came to a stop. I conjectured that I must be in an underground garage of some sort, judging by the movements of the car. I was lifted bodily out of the back seat, and carried to some kind of loading platform at the side of the garage area, where I was placed. I looked warily about me, careful to ensure they didn't see me do it.

'Before I had time to consider further, the men came over to me and helped me stand, before making it clear that I was to follow them. We went down a few steps to the right, then walked a few paces right again. I almost fell down another couple of steps, emerging suddenly into a long hallway. We passed a door on the left and came to a second door, where we stopped. It was a double door: the outer one was sheet metal, the inner one a normal wooden door. It was obviously underground. I looked down the length of the hallway, which was drab and dimly lit.

'One of the abductors leant across me and pushed the door open. I walked inside and stopped wearily. Four new walls to look at. For how long this time?'

FOUR

Counting The Days: Doha

'I entered my new prison, feeling strangely detached. I examined my surroundings as if I was recording the details for someone else. It seemed as if I was in some kind of underground office. The room was shaped like an L, around four metres square with a bite taken out of it. Into one corner was built a structure which housed a pump. Its door was locked. There were shelves on two sides of the room, full of files. A desk stood in the centre of the room, bereft of the usual telephone one would expect to see on it, but piled high with papers, seemingly dumped with no particular order or method. This area was fenced off with two large pieces of plywood and I was told not to go near it, not to look over it or go behind it. By blocking off this area the room was effectively made much smaller.

'The pump was needed to take water from the bathroom just next door up to a higher level, which convinced me that my assumption that the garage was underground had been correct. The pump was electrically operated and the switch was over my bed. Two or three times a day my captors would come in, unlock the door to the pump and lean across me to switch it on. Then would follow a scene straight out of a slapstick comedy programme: one fellow by the pump would be calling to another in the bathroom watching the water level and shouted instructions in Arabic would often be followed by a volley of curses when one or other of them misunderstood or made a mistake.

'I wouldn't have ever dared to laugh or chuckle, except inwardly, because they would have immediately taken it as such an insult, and retaliated. But there were numerous times when I was secretly amused and I could inwardly laugh at their stupidity and incompetence. It helped keep up my morale, when I considered their inefficiency and at times imbecility. They were really peasants – apart from the educated few who ran the operation – and they behaved like peasants, in a half-witted, country-boy sort of way, rather like caricatures of West Country lads in a *Two Ronnies* sketch. They were so amateurish – they obviously hadn't held a hostage before – and I frequently found myself saying "Bloody fools", and laughing under my breath.

'I was always instructed to cover my head with a towel when my captors came in to switch the pump on or off, so that I couldn't see them. If they thought I had, they would shout at me and on some occasions hit me with the flat of their hands. Whenever that happened I'd shout and create a terrible fuss, as if I'd been badly hurt, making as much of it as I could. If I made enough noise someone else would come in and take away the man who'd hit me. I'd do anything to attract enough attention for someone to intervene, although they rarely hurt me; it was more the indignity which caused me to rebel.

'During my time there I managed to look over the make-shift fence and saw the hundreds of files on the shelves. One shelf held folders, the other ring files. When my guards were inattentive, I was able to see that each file was for a different month – January, February, March, April, May and so on. They had newspaper cuttings in them, all in Arabic which of course I couldn't read.

'On the lower levels there was cupboard space, but the doors had been taken off. I was able to probe into them and amongst other things I found a yearbook of the American University of Beirut, dated 1985. Days later, when I was sure I wasn't being observed, I was able to open and look through the yearbook, and noticed various pen marks at points in the book, as if someone had gone through it making notations. There were also some blank spaces, as if certain pieces of information, or perhaps photographs, had been ripped out. It had all the photographs of the professors and students graduating that year. I thought of the American professor, Tom Sutherland, who had been seized in 1985, and the other fellows of the American University who were taken later. A new fear raised its head like a serpent inside me, and I tried to quell it. These men, it seemed to me, were connected to the missing academics. Was there more to my kidnap than ransom?

'The conditions at this second place were worse. It was as if my captors were saying: "Playtime's over. Let's get down to business."

'That night my legs were chained and later they were to remain so for much of the time. One chain was wrapped around in a figure eight about my ankles and fastened with a padlock. It was firm, but not so tight that it bit into my flesh, although the weight of my own body made it uncomfortable. There was no freedom to move. When I was placed inside the room the first evening, I was made to cover my head with a double layer plastic bag, encasing my whole head, right down to my shoulders. A guard sat in a chair next to me the whole night, his gun pointing towards my head. Occasionally I lifted a bit of the bag, to get a breath of fresh air. It wasn't tight, but it enclosed my whole head so that at times I felt as if I would suffocate. The moment I lifted it or even angled my head so that I could see through the gap at the bottom, the guard barked at me "Pull it down!" I would do so and wait for another chance, but he never took his eyes off me. The artificial light was permanently on. My bed had been moved with me, both layers of the yellowing foam mattress, and I lay on it, chained like a dog, my head covered, wondering how much worse it could get before my body simply gave up. My spirit was still strong. I was determined I would live.

'The next morning, the bag was removed from my head, but I was given strict instructions not to look at my abductors. I complained about the chain on my legs to a man who appeared to be the leader of this group and a short while later he had it removed. I wasn't chained again at this place, which I later found out was called Doha, although subsequently I was kept almost permanently chained. Typically of them, the discarded chain and bag were simply dumped in a corner of the room, where they lay ignored. My abductors never removed anything when they had finished with it; it would just lie and fester where they had left it. Eventually I tired of seeing both bag and chain lying there and put them both into an empty drawer which I'd found, to get them out of my sight. No one noticed. It never occurred to me to use the chain as a weapon myself, although even if it had there was little I could do, with guards posted outside the room. After that first night, there was no guard actually in the room with me, which was what gave me the chance to examine the files near the desk. I supposed they knew how unable I was to escape, and my powerlessness filled me with anger.

'There was an air-conditioner mounted on the wall of the room where I was being held, powered by a hidden generator. I was able to control it myself, and later the switching on or off of the light. That small amount of control over my own environment meant a great deal to one as deprived of free will as I now was. There was also a small fan. It was the end of May and Beirut was beginning to get warm. I was glad of the chance to ease my discomfort in the heat.

'I discovered my watch was missing, taken from my discarded trousers whilst I slept. I complained vociferously, since without any way of telling the time my perception of reality would be even more distorted. After two or three days they provided me with a large Sony clock, set, I discovered later, an hour fast. I don't know why – perhaps just to confuse me, although many of them couldn't tell the time themselves. I would ask them the time and they'd never know; they'd just tell me some absurd hour like two in the afternoon, when I knew perfectly well it was at least six or seven in the evening. Without even a glimpse of daylight, it was impossible to keep track of the hours without a clock.

'I had nothing to do but think. I had no books or anything else with which to occupy my mind. When I asked for news, they brought me a radio, tuned into an FM music programme. I asked them to allow me to retune it, but they refused. I hated the loud, brash music and resented it mocking my need for some sort of contact with the outside world. I craved just a short bulletin on the BBC World Service. Occasionally I could hear explosions in the distance, once quite near to where I was being held. I could even feel the vibrations, and heard heavy continuous rumbling which I at first took to be aircraft noises, but subsequently decided must be tanks, since the noise would approach, remain stationary for a time and then move forward. I wondered what was happening in this volatile country. Denied news, I insisted the radio was taken away.

'Around the third day I was there – ten days after I was captured – I was visited by one of my abductors, a self-confessed Palestinian. He came in and crouched down near me, regarding me intently. I asked him if he was the boss, since the people around me seemed quite different from those who

61

had held me for the first week. He held up one hand, with three of his fingers extended. His eyes never leaving mine, he counted his fingers: "One, two, three." Then he said, "This is me," and pointed to the third finger. It appeared he was third in their chain of command. I asked him his name and he said it was Abas.

'It was the first sort of conversation I had held since I was kidnapped and I suddenly realised how much I missed ordinary human contact. I had never been a gregarious person, although I enjoyed mixing with people occasionally, but I don't think I knew how much I needed the simple encounters with people one ordinarily takes for granted. I asked Abas if he would come again, and he said he would; I looked forward to it. His English was fairly good, since he was an intelligent man. He wasn't an intellectual, but neither was he a thug like so many of the others who held me.

'I thought how much I missed everything I had begun to take for granted. Sunnie, my ordinary life, my friends – even my beer. Lonely suddenly, I asked Abas the question always on my mind.

'"How long will I be held a prisoner?"

'Abas shifted, and furrowed his brow. He looked straight at me. "I don't know," he said, eventually. "It depends on when my friends are released."

'At that moment the last shreds of illusion were torn from me and I faced up to the truth, which I had known for some time, but refused to acknowledge. I hadn't been abducted for my money, nor was I being held for ransom. I was a political prisoner, like John McCarthy, Terry Waite and those who had gone before me. Some of them had already been held for more than four years. Now it was happening to me.

'I looked directly at Abas and asked him again how long.

'"It might be one month. It might be two. Maybe longer."

'There was understanding in his eyes, but no compassion,

no sympathy. To him I was a victim of a war he had not chosen but was determined to win. It could just as easily have been his life – it happened to be mine. There was no malice, but the determination was unrelenting.

'I complained to Abas that I was not able to exercise enough because of the smallness of the room. He told me he'd been imprisoned for a year with twenty people in a room no bigger than mine. He seemed genuinely surprised that I was complaining. Was I not pleased to have the whole room to myself?

'I realised then how little I knew about this war.

'I had been in the middle of it for years; I had orchestrated my life around the shelling, endured air raids and bombing, learned to deal with shortages, no water, no power. Yet I had learned nothing of the causes of all these things, although I had experienced their effects. I had learned to differentiate between the various militias and factions, with no real under-standing of the ideals for which each one fought. Now I was a part of it, a direct player instead of a spectator.

'I sifted through the bits and pieces I could remember from newspaper reports. I seemed to remember some issue involving Palestinians held in Britain. Abas' English was very good; could he have been held there? Were those the friends to whom he referred? Mrs Thatcher was brought up frequently and very acrimoniously by all the kidnappers who held me at one time or another. Their language was the colourful hyper-bole one came to recognise in this part of the world, hostile and vengeful against the British Government but Mrs Thatcher in particular.

'After I was released, I learned that around this time there were seventeen Arabs being held in Kuwait who were alleg-edly responsible for the bombing of the American and French Embassies in Kuwait in 1983. The issue was connected to the Western hostages for a long time; the kidnap groups wanted the release of the seventeen Arabs in exchange for some or all of the hostages. At the time I knew nothing of this; confused, I still associated myself with Palestinians being held in Britain.

'Abas came to see me again and we talked about things in general; it was the only tenuous link I had with normality. He never hid his face from me, and with him I didn't have to hide mine. Later, the kidnappers would force me to cover my face with a towel whenever they came in, and I would go for months without ever seeing a human countenance. After I left Doha, I never saw Abas again. Months later, when I was at Kaslik, one of the kidnappers came into my room and asked me if I would work with them.

'"Doing what?" I asked.

'"We want you to go to Israel," he said, "and bring back one of our men for us."

'"What will you do with him when you get him back here?" I said. "Will you kill him?"

'He was silent for a moment and then nodded. "Yes," he said.

'"I'm sorry," I replied. "My killing days are over. I can't do it."

'Two days later, I gathered from the conversation around me that the ridiculous notion of using me had been dropped and that instead the leader of the group at Kaslik recruited a young Palestinian, a boy who owned a motorcycle which needed a new battery. Apparently, the boy was told he'd be given a new battery if he'd help them. Two days after he left Lebanon, a building was blown up in Tel Aviv, killing both the boy and the man he'd been sent to find, Abas.

'I found it difficult to believe they'd actually asked me, that they would even contemplate letting me go, never mind sending me to Israel to help them kill one of their former soldiers. Yet they seemed serious and their actions were so bizarre I had no choice but to believe they really considered recruiting me.

'With the new realisation that I was a hostage came a new determination to survive, no matter the circumstances. Previously I had held on to the hope that my release was imminent. Now I had to face the fact that it could be months and adjust my mentality accordingly. Conditions were worse than they had been during the first week, at Sidon, but they were by no means inhumane at that stage. I had to live each day as it came, in the present, however unpalatable that might be, rather than in the future, which for now had been frozen. I began to keep a conscious diary, marking a tally on my cell wall. I tried to memorise as many details as possible, as much to fill and occupy my mind as to bring my captors to justice when I was released.

'The electricity power supply was usually on for most of the day; for three hours in the morning and two in the evening it was off. At first I thought it was from eight until eleven, but when I realised my clock was an hour fast, I adjusted my assumption. Details began to matter. I'd have to light candles when I had no power, since being underground there was no natural light, and I had no wish to be in the dark. There was never any objection to my using candles, which they provided, and I was given matches with which to light them. Again in the evening, from five to seven, the light would go off and I'd light my candles.

'The food was unremarkable, but edible. Arabic bread was served with everything: breakfast, lunch and supper. I hated it, and I was always given more of it than I could or wanted to eat. I'd tear off a large piece and preserve that to nibble on during the course of the next several hours – it was like tearing off heavy-duty paper, and tasted no better – since it was the kind of food that quickly assuaged one's immediate hunger when the meal was served, but left one feeling a little peckish an hour or two after having had the meal. I was never really happy with the food I had the whole time; despite forty years in

Lebanon I loathed Arabic food and was still a bacon-and-eggs man. It wasn't very satisfying either, but I would eat as much as I wanted and throw the rest into the wastepaper basket which they'd left in the corner of the room for me.

'I didn't eat a great deal and always ended up throwing food away, which I rather resented. I wasn't being starved, but I certainly wasn't overfed, and I hated throwing away food which, had it been more palatable, I would have eaten. It was usually an excess of rice, beans or corn which I discarded; numerous times they served me a plate of boiled corn, very badly cooked – lumpy, unpleasant to look at and not particularly satisfying in terms of diet. A great deal of that met its fate in the wastepaper basket. Alternatively they'd serve me a great deal of rice, and nothing else, which came to a similar end. I tried countless times to tell them they were giving me too much Arabic bread, which I was throwing away, and for a time they reduced the amount they were giving me, but always forgot and returned to normal after a while.

'On one occasion, much to my astonishment, I was provided with a very good meal of Dover sole, beautifully prepared and garnished. I couldn't understand it, and vacillated between thinking it was the last meal of the condemned man or a signal of my release. Of course it was neither; it had been prepared for someone who didn't arrive and given to me because it was spare. It happened once or twice more, and was always a prominent event when it did.

'They were very regular with my meals, then; I only had to knock on the door and ask for food once or twice, each time in the evening. Breakfast was around nine o'clock in the morning, I had lunch around one, and supper at about eight or eight-thirty in the evening. It became my only way of telling the time when they took from me the Sony display clock, which they had given me when I arrived. They became obsessive with me not seeing their faces and I had been using the reflection in the clock to see parts of the room which I was unable to see directly, if they were present. Once or twice it was moved to an angle where I could see nothing of interest in the reflection, but eventually they tired of this game and took the clock away altogether. I had no way of knowing whether it was day or night, except for my meals and the regularity of the power being cut off.

'I was given books, to relieve the terrible monotony of my isolation. They were all paperbacks and most of them I read at least twice. My favourite was a Wilbur Smith novel, which I enjoyed reading a great deal. In typical Arab fashion, everything they brought into my room remained there; they never took it out again. The books piled up in the corner, untouched except by me; they got more and more dogeared as I read and reread them, but still they stayed, a tottering column forever threatening to collapse but never quite doing so.

'One of the guards, who seemed more sympathetic towards me, brought me a pack of playing cards at my request, so that I was able to play patience in all the variations which I knew, and quite a few which I invented. It passed the time. The same man used to bring me biscuits once a week, always eleven biscuits and always the same type of shortbread biscuits. Why eleven was a question which mystified and fascinated me. I believe he worked at a biscuit manufacturing establishment in Beirut called Gandour, since they always had that stamped on them. It was possibly part of his take-home ration that he was bringing me. I'd spread the biscuits over two days; fortunately there were no mice or vermin in my cell. This guard was always very good to me, given the fact that we were on opposite sides in this war. Perhaps in another time, another place, we would have been friends.

'I decided when I wanted to sleep or when I wanted to read. There was a steel or chrome chair there the entire time, so sometimes I'd get up from my mattress and sit in it and read.

It even had a soft seat, so that it was reasonably comfortable for me. I had complete choice over my environment, as miserable and small as it was. I could do as I felt like within the limited confines of my existence as a prisoner. I developed a routine of a kind; I'd eat breakfast, then exercise myself in this small area. I'd pace four or five steps from one corner to another, then turn round and pace four or five steps back. I'd criss-cross back and forth, slowly, since I couldn't walk too fast at the best of times. My impromptu exercise class would last for ten or fifteen minutes, before I had to rest, but its benefit was twofold: I was keeping my muscles moving so that they didn't atrophy in my confinement, but I was also making a positive gesture, more to myself than to anyone else. I was saying that I would survive this, that I would come through. As a Battle of Britain pilot I had been shot down half a dozen times, and endured horrific burns and reconstructive surgery. Living in Beirut I had dealt with shelling, air raids and invasions. I was not about to crumble now.

'I decided to examine the lock on the wooden door, aware that even if I managed to break through it there was still a steel door on the other side. Brushing that thought aside, I bent down to look. I straightened up suddenly, then crouched down again for a better look. There was no doubt; I could actually see the bolt which should have been firmly anchored into the gate in the doorpost. It wasn't. It was quite definitely loose – my captors had failed to engage the bolt properly. The wood was old and very badly worn – it looked as if it had been hacked at some stage in its past. Beyond it, on the outer steel door, I could see the catch of the yale lock which fastened it.

'Adrenalin pumped through me and breathless and excited I began to fiddle with the bolt, which was just within reach. I was terrified I would be discovered, but determined to see this through. My fingers seemed even slower than usual, fumbling with the lock. Every rasp of the metal appeared as loud as a drum roll; I was sure the noise would bring hordes of armed guards rushing to my cell. Nothing happened. I continued working the lock, slowly, carefully, holding my breath. I had nothing to work with and cursed my clumsiness. Just as I was about to give up, there was a quick rush and the bolt slid back. I stared at it a moment, stunned, then I was galvanised into action. The yale lock took but a few moments more, and it was undone. The doors were open. I could just walk out of my cell.

'Gathering my courage, I eased the doors open, and peered into the corridor. There was no guard outside, and the place seemed unwatched. Boldly I stepped into the hall, and started walking towards the front door. I was going to make it. Freedom was just ten feet away . . . nine . . . eight . . . just seven feet to go. I pushed my stiff legs to walk faster. Daylight, liberty, the world just five feet from me . . . four . . . three . . .

'"Get back! Get back! What are you doing? Get back!"

'I froze. The guard behind me was running, screaming in Arabic and English. I turned round slowly.

'"I needed the toilet. I hammered on the door, but nobody came." I looked at him in as innocent and casual a manner as I could manage. He didn't seem to be reaching for his gun and I continued. "What was I to do? I called you, I needed the toilet urgently." I paused, and held my breath. Had he believed me?

'Angrily the guard gestured towards the bathroom. I moved towards it, relief flowing through my veins. I couldn't think how close I had come to freedom; I shut my mind to it. Instead I concentrated on how lucky I was to have got away with an attempted escape undetected. After I had finished in the bathroom, I was escorted back to my cell, which I entered with resignation. The doors were firmly locked behind me and the guard jiggled them both suspiciously to make sure.

'I sank down on the mattress, and a sudden wave of fear swept through me. If the guard had thought I was escaping, he could well have simply shot me and asked questions later. I hadn't even had any idea where I was running to; my instinct for liberty had overridden practical considerations. My cell seemed smaller, the four walls closing in. It was hard to have a glimmer of hope, even wild, unreasonable, impractical hope, only to have it dashed. Eventually, exhausted, I slept.

'The next day I was visited by someone whom I knew to be fairly senior in the movement, a man called Abdullah Ja'far. He was the President of a group calling itself the Union of Palestinian Refugees in Lebanon, or so I believed. He came in and sat down in the chair near my mattress, and regarded me solemnly.

'"Yesterday," Ja'far said. "Tell me about yesterday."

'I took a deep breath and told him the same as I had told the guard the previous day: that I had been trying to go to the toilet. I said I knocked on the door and my other hand had fallen on to the inner door which had opened. It wasn't too far from the truth; several times before I had hammered on the door when I wanted to go to the bathroom. Usually I would be answered immediately and told not to hammer, although how else I was to attract their attention I didn't know, and they offered no alternative, so I continued to knock. I could tell Ja'far only half believed me, but I didn't have to try too hard to convince him, and he swallowed my explanation.

'Then I learned why.

'"I want to sleep with you."

'It came out of nowhere, and I started as if an electric shock had been passed through me. He simply came straight out and said it, as if he expected me to say yes. I stared, revolted.

'Ja'far took my silence to mean I was considering the proposition. "I can release you," he went on, meaningfully.

'I could think of nothing to say, and irritated he barked, "I can force you, you know."

'Stung, I replied, "I'd rather you didn't."

'"I want to sleep with you," Ja'far repeated. "I can release you, if you say yes."

'"So you say," I argued, unsure how to deal with this and still survive. "But what guarantee will I have if I allow you to sleep with me that I'll be released?"

'He leapt up as if he'd been shot. "Guarantee?" he shouted. "What is this 'guarantee'? 'Guarantee'? What does this mean?"

'I tried to explain, but angrily he rushed out into the corridor, still shouting "Guarantee? What is this 'guarantee'?" I could hear him as he ran down the hall, calling to his fellow guards.

'I sat still, too shocked to move. I had had no training or preparation for anything like that in my war years or indeed at any other time in my life. I was revolted by the whole thing. I wasn't afraid, but my hostility towards the group as a whole increased, if that were possible given that they had already deprived me of my freedom. I wondered if that would be the end of the matter or whether this Ja'far character would return, and with some trepidation I waited. He didn't come back whilst I was at Doha, although he was to try again months later.

'With so little to occupy my mind, the smallest event took on the greatest significance and I would worry away at things that puzzled me for hours and days, trying to learn enough to be able to file them away as explained. I had so little access to any source of information, many of my hypotheses were pure conjecture, though sometimes I would learn the solution months after the incident which mystified me. Fairly frequently I heard Morse code being used to send messages, but it was too fast for me to read. Frustrated, I could work out a few letters, but rarely read any words. During my flying days

71

I'd picked up enough to get through the test I was required to pass, but it was only a speed of eight or ten words a minute, and this was much faster; even if I hadn't been so rusty it would have been too difficult for me. Strangely I only ever heard outgoing messages, never incoming ones.

'I used to hear strange knockings on the wall next door to mine, which at first I was unable to identify. It transpired, from snippets of conversations I overheard, that one of the Palestinians there had spent seventeen years in South Africa, teaching French I believe, and was now giving French lessons to the lower echelons of the people who were holding me. Sometimes when the classes ended I could hear his pupils calling "Thank you, professor" or "Goodnight, professor". Not long afterwards, I heard a good deal of hammering in the corridor, and I asked what it was. The guard nearest to me said they were putting on a new door, a steel one, similar to the outer door on my cell. He didn't specify where it was being put, but it soon became obvious that it was the room next to mine. I wondered if they were preparing it for another prisoner, since they were going to so much trouble to make it secure, but I never found out.

'My morale was still quite high and I still hadn't lost hope of being released soon, despite Abas' warning that I would be held until his friends were free and my knowledge that the British Government refused to deal with kidnappers. I even entertained hopes that I might be rescued.

'These hopes were bolstered one day when what I believed to be officials of the legitimate Lebanese Army made an inspection tour of the building in which I was being held. I'd been a prisoner for four or five weeks by then. There was a terrible furore outside the building, which I could hear, even underground as I was. It seemed the military forces who were looking for me wanted to search the place and I held my breath in suspense. But it was a nightmare repetition of the day I'd been captured, when we passed through each checkpoint and the car was never searched. The soldiers were no more than ten yards from my room, yet they didn't search. The kidnappers must have persuaded them it was unnecessary; they were consummate liars and obviously convinced the soldiers I wasn't there. As I heard them leave, the disappointment was almost more than I could bear.

'Shortly afterwards, I was awakened at two or three in the morning. Once more we were changing location; perhaps the brush with the military had unsettled my abductors and they thought it better to move. I had been at this second place, Doha, exactly a month, and a prisoner for five weeks. By my calculations it was now the 18th of June. My wedding anniversary.'

For Sunnie it had been the longest five weeks of her life. Determined to keep the vow she had made to herself the first morning after Jackie disappeared, she resolutely refused to leave Beirut. Whenever someone tried to persuade her to go, she cited the dangers she had already withstood. She had been kidnapped herself briefly, a number of years before, by a group who mistook her for a woman involved in the blowing up of a top PLO leader. Sunnie had been interrogated for five terrifying hours before one of their leaders arrived and recognised her from the riding school. She was released, shaking and afraid, and thoroughly rebuked by Jackie for putting herself in jeopardy by her constant trips across Beirut.

'I had been held for five hours, and I was literally shaking from head to foot with nerves when they let me go. Jackie had now been missing for five weeks. How on earth would he be coping?

'The first week after Jackie was taken, I was in pieces. I couldn't do anything, couldn't see anyone. I could barely dress myself. But then I realised that Jackie's only hope lay with me. I had to make sure he got enough publicity to get the British Government working. He mustn't end up a forgotten hostage, mourned and missed only by me. I looked at how Jill Morrell was fighting for the man she loved; she formed "The Friends of John McCarthy" and hammered away in every way she knew how. Jackie was relying on me to get him out, and I wasn't going to disappoint him.

'I did hundreds of interviews for newspapers, radio and television, of any nationality, for anyone who represented any organisation that could keep Jackie's name on people's lips. I contacted all the people I knew who might have influence, legitimate or otherwise, and called in all the favours I was owed. I even tried to contact the head of the Amal militia, Nabih Berri, although I never managed to see him. I spoke to the head of Syrian Intelligence, who raised my hopes by saying they had arrested one of the kidnappers, but nothing came of it. On Jackie's seventy-fifth birthday, 11 June 1989, I made a fresh appeal, and carried on waiting.

'Up to this point, I hadn't really thought about how I was going to live. My only consideration was what had happened to Jackie, and how I was going to get him released or at least find out what had happened to him. But the rest of the world carried on and I was forced to face up to practicalities. Two or three weeks after Jackie was taken, when the worst of the shock had settled to a dull ache inside me, I pulled myself together and faced facts. I was unable to draw a cheque on any of our accounts, because they were not in both our names at that time. Jackie and I had always had a joint account before, but we had to reconfirm me as a signatory to it by re-signing a form at the bank every year, and back in 1982 we had been about to do this when the Israeli invasion had started. We couldn't get out of the flat, the shelling was so intense and then the bank closed. There was absolutely no chance of having the accounts redone in our joint names then, and that was still the situation when Jackie was kidnapped seven years later. He never really trusted me not to spend it all anyway!

'I spoke to the then Ambassador, Alan Ramsey, and asked him if there was anything he could do to get me some of what was, after all, my money too. He tried, but met with no success. I was unable to use any of our money for the whole two and a half years Jackie was held, although after a year of constant badgering the bank finally allowed me the interest from our capital – a tiny amount – though never the capital itself. I had no pension. I was completely destitute. The first help I had was through the journalist Robert Fisk, who was then working for *The Times*. He wrote an article about me, and some of the paper's readers sent me money with which to buy food, which was desperately needed and much appreciated. The RAF Benevolent Fund gave me a little money too, to help me get by.

'It was hard to think about these sorts of things as the days stretched into weeks and there was still no word of Jackie. The day of our wedding anniversary, I sat in the flat alone, feeling the silence and emptiness echo. At that moment I felt just as much a prisoner as Jackie must be and I wondered when we'd next spend our anniversary together. Where was he? What was he doing now?'

FIVE

Time Passes: Kaslik

'The move this time was a more hurried and tense affair. My abductors seemed more afraid of discovery, and their treatment of me was less indulgent. After I was awakened I was given only a few moments to dress, then bundled out of the room and back down the corridor to the underground car-park which I'd entered a month before. I was pushed against the wall, so that my forehead grazed the uneven brickwork, and my arms were held, firmly but not roughly, behind my back whilst my wrists were tied together with a long piece of cloth. When I was turned around I saw a car with the boot lid already raised and before I had time to protest I was lifted up and pushed into it. There was no question this time of being allowed to sit in the back of the car. I was feeling parched and dizzy, and despite the apparent haste I asked for a drink, to which they agreed. I was handed a bottle of lukewarm water, then the lid of the boot was slammed down and I was left in darkness.

'I could hear a good deal of movement going on around me and lay there listening, trying to work out what was happening, for fifteen minutes or so. Despite the strange thumps I couldn't guess what they were doing. Eventually the car engine was started and I felt the car driving up a steep slope, presumably the exit to this underground garage.

I fell against the back of the boot, uncomfortable but relieved that at least there wasn't a guard in there with a Kalashnikov against my head. They had told me they were taking me to another place, and I had no illusions this time that I was being released. I only hoped that my prison would not be worse than the one I'd just left but, judging by the treatment I was receiving, the regime was getting harder rather than more tolerant. After fifteen minutes' driving the car stopped and I drew a sigh of relief. At seventy-five I felt I was no longer cut out for travelling in this unconventional manner, and my arms and legs ached from being cramped in this small space. The darkness was suffocating.

'There was no movement towards the boot of the car, however, and soon I felt the car jolting as something was loaded up on to it. I conjectured that the noise I had heard before we set off must have been some sort of roof rack being affixed to the car. Whatever they were loading was placed not only on the roof, but even on the lid of the boot. I think it must have been some sort of vegetable produce, which would have made very effective camouflage. It would also have deterred any over-zealous checkpoint soldiers from looking in the boot if they had to fight past cabbages and cauliflowers to do so. After about twenty minutes, I felt the car being pulled down on one side and then the other as if the men outside were tightening ropes. Throughout the operation I could hear muffled voices as the men talked to one another, but not enough to recognise any words.

'Finally the car started again, and I tried to brace myself against the walls of the boot. I felt a clicking in my ears, as one does on a aeroplane flight, and guessed that our altitude was changing and that the car must be going uphill. I could feel the pressure altering as we climbed higher, although I had no idea in which direction we were going. There was a great deal of twisting and turning as we careered round hairpin bends at what seemed like a great speed to me, trapped as I was in the boot. I was being thrown from one side of the car to another, banging my head and jolting every bone in my body as we turned corners. Desperately I worked at the cloth binding my hands, to try to get them free so that I would be able to brace myself against the sides. Fortunately my kidnappers hadn't tied the cloth very securely, and I was able to free myself, which helped considerably. There was no ventilation, since there were no airholes, and my chest was tightening because of the stuffiness. I could see car headlights when they came up behind the car in which I was travelling, shards of light shining through cracks in the bodywork of the car. I tried to think of some way of signalling to someone – anyone – that I was trapped, but there was no way of opening the boot from the inside. Frantically I tried to devise some way of breaking the wiring of the rear lights, to signal or at least break them so that it might attract attention. I pulled several trailing wires from their places but without success. I could feel my slim chances of escape receding with every mile that passed; I was sure my new prison would be far more secure than the previous two had been. This was not to be a brief captivity.

'Suddenly I was thrown against the side of the boot and kept there by force, as if the car was circling. I realised we must be going around a roundabout, but the car did at least three circuits before we turned off, judging from the length of time I was held against the side. Days later, after racking my brains and puzzling for hours, I remembered a very large roundabout on the main Beirut to Damascus road just outside the village of Kaslik. The hamlet was a little way from the main road, but the main access to it was via this roundabout. We went round it at a high speed, judging from the way I was being thrown about, and I could hear the squeal of tyres. Something strange nagged at my memory and I tried to analyse what was wrong. Then I realised: we were going around the roundabout the wrong

way, against the traffic. Fortunately there can have been few
vehicles on the road at that time of night or we would have
caused an accident. It made me wonder what Sunnie would
ever have thought happened to me. How ironic it would have
been, to be kidnapped and then die in a car crash.

'Shortly after we turned off onto the side road, the car
slowed down so that it was almost stationary. Through the
cracks in car's bodywork I could see a wall, very close to
the car. Had I been able, I could have reached out my hand
and touched the brickwork. The car came to a halt, and I felt
the vegetables being offloaded, the suspension groaning as the
weight was lifted.

'Quickly I put my hands back in the cloth binding and
wound the material around them again. I was taken out of
the boot and stumbled against the side of the car. I had been
in it for almost an hour and my legs were so stiff they were
unable to support me. Without my hands to steady myself I
would have fallen if one of the guards hadn't put out his arm
to help me. No one detected that I had freed myself, much to
my relief. I was led down some steps, and one of the men yelled
"Down! Down!" Startled, I ducked my head, wondering what I
had done wrong or what was going to happen. I was pushed in
the small of my back and I paused, unsure what to do next.

'"Down! Down the steps!" the man cried. Suddenly I understood the confusion and started to make my way down the
concrete stairs to a door. The steps turned to the right, and
one of the kidnappers took my arm to guide me in the right
direction. He was trying to be gentle, and they all slowed their
pace to allow me to catch up, since they seemed to realise I
was unable to move any faster. It was dark and as they hadn't
blindfolded me this time I could make out where I was going
by the light of the hand torch one of them held. There was little
to see: I was simply taken into a building, without getting the
chance to observe my surroundings.

79

'I was led into a room and the two foam mattresses which had travelled with me from Sidon to Doha now appeared once more, and were placed in a corner where I was presently installed. My feet were facing a window, around three feet from it, and I was left to sleep, with instructions not to move from my bed. Exhausted, too tired even to be curious, I obeyed.

'The next morning I set about establishing as much as I could about my new surroundings. I walked over to the window when the guards were absent and looked out. I swiftly discovered which direction was east and which west – a hangover from my days as a pilot, I suppose – and then observed the view more closely. To the left I could see there was a small entrance driveway that ended in a cul-de-sac, with a wall. To the right I could see a villa, on a slightly higher level of ground than the building in which I was incarcerated. There was a fig tree roughly thirty yards away from me, probably part of the villa next door, although it was difficult to tell on which side of the dividing wall between the two houses it was, from my vantage point. I used the shadow from the fig tree to tell what time of day it was, since I had neither watch nor clock. The old ways are still accurate. I would wake up in the morning, when the first slivers of light came in from the outside and hit the wall behind me on my left. I would watch the shadows move clockwise around the wall, until it disappeared. Sometimes that was all I did all day. I would mark off the days on a calendar which I scratched on the wall, wondering as I did so if I was going to spend the rest of my life watching shadows on a wall.

'I suppose establishing the direction I was facing, using the sun to tell the time, going back into the past to discover ways to survive the present, was my way of coping. I had been taught virtually from childhood to notice where the sun came up and went down, and my flying days set the pattern in my mind so that now I drew on it almost instinctively. It was natural to me to watch the position of the sun, and I found my estimates of the time of day were very accurate. I allowed for the equinoxes, again a flashback to my RAF training. It's strange how everything in one's life has a purpose in the end, whether large or small.

'Soon afterwards the kidnappers blocked my view of the outside world with a mattress against the window. I was left with a slim angle of vision, through which I could just see the fig tree, until they deprived me even of that.

'I was chained down once more, this time permanently. My captors asked me which leg I would prefer them to chain and testily I told them the right leg, since I slept on my left side because that was facing the door, and having my right leg fastened would give me more room for manoeuvre than if it had been my left. It was a yard and a half in length and attached by a small padlock to a bracket on the floor, then wrapped around my leg and fastened with another small padlock. I counted the links, though I forget their number. Each link was an inch long, and they were electrowelded together – I could tell that by the neatness of the weld. I often complained it was too tight around my ankle, but only once or twice did they ever adjust it. It was tolerable if I stayed motionless, but the minute I moved it hurt and bit into my flesh.

'I was released to go to the bathroom, and once the guard watching me forgot to fasten the padlock afterwards. I slipped across the room to the window, trying to keep out of range of a video camera which they had installed to monitor me from the guardroom elsewhere in the house. No sooner had I moved, however, than I heard them coming to my door; they had seen me. I had a few seconds whilst they unlocked the door in which to dash back to my bed, but they even saw that. Two guards rushed in and chained me down again, shouting and cursing all the time. An hour later they brought someone else who adjusted the position of the bed so that I couldn't see the window.

'They were still not happy with the situation and decided to move the point of attachment of the chain to the floor further away from the window. Originally the end of the chain was fastened to an iron loop attached by bolts to the floor by the wall. Now they wanted to change it to a point in the middle of the floor, two yards away. It was not an easy thing to do. First of all they had to create a foundation for the bracket, which they did using a claw chisel and hammer to break through the tiling and the underlying concrete. Then they took a piece of reinforcing iron and made it into the shape of a horseshoe, before cementing it into the hole they had made in the tiles and the concrete.

'Whilst all this was being done, I was moved to a corner of the room behind the door, with my back to where they were working. They forced me to place a towel over my head, as they always did whenever they were in the room with me. It came down to my nose, so my mouth and nose were free, and I choked on the cement dust. I asked for a cushion or something to sit on whilst they were working, and one of the guards who was actually doing the cementing came over and showed me his hands. He laughed unpleasantly, and passed his hands, covered with soft cement, around my face as if he were going to smear me with it. I ignored him, and he laughed again and went back to his work.

'When the work was finished, I was returned to my mattress, now further from the window, and instructed not to touch the new bracket. The minute they left the room that was the first thing I did, and I wiggled the iron loop around in the hope that it was possible to pull it out before the concrete had set too firmly. It made no difference, much to my chagrin, and I had to accept my new position, too far from the window to see out from it.

'Yet despite all the trouble they had gone to, frequently they forgot to relock the chain after they had freed me in the morning to go to the bathroom. Sometimes it took half an hour for them to realise, sometimes longer. One night they still hadn't relocked the padlock, and I was just about to go to sleep when it dawned on me. Realising the futility of trying to escape, particularly with the video camera in the room, I lay on my back on the mattress and defiantly waved my legs in the air, like a cockroach that has got itself stuck on its back. They saw me on the video camera and I heard them burst out laughing, before they wandered into the room and, still grinning, chained me down.

'I was determined to keep up my routine of exercise, as a way of disciplining both my mind and body. I asked the guards where I could walk, and this provoked lively arguments amongst them as to where the limits should be set. The room itself was only five yards square, so the choice shouldn't have seemed too wide, but they managed to find plenty to quarrel about. I had to walk within the range of this video camera, and one fellow would say, "Must walk from here to here," indicating the limits with his hands. The next day the new guard would say, "No, you must walk from here to here," setting new limits. One said I could walk only the length of my bed, which given the impedimenta surrounding it – my chain, bottles of water and so on – left me less than two paces to walk in each direction. I pointed out the futility of that and sat down on my bed defiantly, refusing to walk two steps at a time.

'Eventually I asked one of the guards to get all the others together for a discussion which would set the limits once and for all. To my surprise, the fellow who had suggested that I walk only the length of my bed smiled at me and apologised. Much to my astonishment, he held out his hand to be shaken. The moment meant a great deal to me; I had been treated as a human being, and for a brief span of time my dignity had been restored. I shook his hand. It was the only time I ever received any kind of apology for my treatment or indeed my incarceration. I settled to my beat, walking from my bed to just beneath the television camera in the far corner – the path all had agreed upon – with a renewed hope in my heart.

'They then installed an intercom system in the room, giving me a small microphone beside my bed, with a receiver on their desk in the guardroom so that we could communicate. If I was walking my beat between the bed and the corner of the room, and I strayed out of the line of sight of the video camera, they would tell me to get back into line on the intercom.

'I had been a prisoner five weeks when I was moved to Kaslik. I had never dreamed when I was taken – or even when I realised that this was no ransom kidnapping but a political abduction – that I would be held for so long. I certainly knew it was no fun anymore. I knew that my incarceration could be just as long as that of the men who had been taken before me and had already been held for four years or more. I could keep up my morale by laughing at the guards, which helped me psychologically; I looked at them and they seemed like ten- or twelve-year-old little boys. But I also knew that the organisers of this movement were danger-ous soldiers fighting a war they were determined to win. I was but a pawn in the game, and I never deluded myself that I was anything more than expendable to them. I tried to suppress such feelings, yet always in the back of my mind was the hope that maybe this was a dream or, if it wasn't, that I'd be rescued.

'During the five months I was held at Kaslik, my spirits were raised many times by the strange trickle of visitors to the kidnappers' headquarters. Their main meeting room was just across the hall from the room where I was being held – which was one of the reasons an escape was impossible –

but it meant that I could often hear snippets of conversations, which were filled out later by listening to the guards' comments to one another. Kaslik seemed to become a focus of interest to various people, much to the kidnappers' dislike. Syrian intelligence officers visited more than once, and there was one Syrian who frightened them more than anyone else. The leader of the group of kidnappers holding me at Kaslik was a man called Abid Awad, and this Syrian officer began questioning Awad quite aggressively. Whenever they had visitors, the kidnappers would always make sure there were at least two of them there, one of them strategically placed in a position of advantage, should the situation get out of hand. On this occasion, Awad had the greatest difficulty meeting the Syrian's questions, and the other kidnapper later told Awad he was on the point of drawing his gun and shooting the Syrian. None of the kidnappers would have wanted to survive discovery and capture by the Syrians; they feared the treatment they would receive were that ever to happen.

'The mere fact that the Syrians came seemed to me to indicate that they either knew or strongly suspected that I was there – if indeed they were Syrians; after all I didn't have the chance to ask them directly myself. I had no cause to doubt it, however; English was always spoken, which I assumed must be their common language – although Arabic would have seemed more logical – and the kidnappers would always announce panic-stricken to one another, "It's the Syrians!", which I'm sure wasn't for my benefit but for their own. I always hoped the Syrians would try to rescue me, but perhaps they were never sure enough that I was there. I longed for the British Government to try to rescue me, since it seemed to me that the kidnappers hated Mrs Thatcher so much the British Government would have nothing to lose by doing so. I had all sorts of grandiose ideas as to what the outside world could do to get me out – I envisioned the SAS diving through windows and replayed their liberation of the Iranian Embassy in London. If they could do that there, where every shot they made would have to be accounted for, how much more could they achieve in the lawlessness of Lebanon? The villa where I was incarcerated certainly wasn't a fortress by any means, although my captors seemed to have every small arms available.

'It seemed so easy to me, trapped as I was with little else to think about. I tried to plan rescue attempts in my mind, but I had no real idea of how it could be done. I knew all the roads which approached the villa were watched from the windows; they could see any traffic in their immediate vicinity and identify it with very little trouble. But after dark, the SAS or the SBS would be in their element, or so it seemed to me.

'The kidnappers were even visited by someone who said he was from Amnesty International. One of the guards watching the road recognised the vehicle from some distance and called out to his fellow, "It's Amnesty International", which was how the visitor later identified himself. He spoke English, and asked various questions of the kidnappers but left without establishing my presence or achieving anything as far as I'm aware. I don't know if he knew I was there or not. I wasn't even sure if I qualified for Amnesty's attention, since I didn't know exactly what sort of prisoner I had to be to come under their remit.

'One day a Canadian man visited the villa, whom I believed to be part of the Royal Canadian Mounted Police. I had a sudden flashback to the days when I'd run a pub in Beirut and one of my regulars was a member of the Mounties, attached to the guards at the Canadian Embassy. One of the kidnappers, a Palestinian, had spent three years in Canada and he asked the visitor where he was from. The Canadian replied "Ottawa" and said he was now seconded to the police in Lebanon for some months, to widen his experience. He was the only person who visited the villa who actually asked what was being held in the room where I was. The Palestinian told him, "It's full of radio equipment." I was listening eagerly to every word and at this point I thought the Canadian must insist on seeing what was in the room. My spirits soared for a moment, and I lay on my mattress willing the man to come in. But despite his suspicions, the Canadian didn't investigate further. It seemed so obvious to me: did he not realise I was only feet away from him? I was beginning to think these visitors wouldn't notice me if I was in the same room as them. I discovered later that a number of foreign agents were seconded to Lebanon to try to halt the drugs runs. It was not impossible for them to have visited Kaslik on a different track entirely, which had nothing to do with me. Not all those who came to Kaslik were potential rescuers. I remember two people who visited, on separate occasions, who made me feel more despondent than anything else. One I know only slightly; we'd never been close friends, but we were on first name terms and I used to see him occasionally in the pub. I remember him well, but I choose not to name him.

He was obviously well known to my captors, and came to identify me. He was brought into the room where I was held, and from the corner of my eye I could see two figures peering towards me. Even though my head was covered with a towel, as the kidnappers insisted, I could peek through it, clearly enough to see my one-time friend point towards me.

'"Yes, that's him," he said. "No doubt at all."

'This had been a friend of mine, now turned Judas, an ally of these men who had deprived me of my most fundamental right, my freedom. I felt disgusted and betrayed.

'The second man who made me feel bought and sold, like so much merchandise, was another man who had been a friend. We used to drink together at my local, the Duke of Wellington, and laugh and joke together. He was Pakistani by birth, from the North West Frontier province. He came twice, and each time was greeted enthusiastically by my captors. I never saw him, but I recognised his voice and knew his name from the guards' greetings. He had been a good friend, and his betrayal hurt me even more. I often wondered if both these men helped identify me, so that the kidnappers could take me more easily, and I felt a tremendous sense of loss and betrayal. I never knew what happened to them. I only hoped they could live with what they had done to me by their complicity and silence.

'Conditions at Kaslik were tougher. I was not allowed to visit the bathroom as frequently as before; instead I was given a plastic bottle in which to urinate. I got them to cut off the top of it, to give me better access to it, and I had to empty it myself once a day when I was permitted to use the toilet further down the corridor. I had another bottle which held water, and both were kept by my mattress. Anything I wanted to throw away, such as excess food, I put into a bag which I was given.

'The box of books which I had had at my previous location, Doha, were brought to my room at Kaslik. Many of them I had read, but there were some which were still new to me. One day the guards came in and simply picked up the whole box of books and took them away, including one which I was in the middle of reading. I protested, but they just laughed and said they needed them, which I'm sure was false – most of them couldn't even read their own language, let alone English. It was just done to make my life more unpleasant. A new set of books were brought instead – all in German. I don't read German, which I told them, but they ignored me. I was never given another book again.

'I still had the old playing cards which I'd been given at Doha. The kidnappers had produced them a day or two after I'd arrived at Kaslik and given them to me. They borrowed them from me on several occasions; after the third time I somewhat grumpily pointed out that they were my playing cards, and had been given to me at Doha for me to play with. Thereafter they left them alone and didn't take them away from me again.

'Those cards became vital to me. As time passed, and it became more difficult to know what was truth and what was illusion, I came to rely on the cards to tell the difference for me. I would play patience, thinking of a certain incident that had happened or something I had been told, and if I managed to win the game then the event or story was true. If I lost, whatever I was thinking of must therefore have been false. I didn't believe the cards had any real power, and I even used to cheat to obtain the result I wanted, yet it was as good a way as any other to determine what was real and what wasn't. I was living in a crazy world, with crazy rules. I was like a child playing "She loves me, she loves me not" with a daisy; even if one believes it to be nonsense, one can't help but listen to the answer. There'd be days when I'd never win, and days when I'd have three or four victories in a row, which to me meant my luck was in that day. It was like a litmus test for truth.

'On one occasion, several guards came in and told me to dress quickly, because I was going to be released. Eagerly, I put on my trousers, which I still had at that stage, and followed them outside my room, not really taking in what was happening. We moved towards the entrance of the villa, men in front of me and behind, when suddenly the one at the front shouted, "Get back! Get back!" I stopped.

'"What is the problem?" I asked.

'"The boss is coming!"

'Moments later, Awad appeared and said to me, "Where are you going?"

'Undaunted, I replied, as I had before when I'd been caught, "To the toilet", and the other guards backed up the story.

'I was sure they were playing games with me. Awad's

appearance at that juncture was too smooth, too well rehearsed, and he accepted the story too easily. I tested it with the playing cards and lost. That meant the event was false, and I believed the cards. My captors could be so cruel sometimes, and yet so human, so normal, at others, when they treated me like a real person.

'One day the father of Abid Awad, the leader of the group in Kaslik, came in to see me, and brought a set of the Arabic chess game – Domar – and asked me if I wanted to play it. I had never played it before – I hadn't even played ordinary chess except once, when I had a broken leg – but I was very pleased to have something new to do, so I agreed and we started playing. Four or five of the guards stood around the two of us and started shouting instructions to me, eager to help me because I wasn't sure how to play. Every time I made a move, there would be a flurry of conflicting advice and criticism as to what I'd done wrong, all of them disagreeing with one another. I lost soundly, but Abid Awad's father asked if I wanted to play again, and this time I simply copied every move he made. If he moved a certain piece, I moved its opposite number. After a while he noticed what I was doing and stopped playing for a moment or two whilst he thought the thing out and decided how to combat me. Normally his response to any move I made was instantaneous, for he was well practised at the game. Finally he figured out what to do, and again beat me easily. It was a moment of relief from the utter tedium of my day that I thoroughly enjoyed; there were few enough of them.

'Unlike the guards, I was allowed to continue smoking, and I was provided with four cigarettes a day. Before I'd not been restricted to a certain number, but allowed to smoke as many as I wanted; here, four was the limit and it was almost always adhered to. The cigarettes would be brought with my breakfast, and I eked them out by smoking half a cigarette and stubbing it out, leaving the other half to light again later. It felt like I was lighting eight cigarettes rather than four that way. I could survive on the limited amount they gave me, but every so often I managed to wheedle an extra one or two from a less strict guard. Awad hated smoking, and banned it from any of his rooms. Because he recognised that I had been a relatively heavy smoker before my capture – it's not unknown for me to smoke fifty a day – special allowances were made for me, much to my relief. They were my one luxury, although they felt like a necessity to me.

'It was at Kaslik that Awad decided he wanted to become a television mogul. He proposed to start his own television station, for which he required a great deal of money, which he estimated to be a million dollars. Initially Awad hoped to obtain that via me, as ransom money, but after a while he decided that Yasser Arafat, the leader of the Palestinian Liberation Organisation (of which the kidnappers appeared to be a splinter group) was a more ready source of income. I heard them discussing Arafat's response: apparently he considered television to be a foolish business and this whole affair to be a foolish idea. Awad was furious, and stamped around the villa yelling, "Arafat doesn't understand!"

'Awad was an ambitious man. He intended first to take over the Presidency of the Union of Arab Refugees in Lebanon and next the PLO itself. He believed that the television station was the means to achieve his ambitions, and finally his father apparently managed to persuade Arafat to loan him a million dollars. It seemed Arafat himself obtained the money from Arabs in the United States, although I was never certain that was true.

'Early in the morning, one day in September, about three months after I'd been moved to Kaslik, a man whom everyone referred to as the Professor came dashing into the room. The Professor – whose real name was the same as mine, Jack, or rather Jacques, since he was of French origin – spoke good English, and seemed to be the accountant of the group who were holding me. He announced, "The money has arrived!", and sat down to apportion it. The cash hadn't actually been delivered, but the promise had been made and, two weeks later, it arrived. The leader who had held me before, at Sidon, Abu George, collected it from Beirut and brought it out to Kaslik. I thought he must have been a well-trusted man, to carry so much money in a suitcase. I heard the astonished gasps when the suitcase was opened and the money was revealed.

'I couldn't believe it: there I was, a British pensioner chained in a cell night and day, held captive by a group of kidnappers who were now setting up their own television station, with money given to them by a man I considered to be a terrorist leader, who had allegedly obtained it from America! It seemed so bizarre, I could hardly believe it was true, but they appeared to be in earnest. It made one wonder where the lines of reality were, and at times I seriously considered whether they, or I, were going mad.

'The next stage seemed to be recruiting people to actually work at this television station, if it wasn't pie in the sky. A number of foreigners started visiting the villa, and came to form this production team, which Awad was constructing around himself. I considered if perhaps I was hearing a radio play, the whole thing seemed so bizarre, but I dismissed the thought. These were definitely human voices in the room next to me – either that or I was indeed losing my mind. They were needed to man the TV unit – technicians, announcers, engineers and so on. Awad appointed himself Managing Director of the station, and gave himself a salary of twelve hundred dollars.

'The whole thing became even more bizarre and surreal: from conversations that were going on in my earshot, it appeared a recruiting station had been set up in Barbados, of all places. In a post office there, a notice had been put on the wall asking for television people to work for this outfit in Beirut. Two visitors subsequently mentioned seeing this advertisement. Later, one of the Palestinians was given a free holiday to Barbados with one of his sons – first-class travel and two or three weeks' accommodation – and he came back laden with cigars. I'm sure all the television recruits were aware of me; I don't see how they couldn't have been. Yet no one ever said a word to anyone else outside my prison. There was no point me calling out to any of these people; they were clearly not on my side. Those who did query my presence – and I heard one or two – were told that I had been sent to Australia to learn about television, of all things. What would I know about television, at my age?'

SIX

Staying Alive

Television was just what Sunnie Mann was having not only to learn about but become an expert on. Three months into her husband's captivity, media interest in Jackie's plight was waning. For a brief moment, when he was captured, Jackie's name had made headlines, but there was little to interest the Press in the lonely, difficult waiting his wife had to endure. Terry Waite's kidnap was a major league media event and John McCarthy was a journalist so his confinement was kept public by his colleagues. But for Jackie Mann there was no such star billing, no posters advertising the number of days he had been held captive. When a service was held to mark a thousand days of captivity for Terry Waite, John McCarthy and the Irishman Brian Keenan were also remembered in the Archbishop of Canterbury's prayers. Sunnie heard no mention of her husband. Jackie Mann had become the forgotten hostage.

Determined to rectify this, Sunnie devoted herself to bringing her husband's name to the forefront of any mention of hostages. She agreed to all and any request for interviews and when the British television network, Independent Television News, suggested a live satellite interview from Beirut in August 1989, Sunnie readily agreed. ITN's Middle East Correspondent, Brent Sadler, was already a good friend of hers and soon became the one person she relied upon during the wait for Jackie's release.

The satellite link-up was a major technical coup for the network. It was the first time any television station had attempted a live link via a mobile satellite from the war-torn city and required a great deal of courage and clear-headedness from all involved, particularly Sunnie and Brent. Before the interview could go ahead, Sunnie had to travel from West to East Beirut via the notorious Green Line, the no-man's-land of rubble which divided the rival halves of the city; gradually it came to earn its name as grass reclaimed what was once the most beautiful part of Beirut. Everywhere were the bombed-out remains of elegant homes, cream and pink stone walls leaning at crazy angles. An orange tree grew through a piano, abandoned when its owners were driven from their home by the shelling. A riot of flowers decorated a sofa. Books, neatly lined up on antique shelves, faced open air instead of a wall blasted away by a bomb. Anyone trying to traverse the Green Line had to take up the gauntlet of rocket fire, grenades and snipers. Aoun's war of liberation against the Syrians was raging. Some of the heaviest tank battles had erupted in the area Sunnie would now have to cross. Snipers were active and few people risked moving out of their homes, let alone across the Green Line.

Sunnie was undaunted by the prospect.

'I couldn't bear being unoccupied, just sitting alone in that awful flat waiting for news. I trusted Brent implicitly. He was one of the very few Western reporters to risk coming to Lebanon at all, let alone into Beirut, and when he later dared to cross from the East – which was dangerous enough – to the West to see me, I knew he was taking a terrible chance, risking kidnap and even his life just to help . It was his support that kept me going through the latest battles in Beirut, alone, desperately afraid for Jackie. Without his inspiration I know I wouldn't have survived.

'Keeping Jackie's name alive served two purposes; it had a very real chance of helping him, keeping him part of any negotiation process the Government or the United Nations were involved in, and it also gave me a reason for living. I knew the chance of making an historic live television interview, from the middle of this war-torn city, was in itself a major challenge. If Brent and ITN could pull this off, I was determined I wouldn't fail them. It would throw some much needed light on Jackie's plight, and it would certainly wake me up and get my adrenalin going.

'Crossing from West to East Beirut where ITN had set up the mobile satellite dish was no easy task, and fired up my adrenalin more than enough. The television crew couldn't come to me, since the risks of kidnap were just too great, and communications from the West even more complicated than from the East. For the same reason the British Embassy was in the East. So I had to go to them. It would have been impossible without ITN's Lebanese cameraman, Mehdi. He was Brent's right-hand man, his eyes and ears in the suburbs of Beirut, an expert at gauging the temperature in the volatile city, and I have no doubt his advice saved both our lives more than once. Mehdi guided me safely across the Green Line to the Montemar hotel in Maameltein, overlooking the beautiful bay of Jounieh.

'The once famous and glittering Casino du Liban lay at the northern end of the bay. I looked at it for a long moment, and it seemed to me that it represented all that had happened to Beirut. This beautiful land had been raped by those determined to have their way no matter what the cost, and my heart grieved not just for Jackie but for the price Lebanon was paying. Samir Geagea's Lebanese Forces militiamen were everywhere, and artillery shellfire plopped lazily into the Mediterranean in front of the hotel.

'I never travelled anywhere without my beloved pet poodle,

Tara, whom Mehdi hated – like all Muslims, he believed dogs to be unclean. Nonetheless he never refused to help me bring her and she was the most war-hardened of us all. Her white fur was permanently grimy because of the city's dust, and I never had enough water to clean her properly. She never flinched at incoming fire, unlike me; even after years of it, I still screamed and covered my eyes, jumping out of my skin if a shell landed nearby.

'Mehdi and I arrived at the transmission point, dishevelled, exhausted but excited. ITN's satellite news gathering equipment was already up and working, a major feat on behalf of their technicians. These things were very sensitive and, despite the description "mobile", difficult to move around, but without them television crews would never have been able to transmit their pictures. Mesmerised, I asked a hundred questions, and patiently the ITN crew explained that we would be beaming the picture they filmed here from the mobile satellite dish to a satellite thirty-six thousand miles away in space, which would reflect it down again to the Goonhilly earth station in south-west England. It would be immediately transmitted to the ITN headquarters in London and relayed to homes throughout the country, even whilst it was happening here in Beirut. It seemed alien and incomprehensible to me then, but I soon came to know almost as much about television as many of their employees and spoke the jargon as if I'd been born to it.

'Brent was fixing his microphone, and preparing to interview me. I spotted a tuft of hair standing up on the crown of his head, and grabbed a brush to fix it.

'"You can't be seen like that darling," I laughed. "You look like a cockerel!"

'The crew fell about laughing and I gathered from their remarks that the journalists at ITN in London could see Brent's impromptu make-up artist at work, since the signal was working, although viewers at home couldn't yet see it. I blasted him with my hairspray and it became a standing joke between us; whenever he went on air I'd always check his hair was smoothed down.

'The interview began and for a moment I felt a little nervous, but then the adrenalin and excitement took over, and I relaxed. I found it easy to pick up the various cues I was given from the crew behind the cameras, and soon learnt the signals which meant I had a minute or thirty seconds or ten seconds, to finish what I was saying. I was able to exploit the camera to make what I was saying more dramatic, knowing that it wasn't what I said but the way I said it that would make viewers listen. Brent said afterwards I was a natural; I just wished television had been around when I was in my twenties, rather than my seventies!

'The link-up worked, literally and strategically. Jackie was no longer the forgotten hostage: his name started to be mentioned in the same breath as Terry Waite and John McCarthy. Many thought he was too old and crippled to survive such harsh treatment, but I knew better. Even though I feared for him, I was sure he was still alive.

'I hated my life in West Beirut. Life had not been easy for the past decade and a half, but at least I had shared it with Jackie. Our relationship was complex; we were not the kind of couple who needed to spend every day and every hour with one another. We led our separate lives; I had my riding to occupy me, and Jackie ran a pub until it was damaged in the shelling, and had his own friends. He liked to go out to parties, whilst I preferred to stay at home. For a while we even lived in separate apartments in the same building, rubbing along together rather than living in each other's pockets. We had both had other liaisons in the past, and had even spent a year apart in the seventies, when I tired of Lebanon and stayed in France and Italy, whilst Jackie remained behind. But we were like bookends – we might be apart but if one of us vanished altogether, the other would collapse.

'It was like that now. I thought back on all our rows with regret and wished I could rewrite them differently. But maybe I'd have a second chance, maybe I would be able to make it up to him, to put him first. I grieved for him as if I had been widowed, but time couldn't heal my pain because there was no end to it. Conditions that had been tolerable when you had someone to share them with became unbearable alone. The shelling still terrified me; each time I heard the hiss and whoosh of one approaching, I braced myself for the impact as it hit, and the rubble which would bury me alive, and the relief as they passed me by lasted only until the next one came. Simply staying alive was a daily struggle for food, water and electricity. The summer heat was relentless and stifling. I was desolate.

'By the end of August, I had exhausted all my reserves. Despite the stamina which had propelled me through a World War, across the world and through Lebanon's civil wars, the Israeli invasion and my husband's kidnap, I felt I could no longer go on.

'The night of 31 August was the worst I had ever endured. Nearly twenty shells passed over my head, and I spent the night lying on the floor. By morning I had decided I had had enough. I lined up a column of strong painkillers on the table, counting them to make sure I had enough. I had sufficient for myself, but not for Tara or Jackie's cat, Sasha, whom I felt I couldn't leave alone in the flat until they died from starvation. I was considering the problem, my mind unemotional and detached, when the telephone rang.

'It was Brent. Tearful and hysterical, I told him I had had enough. He asked me what I meant, and I screamed that I couldn't take the shelling, the shortages, and losing Jackie any more. I was going to end my life.

99

'"Don't be so silly," Brent said. "What's happened to the courageous woman who's lasted this far? What will the world think when it finds out that the indomitable Sunnie Mann has taken the easy way out? Do you want to be known as a coward? And what about Jackie? What will he feel when he is released after surviving his captivity to discover you couldn't take the pace, and left him to cope alone?"

'That brought me round as nothing else could. Brent would always scold and bully me to my senses when I was down, and it was the only thing that made me angry enough to keep on going. For an hour he talked to me, and by the end of it my resolve to stay in the maw of this terrible city was strengthened. I was not going to be defeated. I would survive to see Jackie free. Never again did I ever contemplate suicide.

'Less than a week later, I was told Jackie was dead.

'I was telephoned by someone who said that he had important information regarding Jackie and, even whilst I was sure that this too was a false alarm, I agreed to meet him in the shopping area of Beirut, Hamra, near where Jackie's car had been found. It was a very public place, and I felt as secure as one ever does in that city. The man approached me, recognising me easily, for I was well known in Beirut. He looked respectable, in his late forties, with grey hair and wearing an immaculately tailored suit. His English was impeccable.

'"Mrs Mann, I am very sorry. I have bad news for you," he said, without introducing himself.

'My heart stood still, and I knew what he was going to say before he uttered the words.

'"We have to tell you that your husband is dead."

'I spent the next days in limbo, unsure what to believe. Frantically I contacted the British Embassy, but they had no reliable information. Mehdi was still in hospital, recovering from a sniper's bullet he had taken whilst crossing the Green

Line to do some filming. Once again, it was Brent who lifted the unhealthy deep depression which had settled on me. His attitude was that unless there was some hard evidence that Jackie was dead I should work on the assumption that he was alive. Inside me I felt sure I would know if anything had happened to him.

'During those dark days, it was Brent and Mehdi who helped me pull through, Brent often using his friend as a conduit to pass on messages of encouragement. It was as if they knew when I was particularly low and would arrange something special to lift my spirits. Brent knew my favourite outing was to a restaurant called La Cigale on the East side. It was terribly expensive, and I had to cross that wretched Green Line again to meet him. Yet it was exciting, and brought back my memories of the Blitz in London; one went to extraordinary lengths for a few moments of pleasure. The restaurant was piled high with sandbags to stop shrapnel killing the customers, and the Maître d' recognised me, and kissed my hand. I felt like a queen. They had large shrimps, which Brent ordered for me – my favourites – and I sat back and soaked up the ambience and relished every second of this unaccustomed luxury. Words cannot describe how such an occasion lifted my spirits and spurred me on.

'On one occasion in November 1989, Tara and I had crossed the murderous Green Line and made our way to the Montcmar hotel, to meet Brent and his crew as we'd arranged. Brent wasn't there, and as time passed I began to worry. I'd expected another wonderful morale-boosting dinner and Brent was now three hours behind schedule. It was dark and there had been a great deal of shelling. I had almost given up hope when the hotel doors swung open and in marched Brent and his crew. They were wearing flak jackets to protect themselves from shrapnel, and their faces were grey with dust. They looked exhausted. The cameraman was a young man called Sam King,

whom I nicknamed Joseph Cotten because of his resemblance
to a very handsome American actor of that name. He complained that they had almost been killed and that he had no
intention of going to La Cigale that night, or anywhere else.
He was staying put.

'Brent shrugged off the drama so as not to alarm me. I
knew they were risking their lives to get the latest war news.
I knew I had risked mine for a good meal. I often thought we
were all mad.'

Jackie, alone in his cell in Kaslik, spent many of the long
hours thinking about his wife. He knew she had no way of
knowing what had happened to him or even if he was alive,
and he wondered how she would be coping, enduring the
wars and shortages alone. He didn't even know if she had
stayed in Beirut. Perhaps she believed him to be dead and
had left the country.

'I often asked my captors about Sunnie, whether they'd
seen her. I knew she was well known in Beirut. One of the
guards said he had seen her, and described her as good looking, with a good figure. I knew that was true, but they could
have said that to infuriate me, since it was not a polite thing
to say in their eyes. Whenever I asked about her, they always
said she was fine, and added something silly like "She's gone
off to Germany with a German." Once they said, "She's gone
to England with your best friend," and to test them I said, "Oh,
you mean Fred," making up a fictitious name. "Yes, that's the
one," they replied, and I knew they were lying.

I still loved Sunnie, after nearly fifty years of marriage and
all that we had gone through, and I appreciated her more
when I was deprived of her than I ever had before. Perhaps
we'd been taking each other for granted, living our separate
lives. It was easy to do, given the circumstances in which we
lived. I was still living outside Beirut, at Mechref, when Sunnie

took the flat in the Raouche district of the capital. When I subsequently moved back into Beirut in April 1971, there were two apartments available in the building, and because we enjoyed our independence and privacy, I chose to take one of them instead of moving into Sunnie's somewhat cramped flat. Hers was on the fifth floor, and the two available apartments were on the fifth and the second. Sunnie wanted me to take the one on the second, which would be easier for me to reach as I had previously broken my left leg but I preferred to be above the traffic noise despite the extra stairs. I didn't think of those ninety-nine steps; I wanted us to have adjoining apartments, which is what happened.

'We lived our lives, Sunnie involved with her horses, going out morning and afternoon, and staying at home in the evening, watching videos. I enjoyed my own life in Beirut, shopping and having a drink at my local pub, the Duke of Wellington. Sometimes Sunnie would join me, but more often she didn't, and neither of us minded. If we were invited to parties, I usually went alone. On one occasion, when I attended a party given by the then British Consul, Terry Gardner, Sunnie refused to go. Terry Gardner seemed much offended and said, "When I invite people to a party, they come," which angered me. I said, "Sunnie is one of those people who makes up her own mind, and she chose not to come, but I'm here." It was just the way Sunnie and I were. We existed separately but under the same roof, and continued our normal married life – as normal as anything could be in Beirut.

'In 1975, when the Lebanese civil war started, the shelling upset Sunnie a good deal. She endured it for a while, but finally one day in May simply packed up and left, desperate to get out of Beirut. She stayed with her daughter Jennifer and her two grandchildren, I believe, in France, for six months, and then Sunnie moved to Rome for a further six months. She even wrote to me saying she was never coming back to Beirut, but she did return after a year's absence. By that time the flat she'd had was empty and had been cleared out, so she had no option but to move into my flat, and we lived together again. We had good times and bad ones, but we still stayed together.

'I frequently wondered what she was doing and how she was surviving. I asked if I could write a letter to her, just to tell her I was alive, but they said no. I then asked if I could at least write a letter to my bank, telling them to give Sunnie any money from my account that she needed, because the account was in my name. Sunnie did have her own account, into which she put the meagre income she earned from her riding school, but it dwindled then dried up altogether as the civil wars intensified. It was too small to live on even when the riding school was thriving – Sunnie ran it for the horses not the money. She had a tiny pension, around three hundred and thirty sterling pounds a year, and that was it. She finally closed her personal account, as it was empty. I knew without money from our main account she couldn't live.

'I was afraid life might be a struggle for her, so I wrote the bank this letter. The guards didn't give me an envelope – they wanted to censor what I wrote – and took it away, telling me the following day that the bank had received it. Sceptically I asked how they had it so soon and was told it had been posted – I knew from experience it would not have reached the bank or anywhere else so quickly if it had been posted. They even said the newspaper had published it the next day, but refused to show me the paper or even say which one it was. They were lying: the letter had never been posted. I thought the bank would be reasonable and let her have access to our funds if she asked for it. I had no idea that not even the British Ambassador had been able to persuade the bank to allow her the money, but it did have a Lebanese manager. If he had been English, as in the past, I'm sure he would have helped Sunnie.

'I had now been missing for nearly six months. I had been taken on 12 May 1989, and it was now November. I knew it must be difficult for Sunnie, but at least she had friends on the outside and she was a resourceful, courageous person. I was alone and had only myself to rely on.

'Early one morning, before dawn, I was awakened by a good deal of noise, and to my surprise the kidnappers came into my room and put a bed there – a proper bed, unlike the mattress on which I had to sleep – and screened it off with some sheeting. A man came in, leading a young boy of about thirteen or fourteen, who seemed to have an injury of some kind. The bathroom which I was allowed to use was immediately adjacent to the area in which the boy was staying, and every time I was taken to it I was strictly instructed not to make any noise. Frequently even if I was making no sound at all they would hammer on the door and tell me to be quiet. An American doctor came every day to treat this boy, and whenever he did so the kidnappers switched on the generator, which I could hear. Over the noise I heard what sounded like a saw going, and I wondered if they were doing amputations of some kind, though I have no idea what it was. The doctor spoke with a New England accent, and I guessed that he must be working at the American University Hospital. His name was Doctor Marco.

'Marco later had a row with the kidnap group's leader, Awad. I heard Marco shouting, "I'm a volunteer, I'm not a Palestinian", and he stormed out of the villa. He was dating a local girl, so for a while he continued to come up to Kaslik, but eventually he left Lebanon.

'It was Doctor Marco who informed the kidnappers of a certain drug. The man who had made homosexual advances to me before, Abdullah Ja'far, had not given up his determination to have his way with me, with or without my consent. The doctor told him of a drug which would put me to sleep and permit Ja'far to do as he wished. I was alerted when one of the men came to me one day and asked me what the word "poesy" meant. I said there was no such word, and he left, returning ten minutes later with a scrap of paper which had the word "poison" written upon it. I was convinced they were trying to poison me then, and took precautions as far as I was able with my food and drink.

'Not long afterwards, I was given some stew, which was particularly thick, and some green salad, and I was exhorted to make sure I ate all of it, leaving none behind. I was immediately suspicious, since ordinarily they didn't care what I ate as long as I didn't starve myself to death. I ate the stew, but avoided the salad because it smelt strongly of some sort of medicament. I took the precaution of drinking as much water as possible before the meal, and during it, hoping to minimise the effect of any drug. Finally they took the empty plate away, along with the salad, which I hadn't touched. I overheard the doctor say, "You should have made him eat all the salad." I had escaped this time.

'I felt sure Ja'far would try again, and I tried to stay alert. Two nights later, I was brought my usual cup of tea in the evening, and again I could smell the medicament in it, the same as I had detected in the salad. I didn't dare not to drink it, so I swallowed half of it, and hid the rest out of sight of the video camera, and finished it in the morning. I hoped that by separating the tea into two halves I would effectively minimise the effect of the drug.

'I had heard the doctor say that the drug took approximately twenty-five minutes to take effect, and anxiously I waited to see if anything happened. I felt nothing, neither sleepy nor lightheaded, and after half an hour it became apparent that the drug had again failed. The strain of monitoring everything I ate or drank was beginning to take an increasing toll on my nerves. Next they tried adding the drug to a glass of Pepsi Cola, but it made the Pepsi Cola bubble and froth like a melodramatic horror film, and I again separated it into two halves, as I had done with the tea.

'After the third or fourth failure, the doctor began to be very puzzled. He was using a drug which proved extremely effective with patients in hospital, putting them swiftly to sleep and lasting twelve to fourteen hours. He brought a stronger medicine, and I could hear him accusing the man detailed to drug me, Taleb, of not putting the correct dosage in the food and drink he was giving me. Once I heard someone ask Taleb where he lived, and he cited Tayouney, an area of Beirut where Sunnie and I had lived for a couple of years. He became Taleb of Tayouney in my mind.

'Still the medicine had no effect, despite the dosage having been increased. Eventually, on about their fifth attempt, I feigned sleep after twenty-five minutes or so just to see what they would do. It caused a good deal of commotion; they obviously didn't expect the drug to work. I could hear them conferring amongst themselves, and after a lengthy debate, when they were convinced I was indeed asleep, four or five of them came into the room. I was facing the wall as usual, but because I was supposedly asleep, my face was not covered with the blanket which they insisted upon when I was awake. The chain around my leg was unlocked, and I was eased away from the wall onto my back by the kidnappers. I opened my eyes very slightly, so that I could just see through the slits. Standing at the bottom of my bed was Abdullah Ja'far, his jacket removed. He was unbuttoning his trousers and unbuckling his belt. He intended to rape me whilst I was asleep.

'I decided not to let this charade go on any longer. I moved suddenly, as if I was waking up, and caused considerable panic amongst the men. Ja'far ran from the room as if the hounds of hell were after him, and after uncertainly delaying for a moment, his accomplices followed him. I had no doubt that had I been unconscious, Ja'far would have raped me, and perhaps others. I was never entirely sure why he didn't force me even when I was awake, but perhaps the repercussions from the rest of the group would have been too great. I was never accosted in that way again, although I always feared it.

'These people seemed to me to have no regard for the usual morals of life. They had kidnapped me and deprived me of my basic human rights, but in a way I could understand that: it was war and I was on the other side. In their lexicon there was no such thing as "civilians"; you were on the side on which you were born, decreed by race and religion. But their immorality went much further. Their sexual adventures had no regard for decency or love. Night after night they brought girls and young men to their quarters. The leader of the group, Awad, was bisexual and had a girl one night, a boy the next. His homosexual activities would take place in front of the other men. I could hear the boy screaming, whether in ecstasy or pain I couldn't tell, and Awad making lewd remarks to the spectators: "Watch out, watch out everybody, stand clear," and so on. The boys got paid for it, so they were clearly willing, in as much as youngsters that age can be considered willing. One boy got only half a dollar, and complained. Half a dollar, that was all.

'These activities happened at least two or three times a week, and once or twice a week they'd have the girls. One of them was an air-stewardess; she even managed to steal 'plane tickets for them, I believe. Only Awad had these affairs; the other guards simply watched. I could hear everything, try as I might to block the sounds out. Once I heard Awad taking a girl into what functioned as his bedroom, and she said, "Where are you taking me?" He said, "In here", and the girl protested, "But I'm a woman." His response was,

"We'll soon find that out," and moments later I heard her cries.

'Some months into my captivity in Kaslik, a rival group of Palestinians moved into the area. The hostility between the two groups was marked. On one occasion one of my captors, a man called Philip, and another man who was neither Lebanese nor Palestinian, went for a drink to a nearby village – there was nowhere to drink in Kaslik. The rival group opened fire on the car in which these two were moving, and hit Philip in the arm and he lost a good deal of blood. He was rushed back to the villa and the wound was dressed. Although it had bled a lot it was fairly superficial, I gathered.

'The feud between the two groups grew and the rival Palestinians increased in numbers as more joined them. They were only a mile away, towards Beirut, and soon numbered three times the size of the group holding me. They contacted Arafat again, and I could hear their side of the conversation from my room. There had been a heavy shooting battle between the two groups, and Awad's men had run out of ammunition. They had called America, apparently by radio, and it seemed they had asked for ammunition to be sent to them by the following Monday, this incident having taken place on the Friday. They were told it would take until at least Tuesday, and had to be content with that.

'Awad began to get nervous and decided the other group was too much of a threat. He made preparations to pull out of Kaslik, but couldn't decide whether to go up the mountains to a village called Sofar or down the mountains towards Beirut. Eventually he rejected moving closer to the city, since the nearer he got to the capital the greater the danger from rival Palestinian groups who were in larger numbers towards Beirut. Awad decided to move to Sofar and accordingly began to negotiate with the owner of a place I believed was called the Marble Arch, a restaurant and bar. The owner came to

Kaslik; he was Austrian–Italian, and spoke quite good English. He was the leader of yet another Palestinian group at Sofar – how he came to be mixed up in such a cause I don't know – but this one was friendly to Awad's group. They negotiated a price; I remember them talking in terms of half a million, but whether it was Lebanese money or American dollars I didn't learn.

'Finally, on 18 November 1989, they pulled out. I had been at Kaslik exactly five months, and a prisoner for just over six. I learned later that the day after we left the villa it was badly shelled and much of it destroyed. Half a million dollars had been hidden in the house by the group trying to form this bizarre television station, and one of them actually returned and retrieved it.

'As usual the move was made in the middle of the night. I was put into the back of a car, not the boot much to my relief, with an armed man on either side of me, and two more in the front. We drove from the villa a short distance to a cemetery, and I could see the gravestones illuminated in the moonlight. My first feeling was that they were going to bury me. I just hoped they'd kill me first.

'Five minutes later a second car arrived and this time I was put into the boot. We drove out of the graveyard to my intense relief; I was more afraid at that moment than I had been since I was kidnapped. The thought of being buried alive turned me to stone. The rest of the journey passed by in a blur, but that incident was carved forever on my mind. The discomfort of being once again confined in the boot of the car, which was even smaller than on the previous occasions, seemed infinitely preferable to being entombed alive. I could see through a chink in the bodywork of the car, and we were going down what must have been a very narrow road, since there were walls on either side.

'The drive was brief and I was escorted, somewhat dazed,

110

into another room where my foam mattresses had already been placed. I was to stay at Sofar for the rest of my captivity, except for the final week before my release. I had no idea when I walked into the building that it would be twenty-two months before I walked out again.'

SEVEN

Flight in the Past: Sofar

'As soon as it was light, I set about establishing as much as I could about my new prison. My first action was to find out which direction I faced – north, south, east or west – as I invariably did. The room was about five yards square, but one part of it had been curtained off, with the material suspended from the ceiling and two wires trailing from ceiling to the walls. The section which was thus barred to me was about a yard and a half wide, and maybe two yards long. What remained of the room formed a passageway between one part of the house and another, and the space which for want of a better word was my bedroom. It had one large window, through which sunshine was now streaming. There was no furniture except my two foam mattresses and a blanket, which I didn't really need.

'This time the kidnappers had moved with me, unlike the previous moves which had meant a change in those who guarded me. In Sofar Abid Awad remained in control. He told me the first time we met, at Kaslik, that I had been entrusted to him because I was an escaper, and he was the best jailer, who would be able to hold me whatever I might try. Awad was a man proud of his own abilities and not at all reluctant to proclaim them himself. He later dismissed all the guards who served under him and replaced them, which

112

effectively meant a different group were dealing with me, apart from Awad himself.

'The new location heralded a new regime, which was much harsher than the previous three. The guards were more adamant about not talking; if someone passed by on the other side of the curtain, and I should happen to ask for something at that moment, they would scream "Be quiet!" or "Shut up!" at me. My eye-glasses had been broken in the move from Kaslik to Sofar. I had been holding them in my hand, but during the move from the first car to the boot of the second, I had somehow dropped them and been unable to find them. My captors initially told me that they had found them and they could be repaired, but later said they were crushed and irreparable. I was without them for the remainder of my captivity, almost two years. Even if I had been given books again, I would have been unable to read them. I did ask for glasses of some kind to replace the ones I had lost, and they brought me a cheap pair of sunglasses, not the thing at all. It was useless. It was a great blow not being able to see properly, or read. Once they brought me a newspaper article which had a photograph of Sunnie, but I couldn't really see it, and they refused to let me hold the paper in my hands so that I could peer closely. It was very cruel.

'Once or twice I could hear the guards listening to the BBC World Service and desperately I would crane towards the sound, trying to overhear what was happening in the outside world. Some of the senior guards could speak quite good English – they used it as a way of proving their superiority over those who couldn't – and they understood the BBC easily. The only time I was allowed to listen to the radio, it was always tuned into an FM music programme, which I didn't particularly care for, and I was never allowed to retune it to a news broadcast.

'I had no idea what was happening in the outside world.

113

Once they brought a television and video into my room, but again I was not permitted to find a news bulletin on it. They allowed me to watch a film, which to my delight was in English, but the fellow who brought the equipment to me managed to knock the television and video player from the table on which he had set it up. The whole lot came tumbling down, table, television, video and all, onto the floor, just as the film ended. He tried in vain to get it working again, but the fall was too much for it, and something had become detached, with the result that it was the first and last film I watched during my captivity.

'My possessions were very few. I had a urine bottle, two drinking water bottles, a wastepaper basket whose primary function was to hold the food which I discarded, a plastic spoon and two cups, one containing sugar which the guards replenished as necessary, and one which I used to drink from. My clothing still consisted of a tracksuit, which they replaced every week or ten days, and a vest and pants. That first winter, of 1989/90, I was given a pair of socks, but they were taken away from me in the spring, and not restored the following year. Most of the time I just wore a pair of cheap plastic sandals, probably made in the shoe factory which the Palestinians ran for themselves, or I went barefoot. I had two blankets, one much larger than the other, which I doubled up to create the warmth of three blankets, in effect. At one stage they brought me an eiderdown, a child's coverlet, printed with nursery rhymes and too small for me. I made myself a pillow by folding a small piece of plastic mattress in half.

'The only place where I had air-conditioning was at the second location I was held, Doha, where I had access to my own unit. Fortunately Sofar was high in the mountains, about four thousand feet up, so it was rarely necessary to have additional air-conditioning. Once or twice I asked if the window could be opened to allow me some air, which they did at my request, and several times on their own initiative. Even when they opened the window, they left the curtain drawn. I never suffered from extremes of temperature. In the winter I used the triple thickness of the blankets I had; in the spring I would reduce that to two, and in the summer I would just use one. When they weren't used I kept them folded in the corner of my room – as usual they never removed anything once they had put it down – and they were never washed the whole time I was there.

'My clothes were cleaned regularly, and when they brought me a change of clothing I was permitted to take a shower myself – or a "douche" as they persisted in calling it. The water was hot only very occasionally; sometimes it was lukewarm, but usually it was stone cold. It was always a shower – I never once had the luxury of sinking into a bath of any kind, and I missed it a good deal. But I was able to stay relatively clean, even when the water was cold. I was used to icy showers, and they had never done me any harm up to now, so I thought it unlikely they would begin to have a harmful effect at this stage in my life, much as I disliked them. I was given soap and a towel, which would be changed with the rest of my clothing, but I had no toothbrush or toothpaste. I often asked for it, but eventually gave it up. They offered me shampoo, but I had spent all my life using soap to clean my hair, and I saw no reason to change now. I just said "No, thankyou" and carried on using soap.

'In the very beginning of my captivity, the first week at Sidon, I was twice permitted to use a razor, though I was not given shaving cream but had to make do with ordinary soap. Again that was no hardship, since I used soap for that purpose too before I was taken. At Doha, I was given a razor on one occasion, in the month I was held there. At Kaslik, the last place before this, I was given a razor on request, once a week, but I was never allowed to keep it. But here at Sofar, I

115

was rarely allowed access to one. Indeed, at one time, there was a period of eight months where I was not allowed to use a razor, my hair wasn't cut and my fingernails were not trimmed. My nails were the biggest problem, because they grew extremely long. I couldn't bite them, because my teeth simply weren't strong enough, and I had few enough of them anyway. I did try to break them off, but all I did was tear the nail to the point where it was painful, so I gave that up. I tried to file them down on the wall, on the concrete above the skirting board, but it wasn't really very effective. It became terribly difficult to pick things up, particularly my food, since the nails curved over my fingers and stopped me from being able to get a grip on anything.

'I was thankful I never saw a mirror. I had no desire to look at myself, at the wreck I was becoming. I was glad too that Sunnie couldn't see me.

'The kidnappers began to take less care with me and I was not only treated more harshly, but I was increasingly neglected. My meals were more irregular – I'd get breakfast any time between eight in the morning and midday. Similarly lunch would arrive anytime between one in the afternoon and six in the evening. For the first twelve months I was at Sofar, supper would be served any time between seven in the evening and midnight. On at least twenty occasions I was given no supper to eat at all. Once I had no evening meal five times in ten days and I complained to one of the guards, who was more friendly to me than the rest, when he visited me one day. He immediately went out and spoke to Awad and told him what was happening. Thereafter my mealtimes were much more regularised, and apart from one short period of time I never went without supper again. I'd never been a gourmand, and had always seen food as fuel rather than entertainment, so I just ate what they gave me to survive, as unpleasant as it was. I didn't fantasise about slap-up meals as one might have expected. I just closed down that side of my life and got on with what I had.

'There was one character there whom I nicknamed "The Prodder", because he used to come in when I was exercising with a stick in his hand. He'd hit me in the back with it or prod my feet or tread on my feet or stick me in the ribs, anywhere he could reach. One day I called him a silly bugger, and this was overheard by Awad, who happened to be standing by the door, and called in three of his henchmen. They immediately tackled me, all three of them together, and tried to wrap a roll of sticky tape around my arms, whilst I struggled and fended them off. They got me firmly on the bed, and I lay facing the wall, endeavouring to protect my head from the blows which they aimed at me, whilst they still tried to wrap this sticky tape around my wrists. I shouted and yelled, making as big a fuss as I was capable of, and eventually they were called off.

'I was often hit at Sofar, which was symptomatic of their new treatment of me. Usually they just hit me with their hands, but occasionally I was punched on the shoulder. Once I managed to upset one of them – I can't remember how – probably over the food he was giving me. The character I'd upset had hit me across the head two or three times, and his legs were near my hands, so I grabbed his leg in both hands and pulled hard. My tea was always served from a hot kettle, and he had this kettle in his hand and I thought he was about to pour it all over me. I dropped his leg quickly, and before I could move out of his range, he kicked me in the right shoulder. It was weeks before I could move it again, and even now I cannot lift my arm up straight, despite a good deal of treatment since I was released.

'One or two of the kidnappers had some sympathy for me, and didn't approve of the way in which I was now being treated or the behaviour of their comrades. But even though some of the kidnappers treated me with more consideration than others, I never deliberately tried to build up a relationship with any individuals. Those who were friendly made the advances from their side, each and every time; I never tried to collaborate with any of them. Occasionally when their "no speaking" campaign was in full swing I'd try to get one of them talking, but ninety-nine times out of a hundred I'd just get a rude grunt. They were told not to talk to me, and I was told not to talk to them, and most of the time that's the way it was.

'The local inhabitants of Sofar disliked the Palestinians who had settled in their midst like a giant cuckoo. They knew I was there, despite the crazy stories Awad repeated to them – that I had gone to Australia to learn about television – as he had at Kaslik. The group holding me used to send out a representative to talk to the villages almost every day and he would address the local inhabitants. I could hear them in the first few months, but after a while my captors must have realised I could hear what was being said and thereafter they moved further away.

'Before they moved out of earshot, I heard several conversations. One man, a villager, told whichever Palestinian had been sent out to represent my captors on that occasion, "We are a village of two thousand people, and you are intruders." Their obvious dislike was almost tangible. There was a girl, a teenager judging from the sound of her voice, who every time she saw Abid Awad in the village, would run to him shouting "You're a bastard, you're a bastard" at the top of her voice. Awad loathed it, and it would send him into a frenzy. He'd lose his temper when she started, and shout and scream almost uncontrollably. After six months she was moved to Damascus, probably for her own protection, and a younger girl took up where she left off. I would hear this child, who could be no more than ten or twelve from the sound of her, shouting "You're a bastard, you're a bastard"

118

1 and **2.** The Battle of Britain fighter pilot
with his faithful dog, Vixen.

3. Jackie miraculously escaped from this blazing Spitfire in 1941

4. On holiday with Sunnie's father.

5. Riding at the Beirut racecourse.

6. Behind the bar at Jackie's pub in Beirut, The Pickwick.

7. Sunnie alone in her apartment
shortly after Jackie was kidnapped.

8. Walking along Beirut's Green Line.

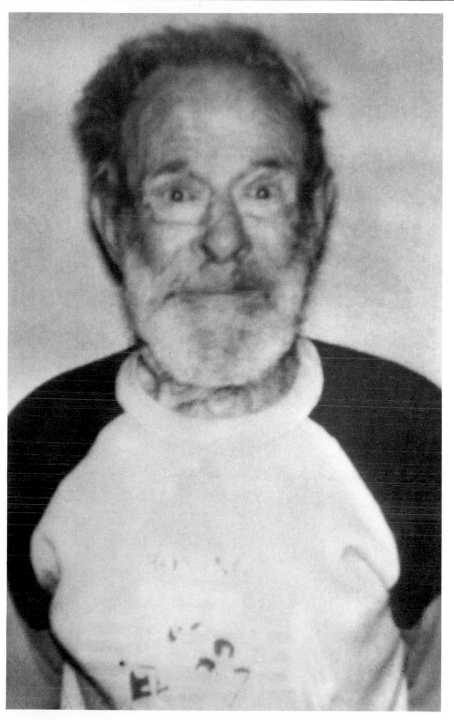

9. The only photograph released of Jackie in captivity.

10. The riding instructor.

11. 865 days of waiting.

12. Freedom at last.

13. Christmas celebrations in Cyprus.

14. A British hero.

15. Recuperating in hospital.

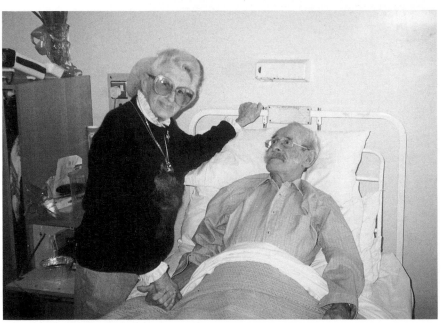

to Awad whenever he set foot outside the building. It seemed to bite deep into Awad's soul, and he resented it to the point of obsession. I was surprised by the effect it had. At one stage Awad simply stopped going out and for nine months he never left the building at all, to my knowledge. He could have eliminated the jeering, I thought, but perhaps he didn't dare risk antagonising the villagers to that extent.

'There were times when I was afraid of losing my mind, and I was aware of the dangers of that happening. Occasionally I would wonder if I was going downhill, but I'd pull myself together and think, "You've got to rationalise things if you want to survive." Survival was always uppermost in my mind, but it did occur to me sometimes that I was beginning to weaken. I had to survive. I tried to remember everything so that I could refer back to it, which is one reason why I can still recall so many things in such detail. I refused to give in to them, mentally or physically.

'The lack of anything to do was the hardest thing to master, and time began to hang very heavily. I was alone and awake for fifteen or sixteen hours a day, and I had no television, no radio, no books, no paper or pencil or any means of occupying myself except a pack of cards. Even more than they had at Kaslik, those fifty-two cards became my lifeline. I played patience a good deal, but my cards wore thin and became virtually unreadable. I had been provided with a small piece of notepaper and a pen on which I was instructed to write any requests I might have. It was a ridiculous demand, since these characters would look at what I'd written, and, unable to read it, simply screw it up and throw it away without ever passing it on to Awad or anyone else who could read English. Eventually my verbal request for a new pack of cards reached someone who had the authority to grant it, and I was given a new set. It was a very significant moment in my life as a prisoner.

'I played with those cards endlessly and in time they too began to fall apart. I knew they would not be replaced, so I had to repair them myself, and I fashioned a type of glue by mixing some of the sugar I was given for my tea with some water. I'd take about a quarter of a teaspoonful of sugar, mix it into a paste, then let it harden a little. I then smeared the paste over the two sides of the cards I wanted to stick together – the backing of the cards tended to become separated from the face with use – and put the two pieces together. It worked. Without those cards I know I would have gone crazy.

'I was an old man, seventy-five, when I was moved to Sofar. I had had a long life and done many things. I had lived in England, in Cyprus and spent the last forty years in Beirut, watching and experiencing all the changes and upheavals there. I had no outside stimulation or occupation, but inside my head there were seventy-five years of memories, stories and experiences locked away. It was a mental library, to which I could go and select an incident, and play it back like a film; and most importantly, it was a library which no one, not even my captors, could take from me. I am sure it would have been much harder to endure solitary confinement for the best part of three years if I had been twenty-five, with my whole life before me, as yet unwritten. But at my age I could review my life and assess what I had done, as anyone who approaches their last years does. It made me a more introspective, contemplative person, and I weighed up how I had lived in a manner I had not done before.

'I deliberately relived my life, watching it two or three times over during the course of my captivity at Sofar. I would select a phase and examine it closely, mentally switching off my surroundings and losing myself in my past. I saw my schoolfriends and tried to remember their names. I watched my teenage years, and looked at the things I did then, the people with whom I mixed. But it was my RAF days, my time as a Spitfire fighter pilot during the Battle of Britain, which inspired me most to survive.

'One day several of the guards were in my room, chatting amongst themselves. As they got up to leave, one of them draped his arm around his fellow, and they left holding hands. It was a typically Arab gesture – they often walked around holding hands in a way which would be greatly misunderstood in England – and I had sudden image of a different two soldiers walking hand in hand, in a different place in a different time, their officer on the other side of the road as if he didn't belong to them. It was in Brest, in France, three days before the outbreak of the Second World War.

'A friend and I had decided to go to Normandy and Brittany, in the autumn of 1939. He was a few years older than I, and he had a car, a Vauxhall, which we took over by boat from Southampton. We toured around the country, including Mont St Michel, which was incredibly beautiful, situated at the end of a narrow causeway which we had to walk along. We went into Brest, the French naval base in that area, and watched the French ships moving around as if we were observing a film set. It all had an air of unreality about it, despite the numerous uniformed troops walking in the streets, holding hands.

'My friend, a chap called Ernest Millard, and I decided to return to Britain, and on a certain Friday night we found places for ourselves on a boat to Southampton, but there was no room for a car, so we had to leave the Vauxhall behind. The AA collected it the following weekend – a week after the outbreak of war. It was quite extraordinary, how easily they got it back, intact and undamaged. In those days, I was driving a red J2 MG, a two-seater soft top – a wonderful motor car which I drove all through the war. I had it when I met Sunnie which impressed her enormously. I presented quite a

121

picture of the dashing young man, for very few people of my age even had cars, let alone such a sporty one. I paid ninety sterling pounds for it. It was a 1934 model, which had never been driven during the bitter English winters but laid up by the owner, who'd also made one or two additions to it. It was in wonderful condition. It had been fitted with a Burgess silencer, which at slow speeds made normal noises, but over thirty miles an hour it developed a lovely healthy roar. It was a mini Spitfire, and nothing pleased me more than racing it across the country.

'We drove back to Portsmouth, where Ernest lived, and on the Saturday morning I picked up my MG and drove back to my parents. I was with them the next day, the Sunday Neville Chamberlain made his speech declaring England was at war with Germany. I was listening to the one o'clock news on the BBC Home Service with my parents, sitting round the dining table for lunch, as we heard Chamberlain's quiet, grim voice announce the outbreak of war. I turned to my father and said, "I think I shouldn't be here," and quit lunch, then drove back to Reading, where the Volunteer Reserve Centre was. I had joined it eighteen months before, in response to an advertisement. I saw the Commandant, who was ex-RAF, one Monday evening after I had finished work, and I told him about my schooling, my background and my flying experience. He told me to come back on Friday and fill in the forms, which I did, and there I was, a member of the Volunteer Reserves. I was twenty-four.

'I had always wanted to fly. When I was young, a friend and I had contributed to an organisation called the Aviation Book Club and they reprinted the history of World War I fighter pilots, and a number of biographies of famous airmen. It was that which nourished my love of flying. When I was twenty-one I took an apprenticeship in General Aircraft Engineering at Philips of Powys, which built Miles aircraft. Fred Miles was the chief designer and together with his brother George, who was head of the aircraft maintenance section, they looked after the flying school aircraft.

'It was a two-year apprenticeship – you could take a three-year one, but I didn't have enough money to do three years. As it was, it cost a premium of a hundred pounds to buy the two-year apprenticeship, and I was paid ten shillings a week. My mother was a bit apprehensive about me flying, but my father was proud of me. As an apprentice I bought the aviation magazine, *The Aeroplane*, every week, which fanned my love of aircraft and my desire to fly. I shared my lodgings with three other apprentices and one of them decided to join the Royal Air Force Volunteer Reserve. His talking about the flying spurred me on, and on 6 April 1938, I signed up.

'The Volunteer Reserve unit was composed of part-time airmen; we all had other jobs and we flew on alternate weekends. We attended a course of lectures twice a week at the centre in Reading, and held numerous get-togethers. It was a gay time. I had finished my apprenticeship by then, and was employed by Philips in the servicing department, which dealt with the repair and maintenance of aircraft. When I wanted to go to France for three weeks, I had asked for extra leave, which the foreman of the servicing department refused to give to me. Never one to bow to authority, I quit. When I returned from France I was without a job. The outbreak of war couldn't have been timed better for me.

'We had two types of aircraft at this flying school, Tiger Moths and Miles Magisters. They'd originally used Miles Hawks, but it was later replaced with the Magister, which was more advanced. All were two-seater aircraft with open cockpits. The Tiger Moth was a biplane, slightly slower but in many ways more manoeuvrable than the Miles Hawk and Magister, which were both monoplanes with a speed somewhere in the region of one hundred and twenty-five miles an hour. I was put on first the Hawk, then the Magister, which pleased me because it was more of a fighter type of aircraft than the Tiger Moth. By the outbreak of war, I had a hundred and fifty flying hours behind me, which made me relatively experienced, so I expected to be in action very soon.

'When I arrived at the centre the following Monday morning, they said, "Where have you been? You were called up on Friday." I said, "On Friday I was in France," and I was forgiven.

'Nothing happened immediately. I spent four or five days filling sandbags and finally asked if I could drive back home. I was asked if I was on the telephone and, when I confirmed that I was, I was permitted to go on condition I was ready to leave at a moment's notice. My parents ran a pub in Northampton then, called The Windmill, – I don't know why, there wasn't a windmill in sight – which was about a hundred years old, small and cosy. They welcomed me back, and for ten days life carried on as if nothing untoward was happening in the world. Then I got a telephone call, telling me to return to Reading. I gathered my courage, and thought, "OK, they've called me up again, this is it," and dashed back to the centre.

'I rushed into the main building and asked my superior, "Where am I going?"

'"Going?" he said. "Nowhere. It's payday."

'They'd called me all the way back from Northampton to Reading to collect my fortnightly pay. It was twelve shillings and sixpence a day, with five shillings a day flying pay added onto it, which made a grand total of seventeen shillings and six a day for so far doing nothing. It was a lot of money in those days, relatively speaking. Two weeks later I got another telephone call, and again I hotfooted it back to Reading in the MG, and it was payday again. Tiring a little of this game, I asked if the money could be paid into my bank instead of calling me back every fortnight, and they agreed.

'I didn't hear any more from them until December 1939. I was called up again and told to report to Hastings, on the south coast. I arrived there a day or two late – I was often late in those days, simply because of lethargy on my part. It didn't seem to matter to me then, although later I became very particular about punctuality. I was tardy so often then I became known as the late Sergeant Mann.

'I made a number of friends in Hastings and in the early days of 1940 we used to go out together, marching up and down the seafront and attending the odd lecture or patronising local pubs. In March that year, I was posted to Hullavington, an advanced flying unit. I had already converted from the Miles Magister to the biplane Hart aircraft, of which there were four or five variations. I was used to the Hart, Hind and the Audax, which were two seaters – a pilot and a gunner. They were not much more advanced than the Sopworth or the Camels of World War I. I continued to fly Harts at Hullavington. I had done only one or two cross-country flights in those days and we were now sent on more advanced exercises, although still no combat training at this stage.

'We were taught how to drop bombs. We had four practice bombs on a rack, two on each side, and the idea was to drop them in the centre of a white circle which had been painted on the ground which made up the bombing exercise range. Once one of my fellow students had a practice bomb which hung out but didn't drop, so he returned to Hullavington. As he landed, he miscalculated and either came in too fast or touched down too far down the airfield. At that point the bomb which hadn't dropped exploded, giving off smoke. The pilot choked to death.

'One day I was performing just such an exercise, when one of my bombs failed to drop. I had dropped three, and the fourth didn't show any signs of either exploding or falling. I made another run over the bomb range to try to dislodge it, but it still refused to budge, and a red cartridge was fired from the ground telling me to bugger off. I had no intention of returning to base with the thing still stuck beneath me and having the same thing happen to me as had happened to my friend. I made another pass, and this time the bomb fell. I was reprimanded for ignoring the red signal, then asked for an explanation. I gave one, and the matter was dropped.

'Amongst our number at Hullavington was a volunteer reserve, a wealthy young man by the name of Sidebottom. He asked me one day if he could borrow my MG to drive to London, which I agreed to as long as he replaced the petrol, which was rationed then. He drove off in the MG, but returned after hours, which meant the gate barriers at the entrance of the base were down. Sidebottom stopped, and the guard lifted the barrier to allow him to advance a little, but he drove straight through. The guard had no idea who was driving it, but he recognised the red MG as being mine. The next day I was called up to the station commander's office and asked why I had ignored the sentries. I explained to him that I had loaned the car to someone, and hadn't actually been in it that night. Fortunately for me I had spent that evening in a local pub with a fellow called Eric Edsall, who was subsequently killed in the Battle of Britain. I gave his name as an alibi and the station commander then demanded to know to whom I had loaned the car. Naturally I wasn't going to tell tales out of school and, much as I was annoyed by Sidebottom, I didn't want him to get into trouble. The station commander accepted my explanation and didn't push the matter further.

'Sidebottom was known as a London playboy. At that stage we were all Sergeant Pilots, but when he went to London, Sidebottom would wear a Pilot Officer's uniform, with wings, and pretend he was an operational pilot to pick up the girls. It annoyed me intensely; I didn't approve of the deception at all. Eventually he was killed, still a Sergeant Pilot. It seemed fitting somehow, that he should die without ever having gained the honours he pretended to have, though I mourned the waste of his life.

'I didn't get a commission at Hullavington, principally because of these two incidents. The refusal to obey the red cartridge signal when I was practising dropping bombs, and my refusal to disclose the identity of the car driver, both seemed to show an unwanted bucking of authority. It was recognised that neither was my fault, and no action was ever taken, but it reflected badly on me. A number of people on my course at Hullavington were commissioned, and although I didn't actively seek one – you were always selected – I felt a little left out. I was an above-average pilot, I knew that, and had always had glowing reports as far as my flying ability was concerned, but I was passed over. I was disappointed, but not resentful, since it was justified to an extent – after all, I had been uncooperative in two separate instances. It was something I regretted.

'In late June 1940, I was posted from Hullavington to Aston Down, near Stroud in Gloucestershire, which was an operational training unit. The instructors there were all from Number One Squadron, which had come back from France where they were flying Hurricanes. The chief instructor was a man called Halahan, known as "Bull" Halahan because of his strength as a commander.

'I had over a hundred hours of training in a Hart under me. I now had to convert to a Spitfire. I first spent an hour flying dual in a Harvard, an American-built aircraft which had a retractable undercarriage and a two pitch propeller. I then soloed in a Miles Master, which had a Rolls Royce Kestrel engine and again a retractable undercarriage. Then I was allowed near a Spitfire.

'The first time I sat in a Spitfire I felt a certain amount of trepidation. I knew nothing about its combat experience, and as far as I was concerned then it was nothing more than just another aeroplane – a more powerful one, of course, but just another 'plane. There was much less room in the cockpit than in any other aircraft I had been in. The Miles Hawk and Magister were both fairly small cockpits, but there was so much more equipment in the Spitfire one felt cramped. It was more or less shoulder width. I had been told of any swing it might have when I was flying, and many more technical details which I didn't take in then and don't remember now. I was told how the undercarriage retracted and was put down, how the flaps worked and so on; the internal controls were pointed out to me. At that time the undercarriage was hydraulically operated. One needed three hands to operate it: one on the control column, one on the throttle and one to operate the undercarriage and flap levers. There was a tension device on the throttle, which one could tighten to hold the throttle in, and one had to do this, hold the stick with the left hand and pump the undercarriage up with the right hand, then change back again once you took off. It was an awkward affair, even though one became accustomed to it in time.

'The aircraft was fully equipped, apart from the ammunition. My first flight was simply a take-off, a circuit and landing again. I was going from the 120 horsepower engine I was used to, to a 1050 horsepower one, quite a jump, and the roar was incredible. After my first solo flight I went up again with an instructor flying a second aircraft, and we did some combat exercises. Finally I was given an aircraft with twenty rounds of ammunition in each of two guns, and told to go and fire them into the sea for practice. When I opened up the guns for the first time, I was surprised by the noise, even though twenty rounds is spent in a moment, almost quicker than one can register. I was using two guns instead of eight, but the whole aircraft vibrated.

'The instructors' Spitfires were always fully armed, and

carrying a full load of ammunition just in case they saw action. On one occasion, an instructor was up with two trainees, when a German Dornier 11 came over. The instructor shot it down, just as I was taxiing up for take-off. I saw the aircraft spin in and crash, and one of the crew members bailed out, but his parachute became entangled with the tailplane, which caused it to spin. All I could see was this aircraft spinning in and crashing; I didn't know it was German. I thought it was one of our aircraft.

'I didn't actually sit and contemplate death, my death, but it did cross my mind. I don't think one ever thought about dying, in that sense. My attitude to the war was that we had to stop these bastards, whatever the cost, even my own life, although I never expected to be killed – one didn't. My one fear, the one thing I disliked more than anything, was the idea of becoming a prisoner of war.

'As a child, when I was eight or nine, my mother's parents always had a family get-together at Christmas time. All my mother's brothers had been soldiers during the First World War, including one who was taken prisoner of war. This brother had managed to escape from the prison camp with two friends, and the three of them were walking down the road early one morning after they'd broken out. They met a German walking down the road towards them, who said *"Guten morgen"* to which one of my uncle's companions replied "Good morning" in English. It was like one of the scenes from the film, *The Great Escape*, where an escaping prisoner gives himself away by speaking English. The German reported the incident to the next police station he came to and within half an hour all three were captured. My uncle was taken back to the prison camp where his hair was shaved off, except for a tuft on the top of his head. Thereafter his head always had that tuft on the top, even when the rest of his hair regrew.

129

'My five uncles would gather together after lunch and start exchanging their war experiences and that sort of thing. There was always a barrel of beer in the house and I was the beer boy. They'd sit in the parlour and one would empty his glass and call "Jackie! Beer!" and I'd take the glass and refill it. I heard all the wartime reminiscences, and my uncle's prisoner-of-war tales made an indelible impression on my mind, giving me an intense fear and dread of being captured. I knew Sunnie would remember this fear of mine, now that I was being held prisoner of a different war, and my anxiety on her behalf was worse than the captivity in many ways.

'I did very few hours in the Spitfire in the operational training unit – maybe eight or nine. A notice was put on the board saying which Squadrons required how many pilots, and we could apply for any of them we wanted. Some were in Lincolnshire, number 12 group, some were 11 group which is mainly Kent and Suffolk, some 10 group which is the West Country, some were even group 13, which covered the North. I chose 64 Squadron, which was in 11 group, along with two colleagues.

'There was no glory attached to us, at least not then. It was just a job to be done and we had to do it. That was the aim of every one of us. We had to stop the Germans, and it was the greatest incentive. There was no glory in action, although there was pride if you shot something down, of course. Every time we went into combat we were outnumbered, sometimes as much as ten to one. We always had to fight dozens of aircraft, and we would be at most a Squadron of twelve, and more usually three, five, or eight. We were outnumbered before we even took off, but we won by sheer determination and having a better aircraft. That was my attitude now, facing my captors, fifty years later. Once again I was on my own, relying only on my wits. I would survive by sheer determination, and because I was better than them. Nothing else was going to get me through.

EIGHT

One Day at a Time

'I was not a serious-minded student, but I was very serious about my flying. I didn't like authority; one endures authority but one doesn't necessarily like it, in my experience. I never deliberately defied those above me – excepting incidents which seemed to me to transgress a higher authority, as when I refused to disclose Sidebottom's name because I didn't wish to tell tales. When I was abducted, I tried to defy my captors as much as possible and still survive; I wanted to make life as difficult as I could for them, without angering them to the point where they'd make my life unbearable or even kill me.

'It was partly that stubbornness in me which had kept me alive during the Battle of Britain. When I joined 64 Squadron, I was posted to Kenley, from where the Squadron operated, although our forward base was Hawkinge, fifteen or twenty minutes' flight away. We would usually take off from Kenley at dawn, when it was just light enough for one to see where one was going on the ground, and land at Hawkinge, assuming nothing happened en route. Although these were operational positionings, we had to be ready to go into action at any time. Once at Hawkinge, we'd be on immediate readiness to be scrambled.

'We had no conversations at such times, sitting in the early morning, waiting to be called into action, from which we might not return. We would mount our aircraft in silence in the eerie grey light of dawn, subdued and thoughtful. Radio silence was the order of the day. We had cockpit radio transmitters, what we called a T.R.9 transmitter receiver. It couldn't do both simultaneously; you had to pull the switch into the mode you required. The waiting wasn't the jovial banter war films suggest; it was war, and you never knew what was coming next. How you felt at any one time depended on how much action you'd seen at that stage, because as one progressed during wartime, the odds shortened. You knew you were flying on borrowed time, and you became increasingly nervous.

'We used to fly in sections: four sections of three aircraft, each in a "V" formation, and one "in the box", the middle of the formation. We might be lead by the Squadron Leader, or his subordinate, the Flight Lieutenant. On my first flight between the two airfields, I was flying at number three position, and priding myself on my formation flying. I tucked myself neatly behind the fellow leading my "V" of three aircraft, a Flight Sergeant, and flew happily for the twenty-minute flight to Hawkinge, where we landed on the grass – Kenley had a runway, but Hawkinge was just a field – and taxied in. As I climbed out of the cockpit, the Flight Sergeant turned to me and said, "That was very nice, Jackie, but you're not going to live very long."

'Stunned, I asked, "Why?"

'"Because you were too busy watching me, and not looking out for enemy aircraft."

'His reply stung me, because I knew he was right. I was more intent on my textbook formation flying rather than fighting enemy aircraft or even looking out for them, and his rebuke stayed in my mind. It was a piece of advice I've never forgotten. Some time later, when our Squadron pulled out of Kenley, the Flight Sergeant stayed behind. He was up one day

133

with some new pilots, as green as I had been on my first flight, and one of the new boys was formatting the same way I had been, paying no attention to his surroundings. He cut the tail of the Flight Sergeant, and the two aircraft crashed. The pilot who hit him bailed out and survived, but the Flight Sergeant was killed. I've always thought the new boy was doing exactly what I had been doing, flying too close.

'We all lost many friends and colleagues during the Battle of Britain. Many of those who died lost their lives simply because they were too inexperienced. One of the men who had transferred with me to 64 Squadron, a chap named Reggie, should not have been allowed to go to Kenley. We had been on the same operational training together and I'd been called into the Chief Instructor's office for some reason at the end of the course. He happened to be absent from his office for a moment, and I noticed a pile of papers on his desk. Idly reading them upside down, I saw Reggie's personal report, which just said, "Below average, but will improve with experience". He never had the chance to get it. Instead of being posted to Kenley, which had to cover London, the most dangerous of places, he should have been sent to the north or Scotland to gain the experience he lacked. On his first trip out, Reggie was in the "tail end Charlie" position, detailed to watch out for enemy attack from the rear of the Squadron. He never returned. He must have been shot down, or come under attack, but all we knew was that he disappeared. It was something that happened; the most vulnerable position was at the rear, because one could easily fall behind and be picked off. He was just twenty-two years old.

'Days after I arrived at Kenley, I had my first kill. It was only my first or second operational flight, and we were flying over the French coast, near Calais, when we ran into some German ME109s. I managed to manoeuvre higher than one of them, but he was out of my range. The ideal range for a Spitfire was about two hundred yards, even though the actual range of the Browning guns with which we were equipped was half a mile or so. We had four guns on each wing, all aligned to converge at two hundred yards, making it the ideal distance. I followed the 109 and at that height I was just about holding my own – he wasn't going any faster than I, nor I faster than he, so I couldn't catch him. Finally he pulled up into a stall turn: pulling up the aircraft until it more or less stalls and then nosing over to go down. In that respect the ME109 had an advantage over the Spitfire, because the 109 pilot could just push his control column forward and dive down straight. It was not something a Spitfire could do because the engine would cut out from lack of fuel. The 109 had a different type of carburettor and could therefore dive faster than the Spitfire, but performance varied at different altitudes. The Spitfire had more manoeuvrability in some situations: it could turn a tighter right turn, enabling you to get a deflection shot inside the 109's turn, though both planes were equal in turning to the left, because of the different torque on the engines. I loved my Spitfire – it was far more than just a tool. When we joined a Squadron we were allotted a particular aircraft, and if it was serviceable we always flew the same plane.

'I did a half-roll to chase the enemy aircraft, turning the aircraft over to go down. I gained two or three seconds, and came within range of the 109. I fired.

'I hit him and he went into a nosedive, trailing black smoke. I saw bits of the aircraft flying off, from the cockpit I think, and went down after him and followed him until I was flying at ten thousand feet. By this time he was well ahead of me, but he kept on going down, and finally I saw him hit the sea. I saw two splashes and I conjectured that the pilot had bailed out or fallen from the aircraft. After we landed the Squadron Leader also claimed a 109 he'd shot down, and we concluded the two splashes I'd seen had both been enemy aircraft. I hadn't even emptied my weapons; I hadn't needed to, because I hit the 109 with my opening burst of fire. I wasn't scared at all – at least I don't remember feeling afraid – but elated, the adrenalin pumping. I didn't rejoice in the pilot's death, but in a job well done. After all, it was what I was there for.

'During our operational training we'd learnt to fly Spitfires, but had very little combat training itself. I didn't even know how much actual ammunition I had. When we'd practised we'd used twenty rounds out of two guns, just to learn how the aircraft felt when one was firing. The first time I was in combat, I had had just the one practice at firing the twenty rounds into the sea; we didn't even aim at anything, just shot straight into the water for a matter of a few seconds. In combat we were supposed to keep track of what we were firing, so we'd know how much ammunition we had left. I didn't know how many rounds we had in each gun. I had fired for twenty-three seconds, I learned later, though at the time it had seemed like one and a half minutes, which was what I put on my combat report. The officer to whom I delivered it pointed out my error, and I realised that when I counted four or five seconds, I'd probably only fired for one second, if that. Time passed differently when you were in combat.

'My second kill left a nasty taste in my mouth, even though I knew it had to be done. I had come across a 109, and after some manoeuvring I found myself immediately behind the enemy 'plane. I opened up on it, from about two hundred yards, and scored direct hits. Bits were flying off the aircraft, and the pilot was still flying as straight and level as I was. His cockpit canopy flew off, to the right of the aircraft as with all 109s, and I assumed the pilot was going to bail out. I stopped firing, and held my position behind him. I waited three or four seconds, and the pilot made no move to get out. I thought he was trying to fool me and opened up again. The entire aircraft exploded in front of me. It didn't even turn into a fireball, it just exploded into a thousand pieces. It has always been on my mind that I should have given the pilot longer to bail out. It was part of my own personal humanitarian code of combat: you didn't open fire on a pilot trying to bail out, you gave him a chance. I felt a sense of guilt that I didn't give him longer, and compassion for him. I was firing at an aeroplane not an individual. I can't speak for other pilots, but it was how I tried to operate. I believe German pilots did the same, despite rumours that they shot deliberately at pilots who had parachuted out.

'It was always safer to be behind the enemy aircraft, because then he couldn't fire back at you. On one occasion I was sitting behind a 109, having opened up on him when he came within range. Bits and pieces of the aircraft were flying off, when suddenly he slowed up. In order to avoid ramming him – at three hundred and fifty miles an hour, it doesn't take long to eat up the two hundred yards firing distance I was from him – I pulled up and throttled back, so that I was just over the top and to one side of him, flying at the same speed. I could see down into his cockpit and I sat there for a few seconds looking down. The pilot didn't move at all; not his head or hands or anything. I suddenly realised he was dead, although he hadn't slumped over the controls. Five 109s were sitting on my tail, like vengeful sisters, and I broke off the engagement rapidly, which seemed the wisest thing to do. It was the closest I ever came to seeing the face of the enemy I was risking my life to defeat.

'I counted six enemy aircraft I shot down, with three others damaged. I was officially credited with five kills, since one was never recorded, four of them during the Battle of Britain, and one later. You could have three or four pilots firing at the same aircraft, which might be damaged by the first one, who probably claimed it, and then the others might continue firing until it crashed, and claim it too. The rivalry meant a kill had to be confirmed by someone else. My last kill was confirmed by the Navy, who reported seeing an aircraft crash into the sea which could only have been a 109. I hadn't shot it down; it had a technical malfunction which meant the pilot was caught in a dive from which he couldn't recover. Since I had caused it to crash, if indirectly, the kill was credited to me. I missed out on being a flying "Ace", since that required six official kills in the traditional lore of combat flying. Many people came through the war without scoring anything; I knew I was an above-average pilot, and all my records stated as much – one even graded me as exceptional.

'I was downed six times between the summer of 1940, when I was posted to Kenley, and the spring of 1941, when my combat career was brought to an end. During that time I served with three Squadrons – 64 Squadron at Kenley, 92 Squadron at Biggin Hill, and finally 91 Squadron at Hawkinge.

'My first forced landing was when I was with 64 Squadron, and came head to head with a 109. We had engaged each other and were now bearing down in opposite directions. Neither of us would give way, because to do so would put the one yielding into a vulnerable position, so we stuck to our courses. We were psyching each other out, and it was a dangerous game. I was flying at between two hundred and fifty and three hundred miles an hour, and he was travelling a little faster since his course was downwards towards me. I fired a short burst, not daring to alter my course which would have exposed me to his return fire. Terrified, I watched him come closer and closer, our combined speeds six hundred miles an hour.

'We passed over each other just at the point when I thought we were going to hit each other head on. I thought his propeller tips would graze my aircraft. Quickly I turned after the 109, but by that time he was half a mile ahead of me, outside the range of my guns, and fast disappearing into some clouds. I couldn't pursue him any further; there's no point following a fighter into clouds because the enemy can do anything and you can't see him. Somehow during the engagement I managed to lose my Pitot head, the device which indicates your airspeed. I couldn't think how, since the 109 passed over my head and the Pitot head is under the port wing, but it meant I had to go back to base. Fortunately no other enemy aircraft materialised, but I was forced to land my aircraft by feel.

'I was on another patrol not long after this incident, manoeuvring my aircraft, when I realised there was something seriously wrong. I had only the tiniest amount of movement on the control column, either forward or back, or laterally from side to side. I had to get back to the airfield before I encountered an enemy aircraft, or I would have no chance of survival. As I landed, I hit the ground with the starboard wingtip and the starboard wheel simultaneously. Fortunately for me the 'plane bounced back on both wheels, and I ran off the runway onto the grass, with no further damage. I was lucky that hitting the ground with my wingtip didn't cause the aircraft to cartwheel, as so easily could have happened. The ground crew mechanics examined the aircraft and found a cannon shell jammed in the foot of the control column. One of them prised it out and gave it to me, and for many years I carried the nose of the cannon shell around with me.

'My first flying injury was in fact an own goal. We had been over to the French coast, where we saw some enemy action and became separated from one another. I was heading back to Kenley, flying at about eighteen thousand feet, when I heard a loud explosion and took immediate evasive action, wondering where the hell the attack was coming from since I could see no enemy aircraft. I saw the black cloud of the shell burst and a white streamer coming from my Spitfire, because the Glycol cooling system for the engine had been hit. Thinking quickly, I checked the IFF radio identification system, which was working; that puzzled me, for if the IFF was functional I should not have been fired at by our side. I was within gliding distance of Hawkinge, so I just throttled back the engine to preserve what little power I could get and took it home, crossing my fingers that I wouldn't meet any 109s. At that time land mines were being laid on Hawkinge's airfield, to prevent enemy aircraft landing, and one of the cable drums was still sitting out on the airfield where it had been left. I had no brakes, and forced the undercarriage down manually. I had flaps, but I was still rolling at quite a speed when I hit this cable drum with my wingtip, which stopped me and swung me round, since I had no steering and no brakes. One of the undercarriage legs collapsed as I turned, but I managed to climb out.

'It turned out that a Royal Marine Battery, based at Dungeness, had shot me down; indeed, they claimed the highest firing record for two years, until a battery in the West Country shot someone down at about twenty-two thousand feet. I'll never know why they shot me down; I was the only aircraft in the sky. I can't believe they had their IFF switched on or they'd have identified me from that. They must have realised I was a British Spitfire when I came low enough for them to see me properly, and I often wondered what they must have thought when they saw they'd got an own goal.

'I ended up with shrapnel in my legs from the Marines' ack-ack, although it wasn't a serious injury and I lost very little blood. The doctor at Hawkinge put a dressing on my legs, and the Squadron sent an aircraft from Kenley and flew me back to the base, from where I was driven by ambulance to the Royal Naval Hospital at Greenwich. I think the theory was that as the Navy had put it in, the Navy could take it out! Most of it was in my right calf, although not all of it was removed, because when I was burned subsequently one or two bits of shrapnel were found to be still there.

140

'I always seemed to come through, even though I had close brushes with death on more than one occasion. At one stage I was even reported killed, before I reappeared from the dead, as it were. When I lay in my cell in Sofar, I wondered if Sunnie knew I was alive. I learned later that she had been told I was dead, and the media reported my assumed demise more than once. But I was a corpse which wouldn't lie down.

'In September 1940, I was on a patrol with 92 Squadron one bright, sunny afternoon. We were badly led, in my opinion, because we climbed eastbound, with the sun behind us, always a dangerous option. We had reached twelve or fifteen thousand feet, and the squadron – still all twelve of us together – was still climbing, when a number of 109s passed overhead, considerably higher than we were. They started coming down behind us, and one by one the sections broke away. I caught up with the fellow leading the squadron and his number two, and I flew as the number three in the section. Moments later number two said, "I've left," and I saw there were two 109s right behind us, and I said, "Sorry, I've left too," and broke away. I turned two hundred and seventy degrees and found two 109s in front of me; whether they were different aircraft or the two I'd just spotted I didn't know. I was within firing range and opened up on them, but more or less as I opened fire I was hit.

'The bullet hit me right in the backside. I remember someone asking me many years later how I knew I'd been hit and I said, "You'd bloody know if you'd been hit with a bullet up your arse!" I managed to get my hand down inside under the harness and my parachute, and under my trousers; when I brought my fingers back again they were covered in blood. I felt as if I'd been kicked, but the pain was dull. I took the aircraft back to my base at Biggin Hill and landed normally, and taxied in. The ground crew came up to me and said, "Did you get anything?"

'"Yes," I said, somewhat irascibly. "I got a bullet up the backside."

'The ground crewman turned to his companion and said, "He's been hit," and I climbed out of the aircraft. More interested in what had happened to the 'plane than what had happened to me, the ground crew gathered round the aircraft and gestured to the hole in the side. It was straight through the roundel, the RAF colours emblazoned on the side of the Spitfire. "It's British ammunition," one of them said, and they all looked closer. It must have come from one of our aircraft which had broken away earlier – the second time I'd been hit by my own team.

'I was put in the back of a truck, as there were no ambulances available, and bumped across the ground. The jolting was excruciating, and eventually I hammered on the dividing wall between the cab and the back of the truck, and asked if I could travel in the passenger seat. The rest of the journey was more comfortable, although I don't recommend a bullet in the backside if one is going to be seated for a while, and we arrived at Farnborough Hospital. I was admitted to surgery straight away, where they operated, removing as much as possible. It wasn't a serious injury, but an awkward one.

'I had given one of the ground crew at Biggin Hill half a crown to send a telegram to my parents telling them what had happened. I gave him the address and said I'd been downed again but I was all right and going into hospital. That was on a Saturday evening.

'The following Monday morning, a local policeman arrived at my home and knocked on the door. My mother answered it and the policeman asked for my father, who was not in. My mother gazed at the policeman and instinctively asked, "It's Jack, isn't it?" and he said, "Yes, I'm afraid he's dead." She got hold of my father and told him, and he immediately contacted an undertaker in Bedford, who arrived with a motor hearse, complete with coffin. My parents and my elder sister, Madge, climbed into the hearse and set off for Farnborough Hospital.

'When they arrived, they asked for the mortuary, since they'd been told I was dead. They told the attendant my name and asked to see my body.

'"We've got five RAF boys in here," said the attendant in charge, "And they all crashed together. Frankly it doesn't matter which coffin you take because we can't identify the separate parts."

'"If one of those coffins contains more of my son than the others, then that's the coffin I want," said my father. "Now find me someone who knows."

'The attendant couldn't help him, but sent him down to the local police station. By chance it happened that the Sergeant in charge of the police station was the same man who had been on duty the Saturday I was admitted to hospital, and he explained that there must have been some mistake. "Your son is in the hospital, not the mortuary," he said, and unable to believe it my parents raced back to the hospital, which of course was where I was lying, unaware of the agony they'd just been put through.

'My mother and father rushed into the ward, crying and laughing at the same time. It must have been like a dream; whenever someone loses a person they hold dear, their first thought is "It can't be true" even while they know it is. For them to discover that the miracle had happened and it was a mistake must have been the most incredible news. I was lying on my face with my bottom in the air, and when they told me all the hoohah they'd been through I turned over as much as I could and announced to the ward at large, "Hello chaps, I'm dead."

'When my family reached their home in Northampton, they found the neighbours had prepared a room with a couple of trestles on which to put the coffin, and wreaths and flowers were already arriving. By this time it was ten or eleven o'clock at night. My sister Madge tore into the house, screaming to my younger sister Betty who was in bed, "He's alive, he's alive!"

'The telegram I'd sent on the Saturday arrived the following morning, the Tuesday. Its delay had caused intense pain and eventually Scotland Yard accepted responsibility for sending the wrong information. It was their role, in those days, to notify the immediate relatives of RAF personnel. I believe they recompensed my father for the money expended on the hearse and coffin, and the drive to Farnborough, although my father always denied it.

'Even in hospital, the war intruded on your life and even threatened it. Farnborough was bombed by the Germans and, although there were no direct strikes, one bomb fell immediately adjacent to the outside wall and exploded at the bottom. It did some damage to the ward on the ground floor, but ironically enough the only patients there were German prisoners of war, none of whom were injured. The upper floors, which were occupied principally by WAAFs and WAAF officers who'd been injured in bombing raids on Biggin Hill, were all evacuated. By this stage I could walk by myself from my bed to the toilet and I managed somehow to get upstairs. I don't know how I did it myself, but I picked up a WAAF who was lying on a bed in plaster from her neck to her knees. She'd had her back broken. I carried her downstairs, staggering because I could only just walk myself, and put her under a bed on the ground floor, where she was safe.

'Along with everyone else, I was evacuated to Orpington Hospital, in Kent. I was told there was a badly burned officer there, and I asked if I could see him. The ward sister tried to deter me, because his face was badly burned, saying, "He's not a very pleasant sight." I insisted, was taken along to see him, and we introduced ourselves. His name was Squadron

Leader Tom Leave, and I had no idea then that we would meet again, when I myself was a burns victim. We spent twenty minutes chatting, then I left since he tired easily. He was a little over thirty years old, and the RAF had just introduced a ruling whereby no Squadron Commander could be over the age of twenty-six. My Squadron Commander was only few months older than I was then.

'I was finally discharged from Orpington and I returned home on leave. My wound refused to heal and since the local general hospital refused to treat me, I was admitted to the RAF at Henlow. I was told to take off my uniform, and wear hospital blue. There was a Wing Commander there who was Russian, and he came round the ward one day with a nurse pushing her trolley of tools. I will never forget him standing by my bed and asking this nurse for a probe. She handed him a probe five or six inches long, and I could feel him inserting it into me, along the track the bullet had carved. I felt him take it out, and he handed it back to the nurse, saying, "A longer probe, please." I thought, "How much longer can you need?" and the nurse handed him another one that was a good eight to ten inches long. The idea of that cold steel disappearing ten inches inside me was not a pleasant one, even though it didn't actually hurt. The bullet had hit me on the lower right-hand side of my buttock, missing my spine by an inch, leaving a scar two and a half inches wide. Apparently there were still some pieces deep down, which they decided to leave since they weren't causing any damage and it was safer to let them lie. I had been incredibly lucky once again.

'It seemed I had been given nine lives. I was serving with 91 Squadron, out on a patrol escorting my Flight Commander, a man called Bob Holland, who earlier had received a DFC in the Battle of Britain. 91 Squadron would patrol in pairs, two aircraft at a time, and Bob was leading against enemy interception, whilst I flew number two to him, protecting his rear whilst he looked out in front. Suddenly we were jumped by two ME109s and I was hit. I switched on the T.R.9 transmitter and called his number – we were all given a number in the Squadron, and he was number four – shouting to Bob, "Lookout four, lookout four," alerting him to the danger. I was later credited with saving him from being shot down, although it was an instinctive action.

'My aircraft went into a spin, and I started going down fast, unable to pull out. I was flying at eighteen or twenty thousand feet, which gave me a little time. I was talking to myself, the transmitter still in functioning mode so that the listening watch on the ground, which monitored all transmissions, could hear me. I was saying over and over again, "I'm going down, I can't see, I'm going down, I can't see." They knew immediately that I must have been shot down.

'I spun down, still fighting to get my aircraft under control, and finally managed to pull it out after falling about fourteen thousand feet. I looked around, and couldn't see any damage on the aircraft, but I found it wouldn't fly under about a hundred and forty miles an hour. If I tried to take it slower, it was impossible to hold a straight and level course. I decided to try to take it back to Hawkinge, the base from which I was then operating, but it had only a small airfield, and I knew I couldn't land it there. My only hope was to find an open piece of ground. As I approached I spied a farmer's field. I had to land with my wheels up, since it was impossible to lower them at the speed I was flying, and the 'plane still refused to fly at less than a hundred and forty miles an hour without pitching and rolling. I came down, and examined the field I'd decided on to find it was criss-crossed with anti-landing wires about eight to ten feet above the ground, to prevent enemy aircraft from landing.

'I had little choice at this stage but to attempt a landing. As I came in I saw one of these wires just where I was about to touch down, and I managed to jump over that one, and down under the next one. I hit the ground at a hundred and forty miles an hour with the wheels up, and came to a grinding halt. I was very close to a British army ack-ack battery on a hillside nearby. Troops from this post came rushing over and were beside my aircraft almost as soon as I stopped sliding. Because I'd tightened up the straps of my safety harness, the moment I hit the ground my legs came off the rudder pedals and were driven up into the bottom of the instrument panel. I stepped out of the aircraft onto the ground, just as one of the soldiers called out "Are you all right?" and fell flat on my face. My legs simply refused to support me. I got up again, because I wasn't really hurt, apart from some shrapnel in the elbow of my right arm.

'I looked around the aircraft, and found a bullet hole on the starboard wing, which had cut my aerolon balance cable. That had meant I couldn't hold the wing, so I'd lost most of my control. Fortunately no flammable part of the aircraft had been hit or it would have burst into flames. The soldiers got a car for me and drove me back to Hawkinge, where I was taken to sick quarters for a doctor to treat my elbow. I went back to my quarters, which had been married quarters before the war, so were fairly luxurious, and much envied. My room even had its own bathroom. I walked in and found someone had already moved into my room. My kit had been divided up and I had generally been written off as dead. It was the second time I had been reported killed and whilst I was glad to be alive, I was a little aggrieved that my demise was so often assumed. They had heard me screaming "I'm going down, I can't see" and had believed I hadn't survived. It was the most terrifying episode of my flying career to date, and I had closed my eyes in shock. I remained conscious the whole time, unable to see, yet wrestling with the controls to bring the aircraft down safely. My instinct for survival was

147

strong. It was partly for that incident that I was later awarded the DFM.

'I had faced death so many times, and I wasn't afraid of it. My one fear was imprisonment, capture as a prisoner of war. That always seemed the anathema to me, to be deprived of your liberty and freedom to make your own decisions. I was a man who liked to be in control of his own destiny, and loathed being forced to do something not of my own choosing.

'Fifty years later, my feelings hadn't changed. When my captors in Lebanon decided the time had come to kill me, I was determined to face the fact with dignity and courage, even while I prayed.'

NINE

Is This The End?

'The leader of the kidnap group now holding me at Sofar, Awad, formulated a plan for my death. He wanted to kill me with the maximum publicity and kudos, and to this end, decided to blow me up in spectacular fashion.

'Awad was still in the habit of going into the village of Sofar, despite the inhabitants' hostility, and addressing anyone who would listen. He now promised the children a "big explosion", which was apparently to be sited in the embryo television studio he and his team had contrived across the road. The explosive device was to be hidden in a television set and detonated electronically, using the aerial of the television set in some way which I never fathomed. The electrical charge required for that was to come from batteries placed in the boot of a car, which was in turn to be placed in the garden of the villa where I was being held. It seemed unreal to me; I was beginning to wonder if I was indeed losing my mind, or if my captors had finally lost theirs. The plans were laid – many bits and pieces I overheard filled in the details – and it seemed nothing was going to deter Awad from going ahead.

'For two or three weeks I heard Awad repeating his promise to the children of Sofar, who were always pestering him for details about the promised explosion, asking again and again when it was going to happen. They seemed to have devised some sort of uniform which I was going to be dressed in, perhaps to disguise my identity, and the intention appeared to be that when the building collapsed, with me inside, all traces of my existence and captivity would be erased.

'The date for the explosion was set. I think the kidnappers were beginning to become as confused about their days as I was, for all of us seemed convinced that Hallowe'en was on 30 November. The explosion was certainly planned for 30 November, and the guards referred constantly to the date as Hallowe'en, so that in the end I too forgot that it falls, in fact, a month earlier: on the last day in October. This detail was forgotten by Awad too. Their plans went ahead regardless.

'There was nothing I could do, except pray. Months before, at Kaslik, I had got into the habit of talking to the saint whom I regarded as my special saint, my patron, Saint Barnabas. He was born in Cyprus, a second generation disciple of Christ himself, and was finally crucified in his homeland. Saint Barnabas' feastday in the Church calendar was 11 June, my birthday, and I adopted him. I am not a religious man in any way, even though in my teens I was a regular churchgoer. I used to be a member of the Church Lads' Brigade, and had to attend every Sunday, despite not being a believer even then. My agnosticism hadn't wavered, and still didn't, Saint Barnabas notwithstanding. But in times of intense stress and loneliness, often feeling I was close to death, I found the presence of a man with whom I identified comforting. I would go through my day's activities with Saint Barnabas, saying, "My breakfast was acceptable, my lunch was terrible, supper was not too bad," and so on. During moments of extreme depression, if things seemed particularly bad and I felt I couldn't go on much longer, I'd appeal to Saint Barnabas, chatting to him as one would to a friend, saying "Please do something about this, I've had enough," and the depression would pass.

'I would never have really described it as praying, although I suppose that's what it was. To me it seemed like a conversation, a one-sided chat. I'd even speak aloud, albeit in an undertone. At Kaslik the guards had introduced a listening device into my room which I detected because I could see a double wire coming through the wall, to a plug which as far as I could see had no other purpose in life. To my surprise, not long after I began talking to Saint Barnabas, I heard my captors referring to him, whom they wouldn't have known before I mentioned him. I concluded that they were listening to what I was saying, and to test my theory one night I called on Saint Sebastian instead. Sure enough, the following day I heard his name mentioned, and I adjusted the level of my conversations, turning my head away from the pickup, so that they could no longer overhear what I said. It wasn't important that they heard, inasmuch as there was nothing secret about my words, but they were private and I resented the intrusion the listening device represented. Soon afterwards, the pickup was turned off.

'November 30 arrived, and I gathered a television camera was placed on the roof of the building in which I was being held, directed, so I understood, at the other building which was destined to be demolished, and me with it. The idea was that the whole thing was to be filmed and shown on their new television station, if and when it started, as a big publicity point. The kidnappers had asked the local police to prevent a crowd from gathering too close around the building they'd targeted for destruction, saying they were going to blow it up as a publicity stunt. The police happily co-operated with them. Everything was in place, and I believe I was as close to death then as I had ever been.

'Then it started to rain.

'I listened to the rain falling and hope glimmered. I prayed to Saint Barnabas, harder than I ever had before in my life, begging, "More rain! More rain, please!" If it rained perhaps they'd have to stop.

'I heard it raining harder and harder. My captors complained that the television camera on the roof was unusable, because of the water on the lens, and the weather became so inclement it was in danger of being ruined or swept off the roof altogether. Reluctantly, the guards were forced to dismantle it and take it down. The crowds waiting outside to see the explosion seemed restless, and impatient. Finally the kidnappers had to abandon the whole attempt.

'I was not safe yet. The explosion was rescheduled for the following evening.

'The kidnappers decided to dress someone up in the costume they intended me to wear, as a rehearsal perhaps, or just for their own entertainment, and accordingly one of them put on the clothes, topped with a large straw hat. I've no idea what the purpose behind it was, but I was grateful that they did it, for the police came visiting that afternoon, and caught the guard wearing the strange ensemble intended for me. Awad decided he could no longer risk putting the scheme into action, and the plan was once again abandoned. The children in the village pursued the idea of the "big explosion" they'd been promised, and for a while Awad fobbed them off with plans to stage the event at a later date. To my relief, it seemed the scheme had been abandoned, once and for all.

'I hated the thought of dying in such a fashion; to the outside world, I would just have vanished, and no one would ever have known what had become of me. There is no instinct greater than the one for survival, and frail as my body might be, the desire to live burned in me as strongly now as it had ever done. I thought back over the moments where I had brushed death in my flying days and I was determined that it should not end now, like this, ignominiously dying a prisoner, with nothing to mark my passing.

'It was not for this that I had survived the Battle of Britain.

'My last flight as a fighter pilot was on 4 April 1941. I was then with 91 Squadron, patrolling as usual in pairs; one of us in front doing the spotting, looking out for enemy aircraft, and one behind protecting his tail, weaving back and forth both to keep an eye on his partner and to watch out for the enemy. That morning I was suddenly scrambled, because two enemy aircraft were reported coming in. My partner was a chap called Speares, known as Dagger, and the two of us ran to our aircraft, which were just a few paces from the dispersal hut where we sat waiting. We climbed in as quickly as we could, and took off. The enemy was reported to be over Deal, so we headed in that direction, but before we reached our destination we were told the enemy was now over Ramsgate. Accordingly we changed our course for Ramsgate, but were then told the enemy was once more headed for Deal, and we altered our direction again. Then the message came that the enemy had headed for home, and we relaxed.

'The Sergeants' Mess were entertaining the local police that evening, and I was looking forward to the Mess party. I sat contemplating the green fields below me and the blue sky around me, thinking about the pleasant evening ahead. I was four or five miles from my base, Hawkinge, and I set my course for home.

'Suddenly the aircraft shuddered as I was hit by cannonshell, in the starboard wing root where the wing was attached to the centre section of the 'plane. I took at least eight or ten cannonshells in that one burst, and I could see chips of metal from the wing sticking straight up. I broke off to take evasive action, and peeled upwards. The aircraft was still flying normally, the engine still functioning, and I thought with relief that I could still make it back to Hawkinge. The enemy must have been on my right, judging by the hit he'd scored, but I hadn't even seen him, and there was no sign of him now.

153

'I was only a few miles from my base when I suddenly realised I had a lot of petrol swishing around in the cockpit. The hit was obviously worse than I had thought, and some part of the shells had pierced the petrol tank, which was between the cockpit and the engine. I could feel the liquid sloshing around my feet, and I knew there was a great deal of it. I could smell the fumes, and my heart chilled. It was the nightmare of every pilot: I knew that my life depended on the decisions I made in the next few seconds. I decided I had to land, and aimed for a farmer's field close by me.

'I approached the field carefully, the engine still running, and throttled back. I decided not to try to put the undercarriage down or I'd run out of field before I stopped. I had to make a forced landing on the 'plane's belly and pray I came to a halt before the field did. I was flying very low, around two hundred feet, and slipped the sliding canopy back, which was the worst thing I could have done. Immediately the draught in the cockpit caught at the fumes from the petrol sloshing around, breezing them out of the cockpit towards the exhaust of the 'plane. The fumes ignited in the heat, within seconds the cockpit was ablaze, and me with it.

'I was flying far too low to bail out; I would have been splattered across the field before my parachute even opened. The cockpit was full of flames and I could feel them scorching me. My goggles were perched on my forehead – I'd slid them up when I thought I had nothing to worry about, because goggles were difficult to see through: the least spot looked like a distant enemy aircraft. Now, I was paying the price, as the flames burnt my face and eyes. All I could do was try to hold the aircraft steady as it came down and close my eyes to protect them. I hit the ground with my eyes still closed, and overshot the field slightly so that I actually flew through a nearby hedge. Sheep sheltering under the lea of the hedge scattered in all directions, terrified at this burning wreck hurtling into their midst. As I hit the ground the starboard wing fell away, too damaged by the shells to stay together.

'The danger of being trapped in a burning cockpit was one of the horrors of flying, but I had never dreamed it would happen to me. My only thought was to get out of the blazing aircraft. The metal was red hot but I climbed out, ignoring the stench which I later realised was my flesh burning. My mind seemed to cut out and I went into automatic pilot, mechanically carrying out the escape-drill which had been drummed into all of us.

'"If you land in enemy territory, you must hide your parachute. If you don't, the Germans will find it and know you are in the immediate vicinity. Then they'll search and find you too." I heard the words echoing in my head, and realised I had left my parachute in the aircraft. I climbed back into the flaming 'plane, pulled the parachute out and ran a few yards to the ditch by the hedge, hurling it into the bottom with all my strength. I scrabbled around the ground, flinging brambles and leaves on top of the parachute to hide it. Abruptly I stopped, realising what I was doing. I wasn't in enemy territory; there were no Germans who would be looking for me – I didn't need to bury my parachute. I felt pain in my legs and looked down. They were on fire – the whole of my right leg was ablaze. I began beating the flames out with my hands, which were fortunately protected by silk inner gloves and heavy RAF issue leather gauntlets. My fingertips were scorched where the leather had worn, but my hands weren't burned. As my hands hit my burning clothes I thumped my pocket, and realised my camera was still in it. I pulled it out, ran to a good position near the flaming aircraft, and took two pictures of my last Spitfire, one from the starboard quarter and one from behind the 'plane. It's even possible to see the squadron identification, "DL", on the side of the wreckage.

'I kicked off my flying boots to douse the flames on my

burning trousers and, removing my helmet and goggles, I started to walk across the field. By now my eyes were closing up from burns and I staggered straight into a barbed wire fence, from which it took me some time to disentangle myself. Finally I broke through it and saw a cottage, which I forced myself to walk towards. Every step was painful and each pace was harder to take. I knocked on the door, leaning against the lintel and praying whoever owned the house was in. There was no reply, and in desperation I hammered on the door with my flying boots, which were still in my hand.

'An elderly lady opened the door and immediately presumed I had had a motorcycle accident, what with the goggles and leather jacket and helmet clutched under my arm. I explained what had happened, and she promptly got out her bicycle and started pedalling towards the RAF sick quarters, which were only a mile or so away from her cottage. They'd actually seen me come down from the RAF sick quarters and had already despatched an ambulance in my direction. They passed the lady pedalling furiously on her bicycle, and she turned round and followed the ambulance back. By the time she caught up with it, the crew were already halfway across the field to the burning aircraft. The lady rushed over to them, shouting, "He's in my cottage!" and they ran back.

'I had collapsed in the hall of the cottage and was lying there in great pain when the doctor came in.

'He bent over me as he opened his bag of medical equipment and asked, "Who is it?"

'"Mann," I gasped.

'"Oh, not again," he groaned, and I peered up at him. It was the same doctor who'd treated me for the shrapnel wounds in my legs when the Royal Marine battery shot me down. I learned later his name was Jacobs and he even wrote to me.

'I was given a shot of morphine and loaded into the back of

156

the ambulance on a stretcher. We drove to the sick quarters, where Dr Jacobs went inside, leaving me lying in the ambulance with one of the attendants. I was desperate for the man to keep talking, talking about anything but just to keep talking, so that I would know I was alive and to take my mind off this terrible pain. But all he said was, "Don't worry, you'll be fine, don't worry," until I was ready to scream.

'The doctor reappeared and we drove to the Royal Victoria Hospital at Folkestone. By this time the morphine was beginning to take effect. I was told many years later by a qualified nurse that the shock effect of a severe burn is such that you don't feel the full pain you would in other injuries. I have to say she was wrong. The pain was acute – anyone who says otherwise hasn't been burned. I remember arriving at the Royal Victoria and being taken out of the ambulance, but I don't remember anything after that. The drugs, the pain and the shock combined to knock me out. I had no idea what the extent of my injuries was at that stage, and no inkling of how bad my burns were.

'I awoke heavily bandaged and unable to see. My legs had been dressed with tannic acid, which was the burns treatment used in those days. Its main drawback was that it created a form of artificial skin over the burns area, a hard skin, which tended to break and crack. The only remedy then was to cover the breaks with more tannic acid, which aggravated the problem. My eyes were bathed daily. When I had closed them as I crashed, I had protected them from the worst of the flames, although my eyelids were burned away.

'About eight days after my accident, the nurse was changing the dressing on my eyes as she did every day. As she took the bandages off, I was able to open my eyes. I looked into her face and said the first thing that came into my head, "You've got a shiny nose!"

'The nurse screamed and dropped the dressings in her hand

on top of her trolley, and rushed down the ward crying, "He can see! He can see!" Until that point the doctors had been afraid my eyesight was permanently damaged.

'I was moved from the hospital in Folkestone to the Queen Victoria Hospital at East Grinstead, in West Sussex. It was renowned for its pioneering treatment for burns, led by the brilliant surgeon, Archibald McIndoe, who gave new life to so many burned aircrew. After a night in one of the ordinary wards, I was moved into what was known as Ward Three, which was the specialised burns ward where ninety-five per cent of the patients were burns victims. McIndoe had recommended my move to the Queen Victoria from Folkestone, as he believed he could do a great deal for me.

'He was the first person to come and see me after I arrived, and methodically he assessed my injuries. My legs were severely burned, the right leg worst; it had third-degree burns, the left leg first- and second-degree injuries. I had third-degree burns on the skin around my eyes – they were particularly bad because I'd had my goggles up. My cheeks, chin and ears had been protected by my flying helmet, and my oxygen mask and microphone saved my mouth, although one side of my nose was rather badly damaged. My fingertips were slightly scorched, but the leather gloves had protected them from serious injury.

'I was immediately started on a course of saline baths, to remove the tannic acid, which McIndoe considered outdated. He had noted that pilots who crashed into the sea recovered more quickly than those who crashed on the ground and deduced the healing effect of salt water was helping heal the burns more rapidly. Accordingly all his patients followed a course of saline baths. I began with two a day, one in the morning and one in the afternoon. A special team was trained just to give such baths to the burns patients. The salt water softened the tannic acid so that it could be lifted off, or cut off with a scalpel, until it had all been removed and the healing could begin. It was pioneering treatment, and I became one of McIndoe's so-called "Guinea Pigs", those pilots who benefited from the surgeon's talented hands.

'I had to undergo reconstructive surgery, and two months after I crashed, in June 1941, McIndoe grafted skin taken from my left upper arm to my eyes. All the burned skin was cut away, for by that time the natural skin on my eyes had shrunk as it healed, so that even asleep my eyes didn't close. The skin from my left arm was cut to the required shape and grafted to form my upper eyelids. McIndoe used more skin than he needed, so that after the graft had definitely taken, the superfluous skin was removed. My lower lids were operated on by an RAF Squadron Leader studying grafting techniques, whose name was George Morley. He took the skin from my right upper arm, and from it formed the lower lids. McIndoe had done the upper lids because they were more complex.

'I had two skin grafts on my legs as well. The scarred area wasn't healing well, and a piece of skin from my upper left leg, which wasn't so badly injured, was grafted onto my right leg, which had been burned more severely. My left leg was left resembling a draught board; it still bears seventy-two dots, perfect white circles much lighter than the rest of my leg. They were pinpricks of skin which were cut off in order and then grafted onto the right leg where the third-degree burns were. Each one is about a third of the size of one's little fingernail, lined up in regimented fashion in a large square across my thigh. My chessboard, I call it.

'From the very beginning at East Grinstead, I was given a ration of two bottles of beer per day; it was apparently a great help in recovery, both psychologically and physically. It certainly proved to be so for me. One day George Morley, who was touring the wards after I'd been there about three weeks, decided to suspend my ration, as he considered I didn't need the beer. The following day I was in the saline bath and I had a complete relapse. I had to be taken out of the bath and rushed back to bed, where I was given oxygen and a blood transfusion, the full works. Apparently I was nearer to dying then than I had been at the start of my injuries. I blamed the doctor for taking me off the beer, although he put it down to delayed shock.

'Archibald McIndoe was inspiring. He had great humanitarian qualities, quite apart from his brilliance as a surgeon. On the eve of every operation, he would come round for a chat with you. One day he came to me, and said, "Well, you're for the slab, Jackie" – which was how we referred to the operating table – and I said, "No, you can't, my parents are coming to visit me." He knew it was a long way for them to come, and he said, "Don't worry, we'll take care of them."

'The next day I was given a pre-operation injection to prepare me for the anaesthetic. The nurse came by and gave me this jab, then I was wheeled into the operating theatre. I heard McIndoe say to his anaesthetist, John Hunter, "Just give him enough to keep him under, John, his parents are coming." I fell asleep thinking what an incredible man McIndoe was, to worry about such a thing with all that he had to accomplish. After my operation I was taken back to the ward and came round almost immediately after my parents had arrived, swathed in dressings and bandages, but conscious.

'At one time the Air Ministry commanded that all other ranks should wear a blue hospital uniform, a ridiculous rule I had encountered in my previous accidents. There was a large outcry against this by both other ranks and officers, and McIndoe himself was strongly against it. It was ridiculed at East Grinstead; if you were playing sports or games you didn't have to wear the blue uniform, so characters with their arms in slings and their legs on crutches would wander about in their own clothes, claiming to anyone who'd listen that they were going to play cricket or tennis, or some other game it was physically impossible for them to engage in. Eventually the Queen Victoria's consignment of blue clothing was piled up into the garden and burned, and the order was later dropped.

'After every operation I was given leave, and I used to take my MG – which I still had – and drive home. On one occasion I took one of my fellow patients home, a chap called Paul Hart. He'd had his entire face rebuilt by McIndoe, and his disfigurement was far worse than mine. The day we went home, he'd just had a graft done from his stomach to his face. Two large cuts were made across his midriff, and grafted to his face, the ends still attached to his stomach. One end was then detached and sewn onto his arm, and when that was safely growing, the other end was detached. He looked pretty ghastly. The customers at my parents' pub were wonderful to him, treating Paul like any normal person, which was just the treatment any psychiatrist would recommend. We were very good friends, and he was with me when I later met Sunnie.

'I was at the Queen Victoria in East Grinstead until early November of 1941. When I was discharged, my legs had been rebuilt, with successful grafts, and my eyes now had upper and lower lids. My operational standing with the RAF was as a Sergeant Pilot still and I was posted back to Hawkinge as a duty pilot – I wasn't flying, but I was able to work in the control tower, giving instructions to aircraft landing and taking off. It was a rehabilitation period, and they worked on the basis that because I'd been shot down from Hawkinge, that was the base to which I returned.

'From Hawkinge I was posted to Number One Delivery Flight in Hendon, north-west London. I was given a week's leave and told to report to Hendon on 1 January 1942. I could no longer engage enemy action, but at least I was flying again. I was relieved I could fly and not desperately disappointed that

I'd been downgraded so I could no longer engage the enemy; I felt I had risked my life enough for one war, and I dreaded the thought of any more injuries, for I thought I'd had my fair share by then. As long as I could fly in some form, I was happy.

'I reported to Hendon, where the Flight Lieutenant sent me down to a Spitfire operational unit at Heston, to do a short refresher course as I hadn't flown for eight months by then. He later became my best man. I had been awarded the Distinguished Flying Medal on 25 April 1941, as a result of my previous engagements, and I was recommended for commissioning. As a result of my injuries, I had been graded as being "B2" condition, and the rule in the RAF was that you couldn't be promoted, and certainly not commissioned, if you're not "A1". It was the second time I lost my commission. Instead, I was promoted to Flight Sergeant, and later to Warrant Officer.

'On New Year's Eve of 1942, I drove home to Hendon, ready to start my posting the following day with Number One Delivery Flight, which principally moved aircraft between squadrons. That New Year's Eve, I arrived alone in my MG, parked it and walked into the Mess. Very few people were there – they were all out partying to welcome in 1942. I recognised no one, and morosely opened my post. I found five or six telegrams, all inviting me to a party at the Dorchester Hotel Park Lane. On the spur of the moment I decided to go to it, and after a quick stop at the local pub, where there was still no one I knew, I headed for the Dorchester in the MG.

'It turned out the party was a "Guinea Pig" celebration, much to my surprise, and I joined in with enthusiasm. Amongst the people at the party was a stunning woman whom I'd met briefly once before. We started talking, and the band struck up a tune which Sunnie and I both liked, so we danced.

Yours till the stars lose their glory,
Yours till the birds fail to sing.
Yours till the end of life's story,
This pledge to you dear I bring:
Yours to the end of a lifetime.

'It was a song, and a promise, which became ours.

'Sunnie allowed me to drive her home in the MG, which impressed her a good deal. I returned to the party, which was still in full swing, my head full of her. Paul Hart, my "Guinea Pig" friend, and I decided to spend the night at the Dorchester, with a couple of other people, and we bedded down in the kitchen area, below ground. The party continued the next day, and that night Paul and I slept in the apartment of the McAlpine family, adjacent to the Dorchester.

'On the third day Paul and I were joined at one stage by an Air Vice-Marshal and as we talked he asked me where I was stationed. I confessed that I should have been at Hendon two days ago, and he said, "Never mind, I know the Group Captain commanding Hendon." He telephoned his friend, and said to him, "If you want Jackie Mann, he's with me," and so the party went on, into its third day.

'At some stage we met the man who wrote the famous song, "The Teddy Bears' Picnic", and he took us to his apartment in the Dorchester, where we spent the third night. On the fourth day, Paul and I ran into a fellow who was a very keen professional agriculturalist: he planned and actually made operational an acre of ground in which his house stood. It was self-sufficient, an early forerunner of the *Good Life* television series of the seventies, with a pig, a cow and plenty of vegetables. We drove down to his house in Surrey later, so that he could show us round. When we arrived, his wife was busy packing her clothes, and about to leave him. We talked her out of it, and beat a hasty retreat.

'Sunnie and I met several times during the course of that five-day party, and we fell in love. It wasn't her looks that attracted me to her so compellingly, but her outstanding personality. She was good friends with both Paul and myself, and a number of other "Guinea Pigs", a socialite who wasn't afraid of reality, ugliness or getting her hands dirty. We met again and again, on my trips into the centre of London, and after four or five months I more or less moved into the house she was renting, in as much as I stayed there whenever I came to town. From Hendon I was moved to Croydon, and I'd come up from Croydon, see Sunnie and maybe stay the night and go back to Croydon the following morning. I'd been with her six months before I learned she had been married, and was in the midst of a divorce, and even had a daughter called Jennifer, who was living with Sunnie's parents. It didn't make any difference to the way I felt about her. On 18 June 1943, one week after my birthday, we were married.

Sunnie had a pet Alsatian at this time, Vixen, and she would bound out onto the runway as I climbed into the cockpit of whatever aircraft I was moving that day. When I came back, I would frequently be flying a different 'plane, yet Vixen would always run out to greet my aircraft as I landed. Somehow she always used to know which one I was in. My colleagues used to joke that it was the way I landed that gave the game away.

'I continued flying from Croydon, and was commissioned as a Flying Officer, at last, in the spring of 1943. My medical category was again upgraded back to "A1", but during the course of my rehabilitation I had obviously given the RAF psychiatrist the impression that I felt I'd done my share, been shot down six times, and was lucky to be alive. The psychiatrist took the view that I should not go back into operational combat, but take another job, and accordingly I was given orders to move to India as a fighter controller, based on the ground, stopping me from flying at all. I was devastated. Flying was my life, and always had been, and the prospect of not being able to fly horrified me. I had a week's notice to pack and collect the tropical gear I'd need.

'But I hadn't taken into account the fact that I was married to Sunnie, and neither had the RAF. She refused to accept the order, and got in touch with Archibald McIndoe down at East Grinstead, and somehow persuaded him to use his influence to have the order rescinded. Between them, they managed it, and I never made it to India.

'Instead, I stayed flying with Number One Delivery Flight. In 1945, I managed to get seconded to BOAC and started flying Liberators, a four-engine American-made aircraft, from Prestwick in Scotland to Montreal in Canada. We carried essential military cargo eastbound, and personnel on the return journeys. My aircraft held the record for the shortest transatlantic crossing from Montreal to Prestwick, twelve hours and twenty-five minutes. Coming the other way, I managed to hold the record of taking the longest, seventeen and a half hours, from Prestwick to Montreal. I was promoted to Flight Lieutenant and continued this run throughout 1945. At the end of August I returned to England on leave, where I was when the War ended. As a civilian captain I transferred to BEA in 1946, and two years later I ended up in the Middle East, working for MEA. Forty-one years later, the country I had adopted took me prisoner.

TEN

Despair

For Jackie, the days at Sofar began to merge into one. He tried to keep an accurate record of the date – indeed, when he was released, he was only two weeks out, after two and a half years without a calendar – but it became more and more difficult to distinguish between fact and fiction. Jackie spent many days lost in the past, playing back his experiences in order to keep some grip on his sanity. The activities of the kidnappers seemed illogical and bizarre at times, and there were incidents which seemed to have little rational explanation. During the twenty-two months Jackie was held at Sofar, he even thought he heard English and American voices which he identified as Intelligence officers. Yet no one came to rescue him.

'The local police too had a station not a hundred yards from my cell and they visited very frequently, particularly in the first months. I'd hear them refer to one another as Sergeant, or Superintendent, in English – they always spoke English to one another – which was how I knew who they were. If they guessed I was there, it never reached the ears of the outside world.

'The conditions under which I was being held degenerated even further. Yet Awad's control over his men was like iron, and those who stepped beyond the limits in their treatment of me were swiftly and cruelly dealt with. There was one character who used to indulge in hashish, and one evening he entered my cell, a stocking over his face so that I would not be able to identify him. He was carrying a roll of sticky paper, the kind that one would wrap around a big parcel, and had unrolled about eighteen inches of it. He leant across me, and started trying to wrap it around my face and arms. I struggled strenuously, wriggling this way and that to stop him securing a hold on me, for I guessed that his intention was to rape me. I managed to thwart him temporarily, and he dropped the roll of sticky tape, which spun across the floor, the unrolled section curling up like a piece of ribbon. Undeterred, he reached for it and endeavoured to tie it around my arms, and I started shouting and screaming for help. Suddenly two or three other guards burst in, and hauled my attacker away from me, hustling him none too gently out of the door. They held an immediate court of inquiry on the spot.

'The "court" went into session and I heard the leader of this impromptu jury say, "You know, this man's offence carries the death penalty."

'"Yes," said one of the guards.

'"Do you still have the chains in the other house?" the other man asked.

'There was a silence, which I took to be a nod of the head. Then I heard leader of the jury say grimly, "In that case, you know what to do."

'I never saw or heard of the man who had attacked me again. I had no doubt that they had killed him.

'I decided that if no one was coming to rescue me, I would have to try to take advantage of any opportunity that presented itself to escape under my own steam. I was beginning to feel I had little to lose.

'One morning I was allowed to visit the bathroom as usual. On return the character escorting me failed to fasten the chain around my leg properly. Instead of putting the hasp of the padlock through a link of the chain, he'd put it around the chain, so the links could slide easily through it. I spent the day carefully testing the chain, and found that the loop around my ankle could be slackened, and I could get my foot out of it. I resolved not to waste this chance, which could be the only one I would get. Any escape I might make would have a better chance of succeeding if I scheduled it for early morning, when they paid the least attention to me. I tried not to think about how slim my chances were, nor what would happen to me if I failed.

'It seemed as if the luck was on my side. That evening the guards engaged in a heavy drinking session, and for once I didn't begrudge them their entertainment. They used to drink screwdrivers – vodka and orange – and the aniseed-based alcohol, Arak, a favourite in Arab countries. Arafat, the PLO leader, later issued a directive, ordering all Palestinian groups not to drink, which they reluctantly obeyed at the insistence of their local leaders. Women too were banned, though they did not stick to that so rigidly. I could hear now the laughter and high voices of women, and I prayed the drink and company combined would distract them enough to give me a fighting chance.

'The minutes seemed to pass more slowly than they had ever done before. Every moment I was afraid someone would check on the chain and discover my secret. Gradually the carousing next door quietened, and by three o'clock in the morning, there was silence. I strained my ears, but could hear nothing. Cautiously I eased the links of the chain across my foot and slipped out of it, wincing as it clanked. I crept towards the door and into their living area, my heart pounding. I peered through the door of one room which was already ajar and saw two of them spreadeagled across the sofa and chair, both asleep and snoring, fully dressed.

'I backed away and moved towards another room, listening for any signs of life but hearing only my own heartbeat. There were two more, asleep in the dark, guns in their hands. I left them and made my way to the back of the house. There was one door which led to the outside, but it was locked and the key nowhere to be seen. I slid along the wall, trying to stay in the shadows, to another door. As I reached for the key, I heard voices. They were immediately outside the house, on the other side of the door I was just about to open. I backed away in panic, certain that if they didn't find me, they'd waken the sleeping guards who assuredly would discover me standing in their midst. I raced as fast as I could towards my room, nearly falling over from lack of exercise and weakness, terrified I'd be discovered at any second. I fell gratefully on to my bed, and leant against the wall, panting. I couldn't walk another step. I realised, as I sank down onto my mattress, that even if I'd escaped, I would have been unable to go anywhere.

'My legs were shaking and my heart thumping. I was terrified still of discovery, expecting raised voices and running feet at any moment. I had no plan but to escape – I had never thought about what was outside. My one idea was to get away from the place, perhaps to the police station a hundred yards away, though I had no idea which side they were on. I put the loop around my ankle again and tightened it, hoping that the man who released me the following morning wouldn't notice. The next day, the guard who came to undo it suddenly shook it and looked sharply at me. I adopted an air of innocence and he left the room quickly, shouting in Arabic at one of his companions. Another man came back and checked the chain was now properly fastened, which of course it was, and they muttered to one another in an undertone. They had no idea I had tried to escape – they probably didn't even know I realised the chain had been wrongly fastened.

'I decided that I must improve my fitness as a matter of

urgency, if I was to have any chance at all of escaping. As a boy, I had been a keen member of the Church Lads' Brigade, which used to meet once a week for a drill of physical training exercises. I used to be an instructor and decided to resurrect those skills which had lain dormant for the last fifty years. I set about devising a programme which I could carry out even though I was chained. I remember hearing a Jane Fonda workout programme on the guards' television once, and I thought if she can do it, then so can I. I started off with lying on my back, and raising one leg ten times, then the other. I gradually increased that to fifteen, and then twenty. I sat up to do neck exercises, then my arms – stretching my arms out straight and flinging them to the sides and back to the middle again. I did this early in the morning, before the guards were really awake, so they never even knew I was doing it. After breakfast I was permitted to walk around the room a few times, and I would then lean against the wall, facing it, and do my body and leg exercises all over again, for about twenty minutes. It made a little difference, although I was still terribly weak.

'I tried to keep track of what my captors were up to, although it was difficult since there were so many of them. There was a crowd of mercenaries, all Palestinian, living near-by in Sofar, who were supposedly on call twenty-four hours a day. The first time they were used, there were about a dozen of them. A fee of fifteen dollars each per day was agreed for their mission, which I didn't manage to overhear. They were used a second time, but one of their number was killed, and they refused to work for Awad again. I was surprised, as they seemed ruthless men who weren't easily scared, and I assumed the risk of death went with the territory if one was a mercenary.

'I did hear two terrorist incidents being discussed however, although I was unable to ascertain the veracity of the kidnappers' statements about their outcomes. There was an attack planned on the Bank of Iraq, which is situated at the top of Sadat Street in Beirut. It seemed all five would-be robbers were killed in the assault by the army, who interceded on the Bank's behalf. Their colleagues were tormented with the failure by the villagers in Sofar; I heard them taunting that the Palestinians couldn't even manage a bank raid. I heard Awad say the raiders deserved to die, since it was their own fault for staying too long at the Bank. There was no glory in failure, it seemed.

'On a second occasion, three or four of them were sent down on a raid against yet another rival Palestinian group encamped a mile or so away. One of them was carrying an explosive charge and somehow he managed to detonate it en route, blowing himself to pieces. No part of him was ever found, except the high powered rifle he'd been carrying. I was certain it was no accident. The man who died had threatened Awad's position in some way, I was certain, and Awad had swiftly disposed of him. It was not the first time, and would not be the last. The assault on the rival group was rescheduled, and this time three of Awad's men died trying to run a Palestinian blockade in an area they called Kew Gardens, for some unfathomable reason. Awad's raids rarely succeeded, hampered as they were by bad planning and amateurs pretending to be experts.

'One of the men who died was called Martin. He was one of four sons of a member of the kidnap group, a man called Carlo who was the apparent owner of the restaurant which had become my prison. Carlo claimed to be of Austrian–Italian parentage, and it was he who was given the ticket to Barbados by Awad when the television arrangements were being made. He had another son, Joseph, a Catholic, who asked me the first Christmas I was at Sofar if I would like a beer or a whisky. I said I didn't mind, either would be good, and seconds later his father came rushing in, brandishing a gun which he held to my head and saying, "You can't have drink here! There's no drink here!" I was certain there was, since people came in and out drinking all the time, but I knew better than to argue. Joseph apologised to his father, saying he hadn't realised who I was – he'd assumed I was just another visitor. If only that had been true.

'It was hard to keep going, to continue to battle to survive, but I refused to give up. I never once contemplated suicide, although I knew they were beginning to hope I would. I heard them say as much, particularly Awad, after the attempt to blow me up had failed. I knew I couldn't escape, because even if I hadn't been chained, there were still guards to get past and my own weakness to overcome. Three or four times a day one of them would come into my room with a gun in his hand, hold it against my head and pull the trigger, to scare me. It was never loaded – I was sure that they wouldn't kill me indoors, because of the mess. Indeed, for some reason they were reluctant to kill me directly in any way. I was becoming a problem for them; they didn't know what to do with me. They couldn't let me go, in case I had some information which could be passed on and used against them, and it would have been an admission of failure simply to release me without gaining something in return. I was an embarrassment, and now they were stuck with me. However bad the days were – and some were so bad I pleaded with St Barnabas to help me – I would not help them get out of the corner they were now backed into by conveniently taking my own life. In any case, I had no wish to die. I was a survivor.'

So was Jackie's wife. By Christmas of 1989, Sunnie had been alone for seven months, her only constant companion her faithful poodle Tara. She had learnt to deal with the Press and become expert at handling live television interviews. Her husband had been reported dead, but Sunnie went on believing he was alive, somewhere, and she went on fighting for him. She received anonymous telephone calls in the middle of the night, telling her to leave Beirut for her own safety, and visits from men she couldn't identify trying to talk their way into her flat. Sunnie crossed the lethal Green Line numerous times to plug Jackie's cause and gain a few days' respite from the constant shelling and danger from car bombs. She had virtually no money and, until Brent Sadler bought her a generator as a present, no means of power for much of the time. Sunnie welcomed it with the gratitude most women reserved for a diamond ring; it meant the world to her, representing as it did the power to have light whenever she needed it, instead of having to rely on candles. And through all of this, no word of Jackie.

As Sunnie prepared to mark her first Christmas alone, she relied on Tara more and more to help her through it. Despite everything she was enduring, consoling herself with the thought that at least things couldn't get any worse.

And then they did.

'It was Saturday, 23 December. I was out walking with Tara and we were on our way home, just minutes away from the flat. It was pitch black, since the lack of electricity meant no street lights and no illumination from people's windows. A car pulled up close to me, and a man got out and started walking in my direction. I wasn't particularly nervous, and I carried on walking without even thinking about him. Suddenly he leapt at me, grabbing hold of my coat and trying to pull me towards the car. I panicked, convinced it was a kidnap attempt, and kicked him hard so that he was forced to let me go. I fell away abruptly and he hit my head hard before pushing me into a low stone wall. I stumbled and hit the ground, smashing into my right shoulder, my head hitting the pavement. Dazed, I lost awareness for a moment of what was happening. In that split second, my assailant seized Tara's lead from my hand and ran off with her. He threw her into the car, and it sped away into the darkness.

'I staggered up from the pavement, screaming and crying, but nobody came to help me. Everyone in West Beirut is terrified of getting involved in any trouble for their own safety. Somehow I got back to my apartment, and took refuge with my friend Fadya Arraman, who listened to my story and put ice on my bruised head, comforting me as best she could. I was heartbroken. Tara had been my only constant companion and friend during the past terrible months since Jackie's kidnap. I didn't know how I was going to go on now without her love and affection.

'With my friend Amine Daouk I went to everyone for help, the Army, the Secret Police, the Syrians, but no one held out any hope of finding her. I offered a large reward for her return, to no avail. It seemed she was gone forever. I had lost the two most important things in my life, Jackie and now Tara, and I wondered what was left for anyone to take. There was only me left.

'A week later, the then British Ambassador, Alan Ramsey, contacted me and said he was sending a car to take me to the East Side for lunch, as he wanted to talk to me. Alan was very sympathetic over Tara, but said he was extremely worried over my own safety, and begged me to leave Beirut, at least for a short while. Every other attempt of his to get me out had failed, but this time I was so depressed over Tara I agreed. I felt as if finally I had broken, in a way nobody really understood. Everyone seemed to think I had withstood Jackie being taken, so what was a dog? They didn't realise she was what got me through the loss of Jackie. We had huddled next to each other during the bombing, shared our food and lived for each other's company. Tara was my lifeline and without her I was beginning to sink.

'I desperately needed some care and attention, and it was virtually impossible now. Brent had been banned from travelling to the Muslim side of Beirut by ITN because of the kidnapping threat, and telephone lines were nearly non-existent. Somehow he managed to get special messages recorded on videotapes for me so that I could play them at home and it helped. It was the worst period of my life, and I couldn't seem to do the things I'd done before; I felt older and more tired, my desire to go on living and surviving faltered. Without Brent and his faithful companion, Mehdi, I would have given up.

'Shortly after Christmas, I flew to England, and travelled to my daughter Jennifer, who lives in Wales. I found the bitter cold very draining, and struggled to acclimatise myself and rouse myself out of this terrible depression I was in. Jennifer was determined to lift my spirits and, with the companionship of my friends and family, I began to recover. She spent hours on the telephone trying to find another poodle puppy for me to take back to Beirut, and finally we found one. We went to collect her in my brother's car, his pride and joy, and tried not to think about what the rough farm track we had to drive up was doing to the car. I was introduced to the poodle, a nine-week-old female, adorable and full of fun. We took to each other immediately, and I promised to put an alarm clock on top of the cardboard box where she slept, to remind her of her mother's heartbeat. Her pedigree name was Benigorn Miss Crystal, and she became Missy.

'I returned to London and met with the McCarthy Foundation Group and John McCarthy's father, Patrick, a delightful man with whom I'd had many pleasant conversations. I was very impressed with all they were doing to get the hostages released, and pledged my full support. I also spoke to Anthony Gray, himself a hostage for over two years in China, who was now running Hostages Worldwide. Both these organisations gave me generous financial help throughout Jackie's captivity, for which I was extremely grateful, since I still had no access to our funds in the bank. Without such help, and donations from countless well-wishers, I would have been destitute. David Waite, Terry's brother, met me for lunch and we acknowledged the grim truth together: that there was little hope in the immediate future of the hostages being released. We all continued to pray and tried to keep their names in the public eye, so they would not be forgotten and left to rot in their cells. With no diplomatic relations with either Syria or Iran at that stage, there was little the Foreign Office could do, I knew, but I still felt they weren't really trying.

'My return to Beirut was delayed by an outbreak of fierce fighting in Lebanon between the Christian General Aoun and his opponent Samir Geagea, head of the Lebanese Christian militia forces. Both wanted supremacy in the East side of the city, and I began to think I would never see my home again, as the toll of dead and injured rose horrifyingly. Eventually, I returned, and the life of carrying water up ninety-nine stairs, constant shelling, little electricity and food shortages was resumed. I was glad to be back in Lebanon, despite the privations – I felt closer to Jackie, and somehow it helped.

'Missy was developing a personality and I would take her for walks on the beach, trying to lose myself in her love of life. She was fascinated by the sand and played around until she was exhausted. Although I knew she would never take Tara's place in my heart, she was pretty and full of fun, and she distracted me.

'There was little or no news of the hostages. The Press had forgotten them and so it seemed had the rest of the world. Every so often I would be told there were rumours circulating that there appeared to be a genuine chance of a hostage release, and my hopes would rise. I would be interviewed, and there would be a flurry of media attention. Reporters from all over the world would dash to Damascus, waiting hopefully for a release. Then it would pass, like a parade in front of my window, and I would be left with the ticker-tape fluttering in the wind.

'I still went to my riding club three times a week, but there was little to do, as stray shells fell around it occasionally, and people were deterred from riding there. The time began to hang heavily on my hands, as the situation grew steadily worse. I had trouble getting beer or gas with which to cook, and after so many months of having no one but my animals to talk to, I was finding it difficult to be sociable and pleasant to people. I was withdrawing into myself, and I wondered how Jackie would be able to cope, his situation being so much worse than mine. I did my best, but there were terrible days of depression when I couldn't see any light at the end of the tunnel, and wondered how long I could go on. Then my natural fighting spirit would raise itself again and I'd think, "If Jackie can do it, so can I," and carry another can of water up the stairs.

'I got into a routine of misery as the months went by, and any sudden flash of hope that could mean a complete change in my life only made the subsequent dreariness more difficult to bear. I began to wonder why I didn't just leave and go and wait for Jackie in a more civilised place. But my superstitious nature would nag at me: I was sure that if I left he would know and think I'd forgotten him, and maybe he'd give up fighting for his survival. I couldn't leave. Every so often something would happen that would make me think, "I can do it. I've got this far and I'm not going to give up now." Sometimes it would be something as small as a bath at a friend's house. No one who hasn't had to stripwash in a saucepan of water can know the lure of relaxing in a hot bath with lashings of bathsalts. It was worth more to me than gemstones and gold. It was amazing how ordinary, everyday things made such a difference to whether I wanted to stay in or leave Beirut. When I had water, I felt I could endure staying on. Without it, life and my temper became impossible, and the only thing I could think of was getting out.

'In March 1990, a British journalist was hanged in Baghdad for alleged spying and his "accomplice", a nurse called Daphne Parish, was jailed for life, despite pleas for clemency from governments around the world. It chilled me to the bone, because it brought home to me the inhumanity of the people who were holding Jackie.

'Shortly afterward, I began to be followed by a red Honda car wherever I went. I noticed it as I travelled to the beach with Missy one day and to test my fear I stopped at some shops on the way back. The car was there again. I was desperately afraid. When I reached home I found two parcels left for me as a present by some anonymous donor. I opened them and discovered two exquisite lamps, but I suddenly feared they had been wired to explode on contact, and I had a security guard from the building opposite mine check them out. Of course they were safe. I was appalled at the state of my nerves, but I couldn't help it. The Honda car still shadowed me, and I was on the edge of panic virtually all the time. If someone came up behind me I would literally scream in terror. The constant silence on Jackie's fate was beginning to wear me down and even whilst I prayed for his survival I wondered how he could possibly keep holding on. I met Jean Sutherland, the wife of the American hostage Tom Sutherland who had been held for more than five years already, and gained some comfort from her stoic determination to keep waiting and keep hoping. There would be glimmers of hope, and in April 1990 three French hostages were freed, but Britain still refused to deal with the kidnappers, and Jackie remained a captive.

'The fighting continued, lulls followed by fierce battles

with much bloodshed on all sides involved. No one seemed able to stop the carnage. Ceasefires came and went, lasting little longer than a few days at a time.

'Jackie's first anniversary as a hostage began to approach, and my worries increased. Hidden at the back of my mind, but refusing to stay quiet, was the fear: what would Jackie be like, even if he was freed now, after a year in captivity? I dared not let my doubts see the light of day, but I couldn't help but be aware of the severe mental strain he'd endured. I might one day get my husband back, in that his body would survive – but would his mind? Would I ever have my Jackie back again?

'Just before his anniversary, there was a statement from the kidnappers that the American Jesse Turner would be freed within forty-eight hours. My hopes rose – maybe the logjam would be broken. It was followed with an announcement by the Islamic group supposed to be holding him that America wasn't being co-operative enough, and the release was cancelled. A week later, Robert Polhill was freed. The roller-coaster of hope and despair was still lurching on. Every day there was some new piece of information, good or bad, and the constant living on the edge began to tell on me. I developed stomach pains and headaches, and the depression increased.

'I distracted myself with preparing press releases for Jackie's anniversary, 12 May, and threw myself headlong into interviews, appeals, letters and meetings. I felt quite sick, but carried on in the hope that somehow Jackie would know how much I loved him, and that I was still waiting. I prayed that one day – please God, let it be soon – he would be with me to watch the recording of the television appeals I was doing now. I sat down and wrote the script, the feeling pouring from the bottom of my heart:

179

This is an appeal for the release of my husband, Jackie
Mann. It is now one year since I walked into my
Beirut flat on that terrible Friday evening of May the
twelfth, and realised that Jackie had been kidnapped
and I had to face life alone. He had been snatched
off the streets after a visit to the British Bank, and
disappeared as though the earth had swallowed him
up. No videotapes, no calls for ransom money, and
no identity of the kidnappers and to this day I have
no positive proof that he is alive or dead. Only my
own feelings tell me that he is surviving as he is a
natural fighter and would not give up easily.

I have stayed on in Beirut, always wishing that
one day some news will come through and wanting to
stay as close to him as possible as I feel he will know I
am near him and keep holding on. Every time I drive
round Beirut streets I keep wondering if I'm passing
the underground room where he is being held captive
in misery . . . I pray every day that the countries who
can help in the release of all the hostages will make even
greater efforts to get them set free so they can live again
as human beings . . . I shall go on waiting for Jackie in
Beirut whatever the cost to my health and nerves, and
know that one day we will be together again, and trust
that we will be able to put this tragedy behind us and
live out our last years in peace and love.

'On the day Jackie had been held a prisoner for a year, I
was in Wales with my daughter once again, enduring the
constant merry-go-round of publicity in the hope it would
help Jackie. I collapsed from nerves and exhaustion, and was
rushed to hospital with internal bleeding, where I was given
an immediate transfusion. I was seventy-six, and fighting to
keep going. How much worse it must be for Jackie, and my
worries intensified.

'I met with "The Friends of John McCarthy" once again,

and we agreed that there was little that could be done until the British Government agreed to co-operate with Syria, who at least knew something about what had happened to our hostages. I said as much to the Minister of State for Foreign and Commonwealth Affairs, William Waldegrave, when I met him and he agreed but said the Government was doing all it could under difficult circumstances. It was as much as I could do to point out that the difficult circumstances were all mine and Jackie's, not the British Government's.

'I returned to Beirut in time for Jackie's second birthday in captivity. I didn't make an appeal this time – I hadn't the spirit, and it seemed to make little impact. I kept wondering how he must be feeling closeted away from civilisation and all alone. What could he be thinking, spending such a day a prisoner – did he remember happier birthdays with presents and love from his family and from me? A week later, it was our forty-seventh wedding anniversary, again I wondered how many more we'd be separated for. There was a feature on the news saying Jackie would be released soon, but I couldn't bear to watch. I'd had enough of such media games, and refused to play any more.

'I was beginning to think Jackie was dead, for the first time. I was forced to consider what I was going to do with my life – I couldn't go on living in limbo like this, always hoping for something I wasn't sure would ever happen. But inertia was becoming as difficult as the situation itself, and again I delayed doing anything – I couldn't quite bring myself to abandon hope altogether. More promises of hostage releases were followed by more shattered hopes. They rose like bubbles in the air, and were just as dependable. Gradually, almost without noticing it, my mind seemed to accept that I was alone, perhaps forever. I began to think of alternatives to Beirut, making financial plans and dreaming new dreams. I wrote a children's story about one of my more infamous pets, a dog called Husky, in the hope of raising enough money to find a furnished flat away from Beirut, perhaps in Jersey, and looked for a publisher.

'Towards the end of July 1990, the red Honda returned to haunt me. I was driving back from the riding club on an open stretch of road by the sea, when suddenly the car drove past me and pulled up abruptly in front of my car. I had to brake suddenly in order not to hit him, and Missy was thrown onto the floor, where she hit her head on a crate of beer bottles, which drew blood. I was furious, and when the man driving the Honda came round to the window of my car, I was ready for him with a beer bottle in my hand. I cursed him in English and Arabic and told him if he didn't move his bloody car I would ram it. I started screaming as loudly as I could, and this attracted some of the owners of nearby coffee stores, who crossed the road to see what was going on. The man became nervous, and ran to his car, driving away in a flurry of screaming tyres. Shaking with fright, I drove home, my nerves in shreds. The British Embassy suggested I shouldn't go out, but that's an impossible demand, for who else is there to do the daily chores of life in Beirut?

'Days later, Iraq invaded Kuwait, and I was not to see Brent for many months. Prices of everything soared immediately, and petrol became very scarce, then all but vanished altogether. Gradually my resolve to leave Lebanon hardened, and I decided to create a new home for Jackie in Cyprus. We had discussed moving to the island before he was kidnapped, but our financial situation prevented us. Now, I decided I had no choice. It would not have been my first choice for a home, but it was near Jackie and I couldn't have afforded Europe. As the summer of 1990 drew to a close, kidnapping broke out again in Beirut, mainly militias trying to make some money from ransoms. The heat was stifling and, as the situation in the Gulf worsened, there were shortages of even the most basic foodstuffs. Petrol prices soared beyond my means and I began to seriously consider riding one of the horses around Beirut. Just as I decided to leave the city for good, the Irish hostage Brian Keenan was released. Hopes for the imminent release of all the remaining Western hostages rose, and I dithered once more about deserting Lebanon.

'I had lunch with the British Ambassador not long after Brian Keenan's release and quietly he told me he really feared Jackie had died in his captivity, since it had been impossible to gather a shred of evidence about his whereabouts. I sat there numbly; I was so used to hearing Jackie was dead one minute and about to be freed the next, that I couldn't respond at all. My mind blanked out everything except the smell of the coffee as we sat there, the steam curling up from the small cups. Yet somewhere deep inside me lingered the conviction that my husband was still alive. I knew how cussed he could be. He was not one to give in.

'September came, and with it a statement that the three British hostages would be released by the end of the month. Terrified to pin my hopes on it, I couldn't help but start planning for Jackie's homecoming. I closed my mind to everything else. I would have to fly to Damascus, where they'd be handed over, and then on to Cyprus. His trousers would need washing – perhaps they'd have to be taken in a bit, if he'd lost weight – and his shirts were in desperate need of ironing. I'd be able to iron them every day, when we were in Cyprus, with plenty of electricity and water, and newspapers and television to keep us entertained. Jackie would like Cyprus, I was sure. Perhaps I'd better take a few shirts, in case he didn't like the ones I'd brought, and he'd need shoes – he'd definitely want his shoes – only I wasn't sure which ones, but Brent would help me there. And some chocolate, I knew he liked chocolate . . .

'I could almost feel Jackie's arms around me and I didn't think how rashly I was tempting fate. I gave interviews to

183

anyone who asked for one, full of optimism that after seventeen months of loneliness, my husband was coming home. I should have known better. Again the negotiations, which I never really understood, seemed to stall. Once again, it was all off. My heart clenching in pain and disappointment, I unpacked Jackie's suitcase, and collected his trousers from the dry cleaners, hanging them away in the wardrobe for the next time, whenever it came.'

ELEVEN

The Last Days: Shweifat

'The situation in the Gulf took up every newspaper and television report for months. The interminable days of waiting, as the situation deteriorated and war loomed ever nearer, dragged on. I wondered how long this phony war would go on, with prices in Lebanon rising meteorically. If it had been hard to manage before, it was impossible now. I was literally afraid to go into a shop any more, in case I didn't have enough money to pay the ever increasing prices. I had visions of harnessing Missy to a basket and working the streets of Beirut, begging for money. My car collapsed completely and I was forced to drive Jackie's Simca, which terrified me. I hadn't seen Brent in several months and when we did meet up in the autumn he looked tired and drawn. I dreaded the outbreak of war, knowing he would be in the thick of the action, covering the most dangerous stories. I couldn't bear to lose him too.

'London resumed diplomatic relations with Tehran, and I began to nurse the flame of hope that flickered inside me. I thought it would be a long, slow haul, but Jackie would be freed at the end of it. Once more picking myself up off the floor, I travelled to Cyprus to choose a furnished flat that would be our home and sorted out Jackie's clothes again, repacking the suitcase as I had so many times before. I cleaned Jackie's bedroom in our Beirut flat, something I hadn't done for a year and a half. My life was moving again, and whatever the news that came, I felt that at last I could deal with it. It was almost as if I had been bereaved, but was finally coming to terms with it, and picking up the pieces. General Aoun surrendered and told his troops to lay down their arms: the shelling stopped, the war was over. Life was changing, and moving on.

'For every step I moved forward, I took a step back. I started being persecuted by a man who took to telephoning me in the middle of the night and making obscene remarks, threatening to kill me if I didn't co-operate. I was terrified, since I knew it would be the easiest thing in the world to get into my flat. The outside door of the building is never locked, and the concierge closes his door and watches television all night. Anyone could walk straight in, and the whole city knew where I lived. I spent all night sitting shaking in the dark, too afraid to even light a candle. When I awoke, it was to the news that one of my oldest and dearest riding friends, Danny Chamoun, had been assassinated along with his wife and their two young sons, aged five and six. Danny had been a supporter of General Aoun for some time, and was running a big risk in staying in Lebanon. But to shoot Ingrid and the children? These were the people ruling Beirut now, and I wanted no part of it.

'The calls continued, and one night I was wakened by sinister knocking on my door. The British Embassy arranged for extra bolts to be put on it, but it didn't quell my fear. The red Honda reappeared – I still had no idea who the driver was or what his purpose might be, and I never discovered it – and I was afraid to go out, and afraid to stay in. I longed for my husband so desperately the pain was all consuming. Brent managed to hook up a telephone call to me, and invited me to spend Christmas with him in Cyprus so that we could have a few days' respite before he returned to the Gulf for the war which now seemed unavoidable. I clutched my talisman, a blue bead I wear around my neck, and prayed to God, Allah and any other deity present, to have Jackie with me this year.

'West Beirut was still no place for foreigners, although some journalists were venturing back. I learned that Brent was in the city filming and hoped he would be able to see me on my side of Beirut, at long last. I later learned he was indeed planning to visit the West, with permission from ITN's Editor; in the meantime, he was adventuring on his own.

'Mehdi, his cameraman, hated all dogs, but when Brent was away he was charged with particular responsibility for keeping an eye on Sunnie, and often had to spend time in her flat first with Tara, and later Missy, yapping at his trouser legs. He endured it, as he endured all that Beirut threw at him, but was neither interested nor sentimental about dogs. Yet one day, as Brent was waiting for the OK from ITN to cross into West Beirut, Mehdi came rushing to him with a look of dire urgency.

'"You will never believe it, Boss," he gasped breathlessly, "but I have just seen Tara in a wooden box being carried on the back of a motorbike in the West. I know it was Tara because she's so small and there are no other dogs like her around."

'Brent was sceptical, knowing Mehdi hated Tara, and bemused by his sudden interest in matters canine. But knowing how much she meant to me, he questioned Mehdi further, and concluded there was a good chance the dog was Tara. Mehdi described how he'd followed the motorbike into a radical Muslim Shi-ite area of West Beirut, a slum district with followers loyal to the Hezbollah leadership making up most of the residents. The Lebanese cameraman had tackled the motorbike rider about Tara, and watched as the dog was taken out of the box and shoved into a ramshackle dwelling behind a splintered wooden door. The new owner had bought her for a few dollars some months earlier, around the same time as Tara was taken.

'Brent listened to the details and decided to investigate further. ITN finally gave him clearance for a brief visit to West Beirut, and he set out determined to do all he could to secure Tara's freedom and reunite me with her. He was risking his freedom, if not his life, to help me, although I was oblivious to the drama on the other side of the city.

'Brent, together with Mehdi and his East Beirut driver, Joseph, who was a Christian, crossed the Green Line into the Muslim half of the city late that morning, travelling in two cars – Mehdi driving his beaten-up Mercedes, and Joseph and Brent following in the driver's veteran Coronet Dodge. As they wove through the narrow streets of one of Beirut's poorest neighbourhoods, Joseph was unsettled, wearing the same expression of deep concern he wore every time Brent and his camera-crew braved shell-fire in Joseph's car. Mehdi too was uncharacteristically nervous. Ever protective of Brent, he suddenly felt the risks of retrieving Tara might be too much.

'Before there was time to debate the issue, the dog's owner arrived with the animal at the shack, and Brent watched, silent so as not to reveal his nationality, while Mehdi bargained with the man. The dog ran about the yard, larger than before, her fur untrimmed, filthy and smelly, but well trained and obedient. He saw enough to believe it was Tara, and the negotiations continued. The man wanted two hundred US dollars for her, and furiously Mehdi began to argue. The furore attracted unwanted attention, Mehdi threatening to call the Syrians and have the dog's owner arrested. A pistol was drawn, and pointed at Mehdi, as the unsavoury-looking locals gathered closer. Events were fast getting out of hand.

'Joseph was getting very edgy, watching from his car parked a few feet away. Brent asked how much the man wanted and agreed to pay it instantly; it was becoming too dangerous to argue, and for once the customary Middle East haggling was forgotten. The money changed hands, and the dog was thrown into Mehdi's Mercedes. At this point Mehdi refused to drive with a dog in his car, on the grounds that it was unclean, a philosophy adopted by many Muslims. This time it was literally true: the dog was filthy. The locals were turning more hostile by the second, and fearing for his safety Brent persuaded Mehdi to get into Joseph's car, whilst he took the wheel of the Mercedes alone with the dog. The two cars set off at a healthy speed towards my riding club near the Sabra and Chatila Palestinian refugee camps. They passed through several Syrian checkpoints, fortunately without mishap, although the sight of a Westerner driving a car alone drew puzzled looks.

'In the meantime, ITN's cameraman, Andy Rex, had arrived at the riding club, ostensibly to film me at work. What I didn't know was that he knew all about the efforts to find Tara and was on hand to film the happy reunion.

'I was standing in the ring when Brent walked in, bearing Tara in his arms, and triumphantly came up to me, as the entire club applauded. People realised he had found Tara and shouted "Bravo!" at the tops of their voices.

'As Andy filmed, I greeted Tara, aghast at her condition. Brent put her down and within seconds she raced off in a different direction, clear out of the riding school. Brent, Mehdi and Joseph gave chase, and returned dishevelled and tired an hour later. This time I tried all the tricks I knew to get some response from Tara. Missy was yapping angrily while Tara stared stupidly up at me. She was heavier than I remembered, and surely her ears were longer . . . and her tail shaped a little more . . . suddenly I realised. This wasn't Tara.

'Brent was more devastated than I was. It was an easy mistake; this creature was the spitting image of Tara, but an impostor nonetheless. We decided she must return to her original owner, but I refused to let Brent risk his life twice. Mehdi was sent to rectify matters and the poor dog was returned, no doubt thoroughly bewildered. The owner returned a hundred and fifty dollars, and Mehdi gave him the remaining fifty for his trouble.

'Late in November, it seemed as if someone was at last answering my prayers. Margaret Thatcher, the most hated woman in many Arab quarters, particularly amongst Shi-ite fundamentalists, resigned, paving the way for a new détente which might see the Western hostages released. President Bush met President Assad of Syria, the first time an American leader had met the Syrian for more than a decade. One of the new British Prime Minister's first actions was to renew diplomatic relations with Syria. The political climate was rapidly changing. These developments were followed by unsubstantiated reports that Jackie would be freed on humanitarian grounds, as he was very ill, throwing me into a frenzy of despair at his illness and delight at the possibility of his imminent freedom. The see-saw on which I lived continued to swing up and down, up and down.

'I spent Christmas Day of 1990 alone in bed, trying to blot out the terrible loneliness and fears for Jackie. My mind ranged over all the Christmases we had shared together, and the pain welled up, more acute than ever. On Boxing Day I travelled to Cyprus and spent three days with Brent, worrying almost as much about his imminent departure for Baghdad and the war as I did about Jackie. New Year's Eve I spent alone in my flat again, thinking over our first meeting all those years ago, in the Dorchester, dancing to our song, promising to be together till the end. I toasted Jackie with a solitary beer, and made him a silent promise that next time we'd be together, drinking champagne.

'The deadline for the Iraqi leader, Saddam Hussein, to pull out of Kuwait — 15 January, 1991 — came and went, with all diplomatic efforts to avert war ending in failure. Two days later, the Allied forces started their bombardment, and I thought of Brent, in the heart of enemy territory, somehow getting his reports from Baghdad out to the watching world. The Western hostages had been totally forgotten; everyone was too caught up in those who had been taken hostage in Kuwait and the excitement of using all those weapons they'd been storing up for just such an occasion. It made me feel sick, thinking of all those people risking their lives. The threat of terrorist attacks meant all flights to the Middle East were cancelled, trapping me more than ever in this destroyed city. As Israel was drawn into the war, bombarded with missiles and urged not to retaliate by Western leaders afraid it would split the Arab alliance against Iraq, I feared for my life again. Lebanon was too close to the Jewish state for comfort. I wondered if Jackie knew what was going on.

'For three months it was as if the world was on ice. There was no mention of the Western hostages at all, as the world's media concentrated on every move of the battle. Eventually the war ended, and in April the world sat up and looked around. Life began to move again. The British businessman, Roger Cooper, held in an Iranian jail for five years, was released, amidst rumours that Terry Waite, John McCarthy and my Jackie would be freed soon. I didn't hold my breath.

'Then an Arabic newspaper printed a photograph of one of the Western hostages to authenticate the kidnappers' following statement that Jackie would be the first hostage to be handed back. The first I knew of it was when a television crew arrived on my doorstep requesting an interview, and I was so excited I couldn't speak. I thought for a moment of how Jackie might be with me in a matter of days, and then I remembered the previous false alarms, and I calmed down. If only the photograph had been of Jackie himself, at least I would know he was still alive. The British Embassy said there was hope, after Roger Cooper's release, but told me to wait. I knew how to do that – I'd had enough practice. The second anniversary of Jackie's captivity approached and I wondered for a moment how many more I'd have to mark, before I sternly quelled the thought. I dared not think about Jackie any more or I would start crying.

'What kept me going through those dark days, as I began my third year alone, was my riding club. Once again I threw myself into it, burying any thoughts of Jackie as firmly as I could. Children can be very demanding, Lebanese children particularly, and the constant questions and concentration required to teach them with any degree of safety effectively blocked anything else from my mind. I had a number of pupils who showed a great deal of promise, and it was a joy to me to watch such children ride their horses as if they were one creature, flowing around the ring.

'Interest in the fate of the hostages seemed to revive in the summer of 1991, as the world got used to the new face of the Middle East, after the forging of fresh alliances which were generated by Iraq's assault on Kuwait. The British Government Foreign Office minister, Douglas Hogg, arrived in Beirut for a whistle-stop tour of the city, and the telephone once more began to ring with demands for interviews. A British film crew made a documentary about Jackie, entitled *The Forgotten Hostage*, a title which to my relief was growing more inaccurate by the day. In July, two weeks before my seventy-eighth birthday, I left Beirut.

'I moved to Cyprus to prepare a home for Jackie and myself, and in my subconscious I acknowledged that if he didn't return, it was where I wanted to be. Brent, who lives in Cyprus, was there to support me every step of the way, as he had always been whenever I needed him, and my diary began to fill with social engagements in a way it hadn't done for twenty years. I signed a deal on an unfurnished house and moved in, eyeing the garden wistfully as I pictured Jackie tending the geraniums there. I knew he would love pottering around, and I renewed my prayers that he'd be with me soon. My spirits lifted and the world seemed a brighter place. I went to parties and dined out, and began to feel quite human again. I had to write down my appointments, I had so many; it was unbelievable after so long without a single engagement for months at a time. I could go shopping whenever I wished and wash my hair three times a day if I chose too. Baths were not rationed, there was electricity, and I could watch television uninterrupted by shelling. Food was plentiful, telephone calls were unimpeded, and I had no stairs to climb. The only thing I missed was my husband.

'On 7 August came an announcement that one of the hostages would be released within forty-eight hours – one American and maybe one British. I couldn't think straight, I was so emotional. One minute I was depressed, and the next flying high, walking on clouds. Everybody telephoned – friends, journalists, British Government officials – and I was told to stay in close contact for when something happened. There seemed to be no doubt this time that something would, and everyone was certain it would be Jackie who was freed first, given his age and deteriorating health. I didn't know what to believe – it had happened so often before. Yet this time something was different; even Israel acknowledged it. I prayed as I had never prayed before, and my pleas were answered. A hostage was released. But it wasn't Jackie.

'After five years' imprisonment, the journalist John McCarthy was finally freed, into the waiting arms of the woman who had done more for him than anyone else, Jill Morrell. As I watched their joy on television, the agony of my loneliness pierced my very marrow. Now, more than ever, I found it impossible to believe in a God who could do this to me. I felt insane with nerves and disappointment, but desperately tried to rally my sinking spirits. An American was freed next, Edward Tracey walking into the sunshine and blinking at his liberty. I began to despair of it ever being Jackie, and wondered if he was even alive.

'Brent refused to let me think like that and as usual bullied me out of my depression. In September we returned to Beirut to pack Jackie's belongings once again, amid constant rumours that the remaining hostages would be freed soon. Brent knew if he could get me occupied, it would jolt me back into life again, and we bought a new suitcase ready for Jackie's belongings. I packed three of his shirts, a suit, a sports jacket, a tie and some underthings with his favourite cravat. As I added some soap and a comb, a hairbrush and a toothbrush, I wondered when the last time he had been permitted to use such items was. Judging from some of the details the newly released hostages were revealing, he might have had no access to them for almost three years. We bought him a new pair of light tan desert boots, and I gazed at his belongings strewn across the bed. At last it really seemed as if would only be a matter of time.

'A group calling itself the Revolutionary Justice Organisation, who were believed to be holding Jackie, issued a statement in mid-September saying that a Briton, almost certainly my husband, would be set free within a couple of days. With it was a photograph of my husband. I stared horrified at the photograph, the first proof there'd been in nearly two and a half years that Jackie was even alive. He was heavily bearded, gaunt and pinched, his eyes staring out of hollow sockets, the suffering of his ordeal evident. Until that moment I didn't know if he had survived, and the mixture of alarm and relief I felt as I gazed at that terrible picture is indescribable.

'I was certain this time the promises of his release were true, yet I was so afraid of my hopes being cruelly dashed again. I was staying at my apartment in Beirut, besieged by reporters clamouring for interviews. Brent was at the Summerland Hotel,

194

an oasis of normality in a city long since gone crazy. For a week we were all on a twenty-four-hour state of alert. The Beirut Press – and, indeed, the world's media – were keyed up and hot for news, any news, reporting every statement made by even the most lowly, insignificant Muslim officials, most of whom had no connection whatsoever with the kidnappers. The British Embassy hostage team were on permanent stand-by, the compound ringed with armed guards, and I felt giddy with the pace of events. An RAF hostage retrieval jet was waiting at RAF Akrotiri in Cyprus, and we bit our fingernails, wondering what could possibly go wrong now.

'I was told that the Iranian Government had informed Britain's representative in Tehran, David Reddaway, that Jackie Mann would be released very soon. That information was top secret then, and I hugged it to myself. It was the first time the Iranian leader, President Rafsanjani, had actually named, in advance, a soon-to-be-released hostage. I moved into the British Embassy in East Beirut, so that I would be on hand the minute there were any developments. I paced about the Embassy, taking Missy for walks with an armed guard, and waited, as I had for so long now.

'The deadline for the release had almost expired. It was excruciating and I wasn't in the mood for anyone's company, except Brent's. When we went out to dinner that night, I felt almost at ease, as if I had fought as hard as I could, and now I had to just sit back and let the cards fall. The two of us knocked back a few beers at the bar of the Montemar hotel, then headed for a restaurant a short distance up a hill behind the hotel, called Tony's House. It was run by a friend called Tony Tayeh, who promised to listen to the radio just in case. We put the British Embassy's walkie-talkie on the table between us, ears tuned for the call sign which would signal Jackie's release. Near our table, a pianist in a white tuxedo was playing, and Brent and I waltzed around the floor, blanking everything from our minds but the music.

'It was when we returned to the British Embassy that we learned the RJO had once again postponed Jackie's release. I couldn't contemplate remaining a minute longer in that hated city, the cars waiting to take me to Jackie mocking me as they sat parked outside, unused. I gave another television interview, not caring if the world knew that at last the indomitable Sunnie Mann had given up hope. I had no idea then that just a few miles away Jackie was watching my broadcast, able to see me for the first time in two and a half years. Desperate to get away from Lebanon, in despair Brent and I returned to Cyprus, unable to believe that the past ten days of hope had been extinguished so cruelly.'

For Jackie, hidden from the eyes of the world, those ten days had seemed just as interminable. As Sunnie had been dashing to Beirut, full of hope, he had finally been freed from his prison at Sofar and moved to a new cell in a place called Shweifat. The atmosphere had altered and he sensed a change in his situation which betokened freedom. He had been a prisoner for more than 850 days, and hardly dared to believe his ordeal was coming to an end.

'The regime altered and this time it was for the better. The food improved immeasurably – whereas I'd been given Arabic bread up to now, at Shweifat the guards gave me a French roll with butter, and various fillings, every day. It was ready made, always fresh, obviously bought from a shop outside, which impressed me greatly. It was the first time I'd eaten leavened bread in two and a half years, and it was a tremendous improvement. I knew it heralded a change and, after what I had endured, it could only be for the better. I was fed three times a day, always a sandwich, often with a can of cold Pepsi Cola.

196

'I still had to sleep on that same foam mattress I'd been given when I was first incarcerated, and there was a guard with me permanently, twenty-four hours a day, sleeping on a mattress next to me at night. I was no longer chained, a change I welcomed with relief. It was the first time they'd permanently removed it since the first ten days after I was imprisoned. I didn't have to cover my head with a towel whenever one of the kidnappers came into the room, but I was still instructed to keep my face to the wall, so that I couldn't see them. If I happened to turned over to reach for something beside my bed, I'd hear the same command: "Turn over! Face the wall!" I was permitted to lie on my back and gazed for hours on end at the ceiling, wondering what going to happen next. I became very well acquainted with the ivory paint covering walls and ceiling, as I prayed for my release. I spent most of my time just lying on the mattress in the corner of the room, occasionally changing from lying flat on my back to lying on my side, though both positions were uncomfortable. I hoped the change in my environment meant something good was about to happen, but I was afraid of being disappointed again.

'I was in a single-storey building this time, very close to a mosque – perhaps even next door to it. I'd hear morning prayers every day, sometimes before dawn, sometimes as late as nine or ten in the morning, and they'd go on for over an hour, deafeningly loud. On one occasion I asked for the volume to be turned down, and they indignantly told me no, it was the Koran that was being read. All I knew was that it was very loud. Again in the evening, around dusk, there would be more preaching for about half an hour in Arabic – not preaching in the Christian sense, but readings from the Koran and expoundings upon it. These sessions took place at the same time every evening, and I used to listen for it, as one waits for a bell to chime.

'The room I was in seemed to be a general meeting place, for apart from the guard permanently watching me, the others would meet there, five or six of them at a time, eating and talking. There was no furniture, excepting the mattresses on which the guard and I slept, and blankets and cushions for the other kidnappers to sit on when they met there. I usually lay down when they were there, careful not to turn my head so that I saw them and provoked them into shouting at me. I had no desire to see them anyway. I was never sure if all the people who gathered there were guards or if some of them were guests of the group holding me, for they seemed to change daily.

'I had no reading material and still had no glasses so it would have been little use if I had. I hadn't taken my playing cards with me when I moved from Sofar, much to my regret, and I missed playing solitaire and patience a great deal. It would have been difficult to play anyway, since I used to lay out the cards on the floor beside my bed before, and, given the fact that they used my room as a meeting place now, I would have had to face them to play, which they would never have allowed. I didn't have the option of facing the other way, since my grubby foam mattress was firmly against the wall, leaving no room. Instead I tried to do my exercises, but to my surprise I was stopped the first time I tried with a shout of "What are you doing?" When I said I was exercising, they told me not to do it any more, and surprised, I complied. I didn't understand why my little workout was now forbidden, but I accepted the ban with resignation.

'The bathroom was off a hallway which ran outside my room and I would be ushered there by the guards, who would show me in and shut the door firmly behind me, waiting to escort me back to my cell when I'd finished. It even had a shower, and on the day I was released I was permitted to use it – they even heated up the water so that I could have a hot shower, which I had hardly ever been allowed during my captivity. The toilet itself was an Arabic affair – just another hole with two footprints on either side – and I longed to be able to use the traditional Western arrangement. The only washbasin was outside, in the hall.

'I had the feeling that I wasn't going to have time to get used to my new prison. It had the air of a transitory place, the kind of room one passed through but didn't remain in. I don't think the kidnappers expected me to be there as long as I was; when Sunnie and I compared notes later, it seemed as if the delay over the last ten days was as much a surprise and inconvenience to my captors as it was to those endeavouring to secure my release. Whatever the negotiations were, I had no idea, but the air of imminent change was impossible to miss.

'For the first time, there was a television set in the room with me, although it was not for my benefit but to entertain those who gathered in the room with me, guards and guests. They left it on night and day, blaring continuously. I couldn't see it, because I wasn't allowed to look in the same direction as the television was placed, but I can remember on three or four occasions hearing a physical fitness programme with a commentary in English. They seemed to enjoy it, and I lay and listened: it helped to pass the time.

'One day they brought the television to the foot of my bed, indicating that there was something on it I would enjoy watching. I had to reverse myself on the bed, so that I could see the television without being able to see them. I manoeuvred myself into the right position and I was able to see the screen. I stared at it in disbelief. It was Sunnie. I had no idea what programme she was appearing on, although I guessed it to be some kind of news broadcast. It was the first time I had ever seen her on television, and the first time I had set eyes on my wife in more than two years. When we had the chance to swap stories after my release, we decided that it was about four days before I was freed – it must have been Sunnie's broadcast when, in despair, she returned to Cyprus. Neither of us had any idea how close we were to being reunited and ending this nightmare.

'The following evening after I had seen Sunnie, I asked if I could watch the television again, but my request was refused. I am sure I was only allowed to see her interview because my release was so near, and I sensed the change in my situation. I believe Awad, the leader of the kidnappers at both Kaslik and Sofar, had been told by the PLO leader Yasser Arafat that I was to be released. The new directive to all Palestinian groups to free their hostages was ignored by Awad, but it gave me hope. I overheard my captors discussing all sorts of jobs Arafat had supposedly offered Awad to get him to leave Lebanon and free me – Palestinian Ambassador to the United States or to Israel, based in either Tel Aviv or Jerusalem, to name but two. I was puzzled by the second choice since it was impossible for a Palestinian to be an Ambassador to Israel, until I decided they must mean him to go as the leader of some sort of resistance group and were using the title "ambassador" to make it sound legitimate. Awad had decided to leave, I was sure; I heard him mention South Africa many times, and Australia once or twice. I knew if he went to one of these destinations, I would be freed, and I knew too that Awad wanted out of a situation he had come to dislike. I dared not hope too much.

'Awad visited twice during my last ten days at Shweifat, the only person from the previous places I had been held whom I saw. It was as if things had changed, despite the fact that I was still a prisoner, and he was a figure from my past. He was the most unpleasant man I had ever come across. Most of my captors were simple people, carrying out what they believed to be their duty without vindictiveness or malice; they treated me as if I were part of their livestock, and when they punished me it was as if I were a recalcitrant goat or sheep. Awad was a cruel man, and his torment was deliberate.

'There was one man at Shweifat who was much kinder than the others, and he became my protector there, almost my mentor. I asked him his name and he said, "You can call me Fareed," although I don't know if that was his real name. If I wanted a cigarette, he would light one and give it to me – around the back of my head, of course, to comply with the kidnappers' directive that I should not see them. He spoke a reasonable amount of English, and was the only person I ever had a real conversation with. On that last day, when I was released, a fellow had entered my room and told me I was to be freed. When Fareed came in later, I asked him, "Fareed, I've been told I'm leaving today – what do you know about it?" Fareed said, "I don't know anything about it," and I assumed then it was just another story I was being told. Perhaps Fareed knew but was simply trying to protect me from another disappointment if it fell through again, as it had in the past.

'The date was 24 September 1991. I had been held for eight hundred and sixty-five days, and spent three birthdays – my seventy-fifth, seventy-sixth and seventy-seventh – in captivity. I had been moved four times, and stayed in five different locations. I had missed my forty-sixth, forty-seventh and forty-eighth wedding anniversaries with my wife, and spent two Christmases and two New Year's Eves alone. And those were only the dates I knew I had missed. How many more events had passed me by as I lay incarcerated, day after day, hidden somewhere in this war-torn country?

'Twenty-four hours later, I was a free man. I was hardly able to believe that in the course of just one day everything had changed and my life had been restored to me. The journey from Beirut to Damascus passed by in a blur. Only the moment I was reunited with my wife stood out in my mind. It seemed only minutes before I'd been locked alone in my cell and yet at the same time it felt as if it was more than a thousand years ago. Now I was stepping off the steps onto the tarmac at Lyneham, gazing enthralled at the skies as a Spitfire performed a victory roll. It was the greatest victory of my life: I had survived.'

TWELVE

Rehabilitation: RAF Lyneham

Jackie and Sunnie Mann arrived at RAF Lyneham in Wiltshire at lunchtime on Wednesday 25 September, the day after Jackie was released, to a vast media circus. Their VC10 aeroplane landed just in time for the British television lunchtime news programmes, and was transmitted live around the world. The delay in their arrival caused by their aircraft developing a fault with its undercarriage gave the RAF time to organise the victory fly-past of the World War II Spitfire, creating the moment for Jackie that remained strongest in his memory in the days to follow. It was flown by Group Captain Spink from RAF Coningsby, whom Jackie made sure he personally thanked later. Hundreds of people gathered at and around Lyneham to see the Manns' arrival; they had become national heroes, and were welcomed as such.

As John McCarthy had been before him, and Terry Waite was to be after him, Jackie was escorted to the VIP suite inside the RAF base itself. It consisted of a small sitting room, with an adjoining dining room, and a bedroom and bathroom, all in a separate wing of the building, which gave an added air of privacy and security. The sitting room looked just as one would expect to find in the home of a comfortable, middle-class family; soft carpeting, several armchairs and a coffee table, a television and video perched in a corner, and a long, low bookcase upon which a telephone and video cassettes were casually placed. The dining room contained a table and chairs, and on its far side was a door leading directly into the kitchen, from where a white-jacketed RAF steward served the Manns their meals.

Across the corridor were Sunnie's and Jackie's bedrooms, and adjacent to the main living area was a third bedroom which became the couple's office: there they dealt with the thousands of letters which poured into the base, and replied to the constant stream of good wishes. In the corridor itself a six-foot-square board was erected, with Jackie's and Sunnie's appointments written down in different marker pens. It was an ad hoc arrangement, brought in when the couple decided they were unable to keep up with what they should be doing when, and demanded a simpler system which prevented double booking.

On to this board went Jackie's appointments for the day: the hairdresser was one of the first, since Jackie had not had his hair cut for a long while. A dentist removed the six stumps of his remaining teeth, which were of no use to him, and the two teeth he did still have, and made moulds to cast him a set of dentures. Jackie's eyes were tested, and glasses made to replace the ones that had been broken during one of the moves between his prison cells when he was in captivity. The wife of the British Ambassador to Beirut, Val Tatham, a dear friend of Sunnie's who had journeyed to England to be with the Manns, cut Jackie's fingernails for the first time in many months. They had become hard and very long, preventing him from being able to pick things up with his fingers. Armed with hot water and vaseline, Val soaked them for the best part of an hour before trying to cut them, and the applause was long and loud when she succeeded.

Jackie was given a thorough medical examination and the doctors found that, given his age and the ordeal he had just come through, he was extremely well. His main problem was a lack of mobility – anyone who had spent almost three years chained in one room, unable to exercise properly or even walk a great deal, would be very stiff, and Jackie's problems were exacerbated by his age. Four months after his release, he was still unable to extract a video cassette from its box with his fingers, simply because they did not have sufficient strength. The lack of exercise also explained his breathlessness and the fact that he was easily fatigued; walking from one room to another would be enough to force him to rest.

Into the pattern of medical examinations and necessary chores was woven the debriefing, carried out by a team of psychiatrists who specialised in rehabilitating victims of Post Traumatic Stress Disorder – people who have suffered an extreme traumatic event, such as surviving an air crash, being a prisoner of war or, in this case, a kidnap victim. John McCarthy had been through the same programme six weeks before and Terry Waite was to be treated the same way.

As the psychiatrists explained, Post Traumatic Stress Disorder has three main recognisable symptoms and, to be diagnosed as suffering from PTSD itself, the victim has to have all three. The first of these is a tendency to have severe, abrupt flashbacks to the traumatic event – it will suddenly come upon the victim so fast that they can actually see and smell and hear the event all around them, and it is an acutely disturbing experience. The second takes the form of avoidance: shying away from anything or anyone which reminds the victim of the trauma, including not travelling to the area associated with it or talking to people involved in any way with it. Finally, the victim will be in an extreme state of 'fight or flight' arousal; the least alarm such as a telephone ringing will set them leaping from their seats. In the event, none of the three hostages rehabilitated at RAF Lyneham had PTSD, although all of them suffered both the avoidance and alarm symptoms.

The psychiatrists prepared to talk the Western hostages through their respective experiences following a debriefing pattern which had only been used once before, on the hostage victims held by the Iraqi President Saddam Hussein as a 'human shield' during the Gulf crisis of late 1990 and early 1991. Woven into the psychiatrists' sessions were debriefing meetings with the Foreign Office, who were still anxious to learn all they could about the remaining hostages, and anything else the newly released captives could tell them about their incarceration. The appointments board outside Jackie's and Sunnie's VIP quarters was filling rapidly.

The psychiatrists were stunned by Jackie's mental health. Physically he might be frail, having difficulty walking, but his mental state was sharp and clear. He retained his sense of humour, and initially had no form of anger or bitterness directed towards his captors – an attitude which characterised all of the releases without exception. The debriefing team consisted of two men, who worked very closely on a one-to-one basis with Jackie and Sunnie – Wing Commander Gordon Turnbull and Squadron Leader David Stevens, both based at RAF Wroughton, the hospital near Lyneham. Their chief aim was to establish a rapport with Jackie and Sunnie, to enable them to talk through their experiences and adjust to the outside world.

With this in mind, the first task was to secure a private place where both Jackie and Sunnie felt safe and sure in the knowledge that they would be given all the time and space they needed to make the necessary adjustment. RAF Lyneham was perfect: the VIP suite enabled the newly released hostages and their families to adapt to normal life without the strains of dealing with the media, and the benefits of constant care. The debriefing team considered it important for Jackie to be in control, since loss of control and loss of dignity were two of the primary deprivations he had suffered. For Jackie, the RAF

206

base meant far more to him than it did to either John McCarthy or Terry Waite, in that he was an airforce man; coming into an airforce environment was particularly important to him, since a vital part of his past was made up of the days he had spent with the RAF during the war. It was to this period in his life that Jackie had looked for support to sustain him during his captivity. Hence the way of life at RAF Lyneham, celebrity though he now was, struck a chord with Jackie, and its very familiarity was in many ways a very potent antidote to the unpredictability of his situation as a prisoner. The uncertainty he had endured for nearly three years was now countered to a large extent by emerging into not just freedom, but this old, comfortable, well-known environment.

The importance of the relationship between the debriefers and Jackie and Sunnie was vital to the success of their rehabilitation, so the individuals who would work with them were carefully selected to maximise the chances of a real rapport developing between them. David Stevens had a particular interest in the psychiatry of the elderly, and it was felt he matched up well to Jackie's profile as a Battle of Britain pilot of the 'stiff upper lip' variety; David had a polite, public school manner and was a very measured, controlled individual who it was thought would appeal to Jackie, and the two men did in fact get on extremely well. To Gordon Turnbull was left the task of helping Sunnie adjust to the changes in her life, a mission about which he admitted he had some misgivings, feeling Sunnie might be resistant to the idea, as indeed she was.

The aim of the two men entrusted with Jackie's mental welfare was to avoid an emotional catharsis; they wanted to begin with actually getting facts, to get the story down correctly, then fill in the jigsaw puzzle and quietly erode any misconceptions that Jackie might have had about the part he had played in that story. An uncontrolled emotional outpouring would have been too fast, and unproductive in the long term. Turnbull and Stevens felt that the thoughts and feelings which Jackie would eventually expose would rise to the surface of their own accord when they were ready, and if they failed to appear immediately it was because they were not ready to. Many might not surface for months or even years and the debriefers decided it would be dangerous to force the issue. During their talks with Jackie, if they felt he was holding something back, they would gently prolong the debriefing session for as long as it took. Part of their philosophy was that, having established the rapport and trust that the whole work hinged on, they could not put down time limits; it could take a week, it could take four. They deliberately tried to keep the door open for Jackie and Sunnie to return to them for more help if and when they felt they needed it. Their purpose was to create such a situation of confidence and empathy that the couple could choose to return for themselves, a degree of control that was part and parcel of the whole ethos of the ex-captive gaining self-respect – he could decide if he needed to talk things through further.

The debriefing itself was very much a matter of asking two questions: what had happened to Jackie, and how he felt about it. Gradually the story came out in its own time and subsequently, almost separately, Jackie discussed his own reaction to it. He became irritable at times, but never angry, and never once lost control of his temper. The psychiatrists were pleased when Jackie was difficult; if he had been rendered totally passive by his captivity it would have been a bad sign. To be able to muster annoyance meant he was capable of both assertiveness and independence.

'I didn't like the debriefings – it began to get a bit tiresome after a while, because it was such repetition,' said Jackie later. 'They'd hark back to something I'd said before and ask me again, to make sure I'd got it correctly. I don't know anything about psychiatry itself, but as far as I could gather it was very thorough indeed. No one ever interrupted us during those debriefing sessions, which lasted two or three hours in the morning, and again a couple of hours in the afternoon. I didn't object to that initially – I didn't object to anything initially, I was so relieved to be free – but after a while it began to get monotonous. It was almost intrusive, because they were trying to find out what all my reactions were to my hostage experience. At the time, I didn't find it at all therapeutic, but in retrospect it certainly was.

'I didn't mind all the mollycoddling, because it was always done so considerately and with such good intentions, and I appreciated that things were being done for me. But perhaps I was given too much care and attention; it made it very hard for me later, when I left the safety of RAF Lyneham and later RAF Headley Court, to get used to being reliant on myself. Sunnie was too careful of me, understandably I know, but I found it frustrating – if I got up to do something she'd leap up and say, "Sit down, I'll do it for you," and having been an independent person all my life, I wanted to do things for myself if I could.

'When the doctors talked to me I paid attention. Although I couldn't remember more than bits and pieces much of the time, I was very far from disinterested: I was intent that if they were talking about me, they should be correct in what they were telling each other. I know Sunnie tends to exaggerate, but I am a stickler for facts and precise language. It comes from my flying days – you can't make mistakes and stay alive. I was taken to RAF Wroughton near the base for a thorough medical check-up, since RAF Lyneham's function was almost entirely psychiatric, apart from the dental work. We travelled there by helicopter, which intrigued me, since I had never been in a helicopter before but, after flying a Spitfire, a Puma helicopter is just another aircraft.

'Wroughton is a comprehensive hospital, where most of the psychiatrists are based anyway, and they had already treated John McCarthy. The doctors there examined me thoroughly – a brain scan, heart scan and so on – and I was amazed to see my own heart beating on the screen in front of me. After it was all over, I asked the doctor what precautions I should take for my future well-being and he said sternly, "Cut your cigarettes down to one a day!" It was a directive I ignored, and continued with my usual amount, which had in the past been up to around forty per day – I felt at seventy-seven it wasn't much use giving up one of my few remaining pleasures in life. The doctor also told me to take the half dose "baby" aspirin every day, to stop my arteries from closing, but my health in general surprised everybody. By the time I left RAF Headley Court six weeks later, I had already gained seventeen pounds and was well on the way to recovery, although slower than I had hoped.'

Not long into Jackie's debriefing, Turnbull and Stevens discovered a certain patchiness in his memory: there appeared to be a period of a month, in the latter part of his captivity at Sofar, during which Jackie had no real memories at all. It was as if he had lost the month, and had no recollection of what had happened to him during it. Concerned that the cause might be physical rather than psychological in a man of his age, they looked for any underlying biological reason to explain the discrepancy, but found no hard evidence of an event such as a major stroke which would explain it. There was some evidence on X-rays of some small spasm or mini-stroke at some stage in his past, but the signs suggested it was old, and there were no neurological indications to back it up. Instead, they put the memory loss down to the sheer boredom of his captivity. Jackie had less access to reading material than the other hostages, and none at all for much of his captivity. He was kept in total isolation, deprived of all real sensory inputs for most of the time he was held.

'When people are initially captured, they go into survival mode, and their adrenalin increases,' Wing Commander Gordon Turnbull explained. 'Basically what they are doing is trying to survive, and all the hostages described the same sort of thing; their vigilance started off very high, and they were more alert than usual, because they were trying very hard to stay alive. Once they realised it was going to be a longer business, and that not much was going to happen, that each day was going to be the same as the others, they tended to settle down. Jackie's memory was sharper for the first period of time, the initial six months or a year, than it was for the latter part, even though he did have a reasonable chronological record for the later period of time, apart from that missing month.'

In order to cope with the unutterable boredom of their days, all the hostages developed an ability to fantasise, to actually enter a trancelike state where they could leave behind the terrible reality of their cell and their situation, and transport themselves in their minds to other places, other times. Jackie spent many hours reliving his RAF days and the phenomenon startled and intrigued the psychiatrists. It was characteristic of people in their situation, an essential protective defence mechanism for those deprived of any sensory stimulation, but what amazed the debriefers was the hostages' ability to control the phenomenon rather than it controlling them. There was never a question of them crossing the boundary between sanity and madness and not being able to return. It was instead a very real safety valve they could control by will, whenever they were upset or angered, depressed or sad, or simply feeling impotent, useless and worthless for having got caught in such a situation. At times such as these, they used this ability to move away, almost into a state of self-hypnosis.

211

Turnbull and Stevens decided this was what Jackie must have done to lose the missing time; it would be patchy, but enough to mean he wouldn't remember much about that period of time.

The phenomenon fascinated but did not concern the psychiatrists. What they found more disturbing was Jackie's possible misinterpretation of events. They did not fear that he hallucinated, although hallucinations would have been considered part and parcel of the sensory deprivation Jackie was enduring; when the brain needs to have some sort of input and fails to receive it, it makes up stimuli for itself. Their main concern was that Jackie did not so much hallucinate as misinterpret things. 'An overheard remark or a fleeting glimpse of something could be enhanced or exaggerated by him, perhaps overemphasised or misunderstood,' said Wing Commander Turnbull. 'Jackie obviously believes these things happened, and indeed they may well have done, given the strange nature of his experience. But there has to be doubt over certain things because he was deprived of sensory input for such a long time.'

The debriefing team admitted they learnt a great deal from their work with the three hostages, John McCarthy, Jackie Mann and Terry Waite. Whilst they could not prove their method of rehabilitation was foolproof, it did seem to facilitate the ex-hostages' adjustment into everyday life. 'If they hadn't had our debriefing, the consequences could have been similar to what happened to Brian Keenan and some of the American hostages, who had no such treatment,' says Wing Commander Turnbull. 'That's not to say that if we had worked things through with Brian Keenan he would not be withdrawn, depressed, and seeming to have lost his purpose in life. But it worked for the other three. Indeed, when Tom Sutherland was released, he adopted the world's media as his debriefer, ringing up journalists and begging to be interviewed.'

212

Sunnie was fiercely protective of her husband, determined that he would be taken care of in a manner she thought to be best. She angrily shrugged off the attempts the debriefing team made to help her, and rejected the psychiatrists suggestions that she should be prepared for Jackie to develop some or all of the symptoms of PTSD, at any stage now or in the future. On the day after Jackie's arrival at Lyneham, just forty-eight hours after his release, Turnbull settled down with Sunnie and Brent, who at Sunnie's insistence remained at RAF Lyneham throughout much of the couple's stay there. The three of them were joined by the British Ambassador's wife to Beirut, Val Tatham, for a debriefing session designed to help all of them, but particularly Sunnie, understand the possible problems Jackie might face. Gordon carefully explained the characteristics of PTSD, and outlined examples of people who had suffered from it, whilst tea and biscuits were served by the white-jacketed RAF steward. Sunnie grew increasingly agitated, interrupting Turnbull over and over again to insist that Jackie was not disturbed or confused, he had no trouble in telling his story. Finally she erupted.

'There's nothing wrong with Jackie! If you keep telling him all this sort of thing, you'll put ideas into his head!' Sunnie shouted. 'Of course he'll start having nightmares if you keep telling him he will! He's better adjusted than all of us sitting here talking about him!'

With that she swept out of the room, slamming the door behind her, leaving Turnbull sitting stunned and rueful in the VIP suite. Thanks to Jackie and Brent's successful attempt to calm her down, Sunnie regained a measure of friendship with Wing Commander Gordon Turnbull and all enjoyed a farewell dinner together on their last evening at Lyneham. As she later explained, she felt that having endured the past three horrendous years alone, she had no need of psychiatric help now. Sunnie maintained, in the face of all

213

argument to the contrary, that the psychiatrists would do more harm than good, that she had known Jackie for longer and understood how to help him recover better than any psychiatrist possibly could. Jackie himself was amazed by the change in his wife and by her newfound independence.

'Sunnie's new life was totally different from the one we had shared before,' Jackie said. 'She had had to do things she'd never done before. We had been invited to the British Ambassador's home in Beirut before, but we didn't normally mix with the Embassy people, excepting one or two from the lower echelons who were personal friends. Sunnie has changed in that sense – she's a much bigger person now than she was. Before she was only interested in horses and dogs, and now it's much more people who fascinate her. I was always the one who liked the parties; now it's Sunnie who's giving them and mixing with all sorts of people, even the Royal Family, that we would never have dreamed of meeting before. I've moved up in her priorities too – used to be third after the riding school and her collection of dogs, but now I'm first, and made very much aware of it. It is almost overwhelming how much she cares for me now.

'I had no idea how much Sunnie had done for me whilst I was kept a prisoner. It surprised me a great deal – I didn't think her capable of doing what she's done. The person who met me at Damascus is a different one from the person I left behind in our flat in Beirut, and it made me look at her in a different way. I respect her far more. I had a renewed feeling of love for her, when I knew what she had done for me. After nearly fifty years together, any couple begins to take each other for granted and at times I had wondered if she really did love me. What she did to get me free showed me how much she cared.

'Yet at the same time, she was mollycoddling me excessively, almost bullying me. "Don't do that," she'd cry, "Do this!" I am a very individualistic person, and I like to be independent. I didn't relish being governed like a small child, which was the tendency not just of Sunnie, but of all those around me. I realised it was for my own good, as I was simply not capable of doing many of the things I wanted to, yet it meant our relationship was rewritten. It's better in many ways, but in some ways not so good, because before I was very much an individual. Now I'm being treated like a child, and sometimes I can't help but kick out at it.

'Being Number One is a novelty for me. I used to be a private person, and it was a difficult adjustment to make, to get used to being so much in the public eye. It was not without its good points, of course; one evening at RAF Lyneham, I think on the second day, Sunnie and I had had dinner with Brent and a friend of his, just the four of us. We had a message that the Prime Minister was trying to telephone us, but we had no telephone in the VIP suite which took incoming calls, to protect us from being disturbed. We could ring out but not receive calls, so we had to ring Number Ten back, and then Sunnie and I spoke to John Major. He also wrote us several letters, saying that if at any time I needed anything at all, I should let him know and he'd do something about it. He even invited the two of us to Number Ten at any time that we could manage to get there. That same evening, Prince Charles passed through the base and, not wanting to disturb our reunion, left a letter with the RAF officers, signed personally, which was given to us, wishing us all the best and expressing his delight at my safe return. I was thrilled, and said, "Why didn't he come and say hello himself?" I would have interrupted my dinner for the Prince of Wales!

'We were both getting overwhelmed by all the kindness and affection we were being shown. It wasn't just heads of state and the heir to the throne who contacted us and wished us well. We received thousands of letters and gifts which were absolutely overwhelming, and a team of people spent days opening them all for us. We replied to as many as we could, though we didn't have the time to respond in person as I would have liked to do. Many of the cards were of Spitfires, and I received dozens of photographs of the aircraft, which now adorn the walls of our home in Cyprus. I was given so much memorabilia of my flying days – lapel pins fashioned to look like Spitfires, commemorative plates, ashtrays and paperweights, letters from fellow RAF Battle of Britain pilots and even offers of parts from my downed aircraft. Sunnie was beginning to think our house in Cyprus would be turned into a Spitfire museum, and wondered where she'd put her few remaining riding trophies that had survived the Beirut shelling. A Spanish family sent us a picture worth eight thousand sterling pounds. I wasn't embarrassed by it – one can't be embarrassed by someone sending us presents – and it lifted my spirits tremendously. Daily a sack would arrive brimming with post; one day we got a slice of a little child's birthday cake, another I received a waistcoat which I started wearing immediately, as I found England cold after the Middle East. We had drawings painted by entire classes of primary school children, and handmade gifts, painstakingly put together and sent to me. Many people sent us money – one little girl gave me her birthday five pound note – and cheques to help us build our new life, or to "Have a drink on us!"

'I had no idea I'd be the centre of so much attention and no inkling I'd be such news. When we landed at Lyneham I expected a small number of Press, but not the hundreds who were there. It was wonderful to be back on an RAF base, and I had no idea I'd be rehabilitated there. As far as I knew it was just going to be a temporary base, and I would be sent somewhere else to recuperate. I had no idea the RAF would pay for all this for me.

'The people at Lyneham were so kind to me I was overwhelmed and occasionally I was rather embarrassed by the attention I was getting. When I'd arrived I wasn't even allowed to carry my bags inside – I wasn't allowed to carry anything. Every time I picked something up, someone would take it out of my hands and carry it for me. I was treated like an eggshell, and after what I'd been through it was wonderful. We had a VIP suite and a waiter to serve our meals. An RAF wife was on hand near us all day, who found us anything we asked for. Carlsberg sent us a keg of beer, and cooling apparatus and a pressure bottle and serving pump, when it was revealed that Sunnie and I liked a beer in one of the newspaper articles about us. We were also sent two small kegs of Real Ale which was frightfully strong, but not too strong for me, and much appreciated. Carlsberg didn't forget anything – they even included two cases of glasses, some of which Sunnie brought back with us to Cyprus, and very useful they are. It was all rather amusing really.

'One of my problems at Lyneham was remembering things; I could see what had happened fifty years ago clearly in my mind's eye, yet the simplest thing from yesterday vanished. Someone had given me three videos of the 1991 cricket matches against the West Indies, I believe it was, but I had terrible problems trying to manipulate the television and video. I wanted to show a friend who came to visit me one of the videos – it was of Sunnie and me on a news bulletin – and I couldn't work the machine. He got up and tick-tick-tick the video was on and working. He went through the whole process of how to turn it on and rewind and so on, which I memorised at the time, but five minutes after he'd gone I wanted to watch the cricket, and I couldn't even turn on the television. My memory was such that I didn't really absorb

217

things – I memorised them for a few moments but unless I immediately went through them again, I forgot them.

'It sometimes seemed as if the VIP suite was a mainline station. The sitting room had one door off it, and was joined to the dining room which had two – one into the corridor and one into the kitchen. All day someone was passing through – RAF people, Gordon and David, Press people once or twice, visitors, Sunnie's friends, the man with the post, a telephone man to fix the telephone so that we could receive calls – it never seemed to be quiet. I used to sit in a corner in my armchair and watch the activity. It was such a contrast to what I'd been used to. I wasn't kept in debriefing sessions and so on all the time; on one occasion, Group Captain Spink, who'd flown the Spitfire when it did its victory roll, came down to RAF Lyneham again with the aircraft for me to sit in, which was a great joy. It had been nearly fifty years since I'd climbed into the cockpit of a Spitfire, and I had a little struggle to manoeuvre myself into place, but the thrill of being there again was worth it. Memories came flooding back and I sat there quite taken aback by the moment. Then I noticed the gunsight was missing and I asked where it was, to the great entertainment of everyone watching. As a result the makers of the gunsight sent me a handsome leather wallet with a diary for 1992 to make up for it being missing.

'I was taken out to the pub several times, which was a great treat for me. I wasn't exposed to the world too soon, because we always had an RAF driver and security man in the front of the car, with Sunnie and me sitting together in the back. One of the men would always go into the pub first and tell the landlord I was coming, and ask him to prevent us from being pestered. We went to one pub, The White Horse, where they served a magnificent menu. I had a pie, and asked for a small portion, and they brought what they considered to be a small portion, but it was far too much for me. The sight of too much food would make me feel ill, because my stomach had shrunk so much during my incarceration. It was taken away and cut in half, so that in the end I was given a quarter of what one would normally be served, and that portion was exactly right for me. Before I was incarcerated I used to order a pint of beer automatically, but now I found I couldn't possibly drink a pint of beer – half a pint was my maximum. I got round the embarrassment any man feels at drinking half a pint by having it put in a pint glass!'

Sunnie coped with the Press attention magnificently, by now an old trooper at handling the media, and she manipulated the experts as if they were green teenagers fresh out of school. It was at times easy to forget she was a seventy-eight-year-old woman, who had spent three gruelling years fighting for her husband to be freed, close to destitution most of the time, with only a few close friends to help her. At times she tired of the constant supervision and watchfulness of the RAF Lyneham team, caring though it was.

'I was beginning to find the constant monitoring of my every move terribly nerve racking,' Sunnie admitted. 'I'm used to an open air life, and I like to be able to move freely. A few days after we'd arrived at Lyneham, I decided to take a walk outside and go and see the guard dogs kennelled at the station – I longed to see Missy desperately. I was just going out of the back door of the VIP suite when the guard there politely stopped me and asked where I was going. I told him, and he said he'd come with me. It was the last thing I wanted – I was anxious to be alone for a short time, just to be myself without having to watch my every move. But it was no good, and the guard insisted, and reluctantly we set off, with me a few paces ahead of him. I was starting to understand how Royalty must feel, never being free to do impulsive, spontaneous things like kicking at the dead leaves on the ground, or trying to collect chestnuts and throwing them at things just to be childish. It was the end of September and I was relishing the crispness of the early morning, keen to snatch a few moments of silliness to myself, but it was not to be. Sedately we walked on to see the guard dogs, but the morning was spoiled for me. I didn't try walking out alone again.

'The next day I decided that, by hook or by crook, I was not going to stay cooped up in this cotton wool prison any longer, and I announced my intention of going to visit one of the nearby primary schools which had made welcome back cards for Jackie and myself. The medical team were flying Jackie to RAF Wroughton by helicopter for his checkup and, as nothing on earth would induce me to fly in one of those machines, I was given leave to go to the school instead. I spent an exhausting but very happy two hours there, ending with the last class wanting to try on my now famous blue glasses, whilst I hovered anxiously wondering if I'd ever get them safely back.

'The Press were clamouring at the gates every morning for news, and I decided to talk to them myself, as they had been so good to me when I needed them. Jackie wasn't yet up to it, so I had to face them on my own. I was getting increasingly nervous and agitated – perhaps the relaxation of the strain I'd been under for so long was having its own effect – and having great difficulty sleeping. Squadron Leader David Stevens suggested I take a sleeping pill, something I never do, and initially I refused. David explained that these were apparently specially made to enable the Gulf pilots who had fought in the war to free Kuwait to get at least five hours' sleep between missions, and eventually I gave in and agreed to take them, thinking they must be safe enough. I couldn't have been more wrong. I awoke in the morning and had my usual bath, only to find I couldn't get out again. After struggling for ten minutes, I managed to drag myself over the side, and staggered into the dining room of the VIP suite. I thought I was dying.

David dosed me with numerous cups of coffee and when I was collected for the press conference by an RAF officer I had to literally hang on to his arm for support. How I got through that conference I shall never know, but I did so, and apparently most successfully. I returned to the VIP suite vowing never again to touch a sleeping pill.

'Our last evening at RAF Lyneham was tinged with sadness and regret, as well as relief that Jackie was well enough to move on to the next stage of his recuperation. We had made many friends, and sat down to dinner with them all, the RAF officers in their full Mess uniforms, and a special menu of our favourite food. It was a wonderful way to end our very much appreciated stay at Lyneham, as Jackie prepared to make his next step in re-entering the world from which he'd been isolated for so long.'

THIRTEEN

Picking Up The Pieces

On 7 October, just two weeks after Jackie had been released, he said goodbye to Lyneham, and journeyed to RAF Headley Court in Surrey, a defence services medical rehabilitation unit. RAF Headley Court consists of a graceful collection of buildings, the original house dating back several hundred years, with additions made over the centuries, including some facilities newly built. It is set in acres of beautifully manicured grounds, avenues of golden yews flanking rows of walnut trees, rhododendrons bordering carefully mown lawns, and beech trees, cedars, wellingtonias and pines decorating the estate. Great swathes of vegetable gardens provide the recuperating patients with outdoor work, and walled orchards and heated greenhouses are profitably used to provide for the table. The topiary gardens and grassy walks facilitate the exercise much needed by many of those who stay at Headley.

The aim of the unit is to return those members of the Armed Forces who have been injured or seriously ill to full fitness in the shortest possible time. It is technically a medical unit, but not conducted as a hospital; the wards are called wings, and there is a deliberate policy to make patients as independent as possible. The unit functions as an RAF station, and those admitted for rehabilitation are required to take part in station duty as soon as their disability permits. The aims set out by

RAF Headley Court are achieved by a programme of graduated and varied physical and mental activity, supervised and adjusted to each individual's circumstances by experienced medical officers. The residents take part in physiotherapy, occupational therapy, hydrotherapy, speech therapy, if it is needed, and workshops to aid dexterity. The philosophy the doctors adopted was much in line with that of the debriefers at RAF Lyneham: the full effectiveness of the rehabilitation depended on the participant's will to get well.

It was to this environment that Jackie came as a special guest of the RAF, leaving Sunnie to her own devices in London. As at RAF Lyneham, he developed a close bond with a few individuals, principally the station commander, Wing Commander Hamish Grant, and the officer in charge of administration, Squadron Leader Keith Lane, who became Jackie's closest confidant. Squadron Leader Lane was in charge of running the Officers' Mess and had access to the infrastructure of the rehabilitation unit, as well as looking after administration requirements. It made him the ideal candidate to look after Jackie, since he could do everything from providing him with a tracksuit to entertaining him at weekends and dealing with Press inquiries.

Lane's first impression of Jackie was that, despite his frailty, he was sharp and independent, and he was astounded by Jackie's memory and recall. Physically Jackie still walked slowly and with a stoop, but the purpose of Headley was to overcome that problem. Jackie was immediately immersed in the life of RAF Headley Court and, unlike at RAF Lyneham, he was encouraged to dine with the officers in the Mess, rather than eating alone in his room. The idea was to bring him into a greater degree of contact with people once again, after the limited interaction he had had at Lyneham, and Jackie welcomed the socialising. He frequently went to the bar for a drink, and was totally unperturbed by the number of people all around him as he walked from one class to another through crowded rooms. Instead, he enjoyed the anonymity of being just one more patient amongst many after the celebrity status he had been awarded at Lyneham.

A programme was devised for Jackie – hydrotherapy, physiotherapy and occupational therapy to build up his wasted muscles gradually and ease away the stiffness of his limbs with strengthening exercises. In the five weeks he spent at Headley, Jackie gained around ten pounds in weight, and his walking was more sprightly than it had been upon his arrival. His stoop lessened, and he gained muscle tone and stamina. As part of his occupational therapy, Jackie made a footstool in the woodwork classes but, tiring of such pursuits, graduated to working in the garden, always a favourite hobby, and he spent hours planting cuttings of geraniums and pottering about in the greenhouses. He learnt where his limits were, and how to push them a little but not too far.

'I was doing a good many exercises, and initially I wanted to do more,' Jackie recalls. 'But I soon found it more than enough, and at times excessive, which was partly my own fault. I started off the day at nine-thirty in the morning with my occupational therapy and physiotherapy. Then I'd have a break, and a cup of tea for half an hour, before another session of occupational therapy and finally lunch. In the afternoon I'd start back again at one-thirty, usually with hydrotherapy in the unit's indoor pool, which was definitely my favourite part of the day. I left Headley in much better shape, although at the time I was not aware of it. I was there for one purpose – to build up my physical stamina, but I didn't quite make the progress I thought I'd make. I asked if I could have an extra hydrotherapy session, since I enjoyed it so much, and they agreed – but made me start the day earlier to fit it in, so if I was tired I had asked for it!

'I was greatly moved by the extreme kindness I experienced

again at Headley Court, as I had at Lyneham. Squadron Leader Keith Lane organised everything for me, issuing press releases on what I'd been doing that day and how I was progressing, and taking me under his wing at the weekends, when the unit itself closed down. He had just returned from the Gulf, where he'd been during the war, and we used to talk about his experiences there over a drink in the evening. I found his knowledge of the air war in particular fascinating, being an ex-airforce man myself. He told me about the prisoners of war who were taken by the Iraqis, and detailed the experiences of the Tornado crews who were captured, particularly the two men who were made to speak on videotapes by the Iraqis. When Squadron Leader Lane described his time during the air raids on Riyadh in Saudi Arabia, when there were no shelters to protect them, I felt a degree of affinity with him, although my war nearly fifty years before had been very different.

'We rarely talked about my experiences in captivity, not because I felt it was difficult to talk about, but because it never seemed necessary. If I wanted to mention something, I would, but Squadron Leader Lane never pushed me to discuss it. I never felt any need to unburden myself and tell the world about it, and he never felt any desire to debrief me again, as it were. He became my friend and we joked that I was the only Flight Lieutenant in the airforce with a Squadron Leader as his aide-de-camp. If I wanted cigarettes, he would buy them for me – I paid for them, of course – and he used to joke that he smoked a good deal more in my company than he ever had before. He found me an address book, which I needed with all the new people I was meeting, and if I had a weakness for chocolates, particularly Roses, he would find them too. He even got in some Almaza beer, the Lebanese beer I used to drink in Beirut. We'd compose letters of thanks to the people who'd arranged things for me, and I would pick him up on his grammar, in a jokey way of course. I very much valued his friendship, and missed him a great deal when I left Headley Court.

'The station commander, Wing Commander Hamish Grant, was very good to me – he invited me round to his home on several weekends. We used to watch the World Cup rugby matches which were playing then, since he was a very keen rugby man, and he even taped one match I couldn't get to see so that I could watch it later. One evening we went out for a drink after the match, together with Squadron Leader Bill MacKay, to the Fox and Hounds in Walton-on-the-Hill, and I drank my usual half pint in a pint mug. When I was first released I used to make a beer last the whole evening, but I was beginning to be able to down a couple of whiskies too, although I was not a great drinker. People came up to say hello to me, which I never really got used to, but it was always very pleasant to know how much people were thinking of me.

'Early on in my stay at Headley, Squadron Leader Lane arranged for me to visit the Marks & Spencers store in Epsom and I wandered around the shop in delight at being able to buy something for myself at last. I always ran through my checklist of things to take with me whenever I went out – handkerchief, cigarettes, small change, my teeth – and on this occasion I included my chequebook, which I'd obtained whilst I was at RAF Lyneham. I selected a number of things I needed, including some shirts, a jacket, a pair of trousers, some shoes and socks and some good, clean handkerchiefs. The jacket was exactly the same colour and style as the one I was wearing, which was bought from the Northampton branch twenty years ago. It was good to know some things don't change. I added up the total as I shopped, and it came to around two hundred and fifty sterling pounds. When I reached the checkout, a telephone call came through from their head office saying that I wasn't to be allowed to pay for the clothes, they were to be given to me as a welcome back present. I was very much moved; I never expected to be given such special treatment, and I was very surprised and grateful at their kindness.

'My first foray into the real world was the weekend after I arrived at Headley, about three weeks after my release. Squadron Leader Lane telephoned the business manager at the Rugby Football Union, and we were given three tickets to attend a match between England and the USA at Twickenham. We were driven by RAF transport from RAF Headley Court and were escorted to the third-floor VIP box on our arrival. Everyone there was terribly nice, and came over to me to say hello and make me feel at home. Michael Aspel was there and I said, "Aren't you the chap who took over from that man Andrews with the book?" He laughed and said yes, and we chatted for a while. I then met two actors whom Squadron Leader Lane said were from the soap opera *Howard's Way*; Jan Harvey, who plays Jan Howard, was very kind to me, and I liked her immensely. I enjoyed myself a good deal, and I found it strange that they considered me to be the celebrity, rather than I them. During the interval, the announcer, who was in the same box as I, declared my presence in the ground, which I found terribly embarrassing. I was so unaccustomed to large crowds and loud noises after the years of my captivity. At the end of the match, a group photograph of the people present was taken, and I happened to be holding a gin and tonic in my hand when they wanted to take it. They objected to that for a moment, but I was determined not to be parted from my drink, and good-naturedly everyone let me sit down for the picture, still clutching the glass. It was always a surprise that people wanted to do anything for me or wanted to meet me, since I felt I hadn't done anything particularly noteworthy except survive.

'We watched the match from outside the VIP box, on the terraces, which I thought had a better view. The marketing director of the RFU later asked me how I had enjoyed the match, and I had to confess that I was not a rugby man as such. I enjoyed watching it better on television because you can see the playbacks, and to be honest I didn't really understand the rules, although I enjoyed the game. The driver of the RAF car was a Welshman, who was madly keen on rugby, and more than happy to have a free ticket to the match! England won the match, thirty-seven–nine, which seemed fitting, and we left to promises of a ticket to any match I chose in the future. As we left, a chap came up to me and said hello. Surprised, I turned to him and asked, "Do I know you?" It was only afterwards I realised he was just asking me how I was, even though we had never met. I never got used to perfect strangers greeting me as if I was an old friend.

'The next day I was visited by John McCarthy, who had been released six weeks before me, but whom I had never met. He stayed two hours with me and we got on very well, and have since remained in touch by telephone. It was good to have someone to talk to without having to explain what had happened, knowing all the time they couldn't really understand. With John, we had common ground, and we understood each other without having to explain.

'Squadron Leader Lane, ever keen to keep me entertained, arranged another outing for me, this time to Biggin Hill, and we travelled there again by RAF transport. I was greeted by the Wing Commander of the airfield and there was a photographer waiting there to take pictures of me. He wanted to dress me up in an old leather flying jacket, with a helmet, of the type we used to have during the War, but I refused to be tarted up. I didn't want to be dressed as a clown; the RAF rig of 1940 was all right in its day, for its purpose, but not to be put in front of a plastic model of a Spitfire for a newspaper gimmick. I despise that sort of journalism. I pointed out that the model had the wrong sort of markings anyway – it was supposed to be 92 Squadron, but it was marked with the letters "GF", which were not 92 Squadron. I prefer things to be correct and the Wing Commander said he would look into it. I looked around the airfield – I hadn't been back since the war, and it was from Biggin Hill I made the flight which resulted in my taking a bullet in my backside. It seemed strange to sign the visitors' book, fifty years later.

'One Tuesday evening, around the middle of October, there was a "dining in" night at Headley Court, complete with two Air Vice-Marshals. As a patient I was permitted to attend the dinner in my own right, and we were all to wear Mess uniform. I was entitled to wear the miniatures of the medals I had earned during my RAF days, but they had been left in Beirut. Unbeknown to me, Squadron Leader Lane rang Snathes Taylors in Wales, who sold them, and told them it would be my last chance to wear the miniatures, and asked if he could borrow them for me just for the night. Snathes sent them down by courier for the next morning, saying they were a gift and I could keep them. When they were given to me the morning of the dinner, I was terribly moved. It was the most poignant moment since I'd seen that victory roll on my arrival at RAF Lyneham, and as I walked into dinner with the medals pinned to my chest I felt inches taller.

'Three days later, I was invited to the Royal Albert Hall for the massed bands of the RAF concert, as a guest of the RAF Benevolent Fund. Once again Squadron Leader Lane had arranged it all for me, writing to one of the sponsors of the event, a cigarette manufacturer, who ensured that we were both invited to the event on 25 October. Before the band show started, we were all gathered together in a small room. There were one or two very short speeches, and then the cigarette representative said they had a small presentation to make to Jackie Mann, and he walked through the crowded room and presented me with a silver cigarette box, as everyone applauded. I was then seated in a VIP box in the auditorium, and at one stage the Master of Ceremonies introduced my name to the assembly, which was received with great applause.

'The RAF trumpeters played the last post, which had a very definite emotional effect on me. It was an important moment, and very impressive. It reminded me of my lost and fallen colleagues, and I remembered even further back, playing the last post every 11 November in church. I broke down, and held the hand of my companion, Squadron Leader Lane.

'"I'm sorry, I feel rather foolish getting so upset," I sobbed.

'"Don't be silly," he said gruffly. "It brings a lump to my throat too."

'The next day, Sunnie arrived to spend the weekend with me at Headley Court, and we spent a peaceful and relaxing time, sorting out a few administration problems and enjoying the hours together. On the Sunday, 27 October, Squadron Leader Lane took us on another excursion he had arranged, this time by telephoning British Airways and asking if we could be permitted to see Concorde at Heathrow Airport. They agreed, and we were met at the airport by the Chief Pilot of British Airways, Captain Jock Lowe, who showed us around the aircraft. I was allowed to sit in the pilot's seat whilst photographs were taken, which delighted me very much. It was a very impressive aeroplane, although I was amazed to see how long it was, yet how small it seemed inside, but I was enthralled to be able to look around her so freely. As we left, I was presented with a signed photograph of Concorde and a Spitfire flying in formation over the white cliffs of Dover. Captain Lowe told Sunnie he had had a hell of a time flying Concorde slowly enough for the Spitfire to keep up! Afterwards we were given two tickets for America to travel any time we liked to; British Airways had initially offered to fly us to New York for the day, but I had no passport, and anyway I wasn't yet up to flying. I looked forward to the moment when I could; flying had always been a part of my life, even though I was now a passenger, not a pilot. It was a wonderful day for me.'

The Wednesday after Sunnie and Jackie visited Heathrow, they were invited to appear as guests on the thrice-weekly television chat show, *Wogan*, hosted by the BBC personality Terry Wogan. Once again Squadron Leader Lane accompanied the Manns and the three of them nearly failed to make their scheduled slot at seven in the evening because they were caught in heavy traffic.

'We arrived just in time,' Sunnie remembers, 'And we were whisked straight away into makeup, new to Jackie but by now quite familiar to me. I had some doubts as to whether Jackie was strong enough to do the show, but he wanted to be a part of it, and with some misgivings I had given in. It was his first live television appearance, and I thought how different it was to mine, several years before, on a hilltop overlooking Beirut, with Brent asking me questions with his hair all tousled. Jackie was nervous, but Terry Wogan was so pleasant and charming that he was soon put at his ease. Whilst we were waiting for our turn, a member of the audience sent over two red roses for good luck, which matched the new scarlet wool suit I was wearing. Terry told me to carry them with me on the show, and I waved them frantically at the audience, hoping the kind person who had given them to me would see. I think it was the first thing Terry remarked on as he started the interview, and it certainly broke the ice. All went without a hitch – Terry was very proper and gentle the way he asked Jackie questions, and we both enjoyed it. We were giving a standing ovation at the end, and Jackie bore up surprisingly well; he was even feeling well enough to go to a celebration dinner at L'Escargot restaurant afterwards, before heading back to Headley Court with Keith.

'Whilst I waited for Jackie to regain enough strength to come back home with me to Cyprus, I found my life in London moving very quickly. It seemed the more I did, the more people wanted me to do, and I was fast becoming the most sought-after person in the country. I received a letter asking me to be the guest of honour at the Woman of the Year lunch at the Savoy hotel, all expenses paid. I thought about it quite a lot, as I knew I had no suitable clothes to wear for such an important occasion, as I hadn't been able to buy any new things for so many years, and I was far happier in my old jeans anyway. Fortunately for me, a dear friend of mine from Cyprus, the wife of a British diplomat based in Nicosia, Lotty James, was in London, and gallantly offered to help me shop. I accepted the invitation to the lunch with some misgivings, knowing the Royal guest of honour was to be the Duchess of York, and that I would certainly be seated next to her. Lotty and I shopped frantically, running the gauntlet of the pre-Christmas shoppers in central London, and eventually ran the perfect suit to ground at Selfridges. I wanted something well cut and in navy blue, as I had no idea what Her Royal Highness would be wearing, and in true feminine fashion had no desire to clash. It was perfect for me, and I felt as happy as I ever could be in a skirt, instead of my habitual trousers.

'I did several interviews before the lunch, and a press conference – I was beginning to feel an old hand at them by now – and as the time for the lunch drew near, my stomach started reacting to my nerves. I'd never met Royalty before, and despite our newfound celebrity status, I was awed. I needn't have worried. Her Royal Highness had more charm than anyone I had ever known, and soon put everyone at their ease, including me, inviting me to call her Sarah straight away. We went into the Savoy dining room chatting like old friends. I received a standing ovation for my speech and I was quite embarrassed, but Sarah held my hand and said, "I want to give you a big hug and take you on as my adopted grandmother, because you're just the most wonderful woman." The day ended on a very happy note – I was invited to the Palace to meet her children, the Princesses Beatrice and Eugenie, a visit I thoroughly enjoyed. Beatrice was a delightful child; she was playing Tinkerbell in the school play and insisted on being called by that name. Later on, when the Yorks sent Jackie and myself a Christmas card with a photograph of their two daughters, it was signed "Sarah, Andrew, Eugenie and Tinkerbell". It's now framed and has pride of place on my wall. I spent a happy morning at the Palace, and left feeling I'd made a wonderful new friend.

'I was being interviewed by the *Sunday Telegraph* shortly after this and they had requested some photographs to go with their article, to which I agreed. I then had a telephone call asking me if I would agree to Lord Snowdon taking the pictures. Would I! I'd have run twice around the Serpentine at my age for the honour – although I wished ruefully I'd had the chance to have them taken when I was twenty-five! Lord Snowdon wished to do the photographs in his private studio at his home and accordingly we arrived there, with me a bundle of nerves. This soon passed after a glass of champagne and the undeniable charm of Tony Snowdon. There was a great debate over what I should wear, and Tony eventually chose red for one of the three pictures he wished to take. It was a colour I had hardly worn until recently, but to my surprise it was a great success. For the second picture I wore my favourite blue jeans, and a fabulous blue beaded jacket that Tony had obtained for me. It was the most difficult photograph of the three for me, as Tony wanted me to throw my head back and laugh; not being a professional model I found this difficult until

I'd had another two glasses of champagne, when it suddenly became easier.

'The final picture, my personal favourite, was the *pièce de résistance* – me in the riding clothes I was so used to wearing. Tony had sent an assistant to a nearby outfitters for the clothes, which all fitted perfectly except the bowler hat, which was far too big. We padded it up with cotton wool, but even so it kept falling down on my nose. It was a hilarious scene: Tony pushing it up, me shaking my head and down it came again, but after four hours of gruelling work and numerous glasses of champagne, Tony was satisfied with the pictures and we called it a day. As I was leaving he gave me the beautiful beaded jacket as a memento – a treasure to remind me forever of the day I had my picture taken by the man I considered to be Britain's top photographer.

'During one of the many interviews I gave before Jackie was freed, I had mentioned the day we first met, dancing at the Dorchester on New Year's Eve, so long ago in 1941. Somehow that chance remark had reached the Dorchester, and to our great surprise and eternal delight, the hotel invited Jackie and myself to spend our last weekend in Britain at the Dorchester at their expense. It was a tremendous thrill, since neither of us had returned since the day we met – we expected the intervening fifty years to have wrought many changes.

'In that, we were quite right but when we arrived on the Saturday evening, 2 November, we felt a great sense of coming home, despite the many differences. The hotel had been completely redecorated, but it was still very special to us. The manager met us and we were shown into a magnificent suite, complete with a four-poster bed, but it was a long way from the lift. Having walked it once, I realised Jackie would be unable to make the journey very often, so I asked them to find one a little nearer the lift to make it easier for him, which they did. It was not quite as sumptuous, but it still felt very grand to us and had a wonderful view of Hyde Park from the windows. Everything for our comfort was there, including a welcoming bottle of champagne and some delicious but wicked chocolates. We were presented with a photocopy of an old menu printed during the War years:

Dinner . . . 5/–
Dancing . . . 2/6
(Only one main course per diner allowed)

'It was very nostalgic reading, and we remembered the happy times we had spent at this lovely hotel. Before we had dinner, we were taken to meet the head chef in the kitchens, and to sign the visitors' book. It was fascinating to see all that went on behind the scenes, in the two-storey spotless kitchen, which had an escalator connecting the floors. The head chef had a team of sixty-five cooks under him, and appeared in a wonderful white hat to sit down and talk to us. I jokingly asked if he had any lobsters, and to my amazement he produced a live one, which we ate that evening. We had some more champagne – neither of us had ever had so much champagne in our lives as we had at the Dorchester that weekend.

'We entered the dining room and were seated at a beautifully decorated table, and had the choice of a large, extensive menu – very different from fifty years before. Then the most beautiful part of the evening began, as the band started playing the old forties' songs – it was like winding the clock back. We couldn't wind it back in terms of years, either of us, but we remembered our pasts with happiness and nostalgia, tears in our eyes. As we listened, the orchestra suddenly struck up our song – "Yours till the stars lose their glory". They had been rehearsing to an old Vera Lynn recording, and we were overcome with memories, holding hands like two children. It was a very emotional and very precious moment. Amidst

235

clapping and congratulations from the other diners, we left for our suite. It was an evening neither of us will ever forget.

'Sunday was spent with a succession of visitors pouring through our suite. Anthony Gray, the man who'd been a former hostage in China, came to see us, and he and Jackie were fascinated to hear each other's experiences. Brent brought his seventeen-year-old daughter by his first marriage to meet us – Nicola was a beautiful girl, a true credit to him, as I knew she would be; she had his good looks and open, sunny nature, and we liked her immensely. There were some comic scenes as we all settled down in the deep armchairs: I said to Jackie, "Would you like some champagne, darling?" and to our great amusement both he and Brent turned round and said, "Yes, please!" I was so used to calling them both darling, and they to hearing it, it was impossible to separate them out. Monday arrived all too soon, and we left the Dorchester reluctantly. As we passed out of the front door, I gave the doorman a pound coin, much to Brent's surprise, as he'd never seen me tip anyone in the whole time he'd known me.

'"What's going on, Sunnie?" he said. "Didn't the moths hang on tightly enough to your purse to stop you opening it?"

'"Well, I thought he deserved it," I said grandly. "After all, it's not every day one is invited to stay at the Dorchester!"

'I flew to Cyprus to open the house in preparation for Jackie's arrival there, since it had been closed for nearly three weeks, whilst Jackie himself returned to Headley Court for a few days. The excursions had definitely done him good – they were a way of easing him back into the real world without overwhelming him and, as part of his rehabilitation programme, had worked well. He had never found it easy to talk to people, as I had, and was not a real conversationalist, but everyone was so kind it was made easy. I knew he would miss the companionship and familiarity of Headley Court, as

236

well as the friends he'd made there, especially Keith, but I hoped he would soon feel at home in Cyprus. He was a little apprehensive about starting another new chapter in his life, but I had no doubt he would adapt quickly, as he had before. Jackie was becoming increasingly confident, more alert and more decisive day by day, and was beginning to assert himself and say what he would or would not do, what he did and did not like. The psychiatrists were pleased that he was at last able to make decisions freely, saying it showed that he had not been broken by his captivity; as for me, I was just glad to get my old, difficult, contrary but much loved husband back.

'I spent the next three days frantically cleaning the house, and buying the extra things I thought Jackie might need. Missy gave me an ecstatic welcome – I hadn't seen her since the day Jackie was released, three weeks before. She had been staying with Brent's assistant, who always looked after her well – too well, in fact, since Missy always put on weight after she'd been there! The day before Jackie was due to arrive on 7 November, the wife of the British High Commissioner in Nicosia, Susan Dain, telephoned to say she and her husband David would drive me to the Akrotiri RAF base where Jackie's plane – the same VC10 that had flown him to freedom – would land. We left early the next morning, since the drive was nearly two hours; it was a beautiful sunny day, just the sort of day to welcome Jackie home. My heart was singing as the miles sped beneath our wheels. After almost three years of not knowing if he was alive or dead, the ecstasy of his eventual release, and the unreal, crazy whirlwind we'd been in for the last six weeks, Jackie was finally coming home.'

FOURTEEN

Home at Last: Cyprus

Jackie left RAF Headley Court the day before he returned to Cyprus, saying a reluctant goodbye to his friends and the RAF way of life which had encircled and protected him for the last six weeks. He was driven to RAF Brize Norton, outside London, where the VC10 was waiting, and spent the afternoon in the Mess prior to a late-night departure. Air Vice-Marshal Sandy Hunter, based at RAF Akrotiri in Cyprus, was travelling on the same flight with his wife. Jackie spent the evening in a room which he shared with two senior RAF officers, and snatched a few hours' sleep before the flight.

'The aircraft seemed to be full of freight,' Jackie said later. 'There were enormous drums and boxes, and only forty or fifty passengers. I was shown to my seat, across the aisle from Sandy Hunter, who came and sat next to me for an hour, while we chatted about my experiences and what Cyprus was like. The captain piloting the aircraft came back to say hello, and we exchanged a few words, and then I settled down in my seat for the rest of the journey. All I was thinking about was my new home in Cyprus. I had no idea what to expect, although I remembered the time I'd seen Sunnie on television, just before I was released. I had seen pictures of a very pleasant villa, which was now to be my home. Sunnie and Missy had been shopping and she was holding a bunch of grapes, near a stall, picking them up and looking at them. During our flight from RAF Akrotiri to RAF Lyneham, Sunnie had described our new home, and I was very much looking forward to seeing it, despite my faint apprehension at facing something new. I had always wanted to live in Cyprus, although I had never thought we could afford it, and up until now Sunnie had always rejected the idea, preferring Brittany in France. Now, at last, we were to have a home together again.

'Sunnie was waiting for me at the bottom of the steps when the VC10 landed. Air Vice-Marshal Sandy Hunter and his wife went down the steps first – they had been so kind and charming to me throughout the flight – and Sunnie was beginning to panic because she saw no sign of me. I came down in a type of cage, to save me having to negotiate the steps, and with a broad smile on my face I hugged her. She introduced me to the British High Commissioner David Dain and his wife Susan, and after saying goodbye to Sandy and Wilma Hunter, we set off on our trip back to Nicosia, where our new home was waiting. I had no idea what to expect, but whatever preconceptions I had had were surpassed when I saw the villa. The Press were waiting outside, snapping photographs and requesting interviews, and my temper finally got the better of me, and I was rather rude to them. I just wanted to get away from all the questions and publicity, and was tired of living my life under the microscope of television cameras. Sunnie opened a bottle of champagne and persuaded me to go onto the terrace and say a few words to the photographers, and reluctantly I waved and thanked them for coming. I felt a terrible hypocrite, since I wasn't at all glad they'd come, and I just wanted them to go away, but it made everybody happy, so it was worth it.

'Sunnie had organised a small party for me, to welcome me home, and Lotty James and a couple of Sunnie's other friends had spent a frantic few hours arranging everything. But after an hour, I was beginning to tire, since I still didn't have the strength I hoped I would soon regain, and we spent a quiet time together, unpacking and arranging the many presents I'd brought back from England, hanging some of the pictures we'd been given on the wall.

'I was very impressed by both the party and the villa itself – the first thing I noticed were my plaques from the squadrons I served under during the Second World War, hanging on the wall, which Sunnie had brought from Beirut for me. I was pleased she had remembered them, but it was about the only thing she had – all my tools, which I valued so much, she had left behind, since they were too heavy, preferring instead to bring back her horse trophies and pictures. The RAF Benevolent Fund had given her enough money to carpet the sitting room, and Lotty had generously made the curtains herself. It was wonderful to be surrounded by familiar pictures and objects which I remembered, and the villa was luxurious compared to the apartment we'd had in Beirut. We had a large sitting room, with an open-plan dining room and kitchen separated by a breakfast bar. Sunnie had one bedroom, with a double bed, which she kept pristine and neat; I, on the other hand, had a separate bedroom, as we always had in Beirut, with my single bed in the centre of piles of books, papers and notes, a mayhem which drove Sunnie mad.

'Sunnie and I had started rebuilding our lives first at RAF Lyneham, then at RAF Headley Court and the Dorchester, but we were out on our own now. I was in Sunnie's hands, and in some ways I missed the professional care and attention the RAF had lavished on me, even though I knew they'd spoiled me. Sunnie took on a new role for me, which I found a surprise – in the past, I'd always been master of myself in Beirut, but she was now the master here. I was not fully prepared emotionally to endure being ruled by my own wife, and found myself occasionally reacting sharply to many of her actions which I knew were undertaken on my behalf, but which I thought unnecessary. I'd be eating a meal, which admittedly I did rather slowly, and I'd hear a call from the other side of the house: "Jackie! Jackie, come here a minute," and I'd not even be able to reply, having a mouth full of food.

'I knew I was being less tolerant of people, but I thought it would cure itself in time – I certainly hoped it would, because I could hear myself reacting too sharply, even whilst I couldn't seem to stop it. It worried Sunnie when I snapped at her, I knew that, but slowly she adapted to me, as I tried to adapt to her, although it was neither quick nor easy to do – we're both too old to learn how to behave differently. We were now living our life together, whereas in Beirut we had gone our separate ways much of the time; Sunnie spent her days with her horses and dogs, and I spent mine doing the things I wanted to. My kidnapping has taken us thirty or forty years back in our relationship, and while that has been good in some respects, it has thrown us together more than we were ever accustomed to. It's impossible to be married nearly fifty years and not work out a way of living together that suits you both, whatever that is, and our way was to be together but not on top of each other; to live our own independent lives without neglecting each other.

'One day, not long after we arrived, Brent arrived at our house as we were having a hot debate about how high to make the central heating. Sunnie left in high dudgeon to go shopping, and Brent and I settled down with a couple of beers for a chat.

'"Do you still love Sunnie?" Brent asked suddenly.

'I didn't even need to think about my answer. "Yes, of course I do, or I wouldn't be here," I said. We had been together so long, and we'd stay together until the end. Despite our ups and downs, the trials we had endured and come through, the differences we now saw in ourselves and in each other, we were together. I hadn't thought too much about love before I was kidnapped, but I had plenty of time to think about our relationship during my captivity, and I knew that I loved her, and always would, whatever happened.

'Sunnie had made so many friends during the brief time she'd been in Cyprus, that almost as soon as we arrived on the island we were inundated with invitations to parties and lunches. Brent's mother, Ruth, arrived for a visit, and she and Sunnie started a friendly competition to see who could mother him the most. The Press interest revived as Christmas approached, and we did three interviews for various Sunday newspapers, one of which provided a Christmas tree as a background for us to pose against, with strict instructions not to let its rival newspapers use the same tree, but to provide their own. I gave in to this revival of media attention, since Sunnie was set on it, but I was tiring rapidly of being the centre of so much publicity. I knew Sunnie thrived on it, so I endured it for her, but I was happy when it ended. Hundreds of Christmas cards arrived for us, and the social engagements increased in number until I had to put my foot down and refuse to attend any more. I was still tired and suffering from a rather unpleasant virus which was circulating around Cyprus, and the strain of socialising was too much for me. We spent our first Christmas together for three years peacefully, just Sunnie and me and Missy, and it was very pleasant. I gave Sunnie a gold bracelet, which by coincidence was exactly the same as the one Lotty James' husband, Christopher, had given her, which amused them both very much. Sunnie presented me with an anorak, to keep out the cold, and a Dunhill cigarette lighter, which proved very useful despite doctors' orders to give up smoking.

'That New Year's Eve was fifty years to the day since Sunnie and I had first met, and the joy of our reunion was enhanced by the news that I, along with Brian Keenan, John McCarthy and Terry Waite, were to be awarded the CBE in the Queen's New Year Honours List for courage and fortitude during our captivity. I felt terribly honoured, and Sunnie was desperate to tell someone, but couldn't say a word until the official announcement. I think it was one of the hardest things she ever had to do, to keep quiet about something so exciting when she was bursting with news, particularly when we received a congratulatory telegram from the Prince and Princess of Wales on the honour. I elected to receive the award from the British High Commissioner in Cyprus, rather than travel to England to accept it from the Queen at Buckingham Palace. I shunned the publicity that would attract, and anyway I was not physically up to the journey. The anniversary of our meeting, New Year's Eve, we spent at Christopher and Lotty James', celebrating in style, but we left early enough to welcome in 1992 at our own home. It was a special moment, as we started the new year together. Neither of us knew what it would hold, but for now we were standing on the brink of it together.'

The party was over, and finally the world's journalists closed their notebooks, put the caps back on their camera lenses, turned out the arc lights and left Sunnie and Jackie alone, to start their lives over again. After the initial euphoria of being reunited had worn off, they were left looking at each other, and realising they were back together, for better or worse. Jackie's captivity had made both of them appreciate the other, but it hadn't eradicated Sunnie's disregard for detail and accuracy which so irritated Jackie, nor had it removed Jackie's stubbornness, or testy insistence on precision and punctuality which drove Sunnie to distraction. Neither of them were saints, and if living without each other had been heartbreaking and difficult, living with each other was at times testing!

Sunnie could not bear to be idle, and after the frantic

243

rush to get the villa ready and the fuss of Jackie's arrival, the day-to-day peace and quiet left her fretful and keen to be active. She even missed the constant Press attention which had so plagued her for last three years. She found it impossible to sit down, and wandered around the flat tidying, rearranging and moving, always moving. Jackie established his base on a chair by the breakfast bar, and watched her like a spider at the centre of its lair. He held his position for hours at a time, keeping up a running commentary on Sunnie's actions, and asking questions.

'Why are you running the hot water?' Jackie would say.

'I'm washing up, darling.'

'But you're wasting water! You should fill the sink, think of all the water you'll use up.'

'Darling, this isn't Beirut. There's plenty of water, and I'm only doing two teacups anyway.'

'You should still fill the sink. You shouldn't waste water. Could I have a beer from the refrigerator, please.'

'Jackie, you're nearer to it than I am, and my hands are wet. Never mind, I'll get it, you stay there.'

At seventy-eight, Sunnie was unable to provide Jackie with the constant care the RAF had lavished on him, and when she tried, Jackie, in his independence, rejected it. She ate very little herself, and Jackie missed the hot, nourishing meals he had received at RAF Lyneham and RAF Headley Court. Despite the central heating, which was his pride and joy, he insisted on having a small electric fire precariously balanced on top of the breakfast table, one bar on, partly to save money and partly because he was unable to programme the system as he wished. Torn between love and a desire to care for Jackie, and a need to live her own life, Sunnie was frustrated and distraught.

Gradually, Jackie started to do more for himself. At the end of November, three weeks after his arrival in Cyprus, he made his first independent foray into Nicosia, travelling to Woolworths to do some shopping on his own. He opened a bank account and received a chequebook in his own name. He organised the building of a cupboard on the patio at the back of their villa to put the brushes, mops and brooms in. He took over tending large pots of geraniums, which Brent had left with Sunnie to care for whilst he was moving house. When Terry Waite was released, Jackie telephoned him at RAF Lyneham to wish him well, but was rebuffed by the security blanket which had protected the newly released hostages. The message to Terry was never even relayed.

Slowly but surely Jackie picked up the threads of a normal life, and reestablished himself as master in his own household. It was not a situation Sunnie was comfortable with any longer; for the best part of three years, she had had to fend for herself, and had learnt to change washers in taps, organise her own travel, and write her own cheques – all the things Jackie now wanted to take over. Inevitably with two such strong characters the tussles between them grew a little more heated and rather more frequent, and each would consistently take Brent aside to complain about the other. Sunnie would say Jackie resented her friendships and independence; Jackie insisted Sunnie was pushing him too fast, and he wanted more time to readjust.

Sunnie was terrified of crossing Jackie and making him ill, and grew increasingly nervous and anxious, losing weight herself and unable to sleep. The problem stemmed partly from the very nature of their marriage. Both came from a generation when the husband ruled his wife completely, and it was accepted for him to have sole access to their joint funds, and to make the final decision on anything which affected their lives, from buying furniture to the country in which they lived. Sunnie had married Jackie on these terms and, although she rebelled frequently against them, had, until his kidnap, bowed to his wishes. For the last three years, however, she had learnt what it meant to be a woman of the nineties, and having thrown off the shackles, showed no desire now to replace them.

The air was never cleared because both were afraid of arguing, having spent the last three years longing for each other; their expectations of a textbook happy ending had risen so high, neither would admit the possibility of disagreement. Sunnie even contemplated contacting Wing Commander Gordon Turnbull, whose offer of future help she had firmly rejected as unnecessary. It was a situation which could not last, and finally came to a head one evening as the couple sat watching television.

'I'd like a beer please, Sunnie,' said Jackie imperiously.

Sunnie was about to get up from her chair, when she paused.

'There are plenty in the fridge, darling,' she said instead. 'Why don't you get yourself one?'

Jackie did not move, and the impasse continued. Half an hour passed, and Sunnie and Jackie sat there, resolutely concentrating on the television screen, neither of them prepared to give in.

Then quietly Jackie stood, and marched into the kitchen. He returned with a beer and sat down again, saying nothing. The deadlock had been breached, and from then on their relationship began to find its place in the same path it had worn before Jackie's capture. Sunnie discovered a riding school where disabled children were taught outside Nicosia and joyfully enrolled as a tutor; it was the one thing that gave her true independence and fulfilment, as well as an undeniable link with the past.

In the second week in January, Jackie was managing so well by himself that, despite his slight cold, Sunnie decided to spend a few days in London, and both of them relishing the prospect of seventy-two hours' independence, they parted the best of friends. When Sunnie returned, Jackie hurried to the door, as excited as a child, and threw his arms around her and kissed her in his pleasure at seeing her again.

He seemed to be throwing off the cold, despite losing a great deal of weight which he concealed from everyone about him. The next day, a Saturday, he spent in the centre of Nicosia, hunting for material to make a suit in which he was to accept his CBE. He triumphantly returned home with his purchase, and the two of them settled down to a good meal of roast chicken – cooked in their new microwave – potatoes and vegetables. Delightedly, Sunnie watched Jackie devour his heartiest meal since his release three and a half months before.

The next morning, Sunday 12 January, Sunnie got up early as usual to take Missy for a walk. Jackie was still sleeping, and she slipped quietly out into the crisp morning without waking him. On her return he was still sleeping and, slightly puzzled, since he was not a late sleeper, she prepared Missy's breakfast.

Suddenly there was a desperate cry from Jackie's room.

'I ran into his room in panic,' Sunnie said. 'His face was completely grey, and he was clutching his side in agony, crying "Pain, pain" over and over again. I thought I'd lost him. I had survived all of this, we had come through everything, and now I was about to lose him. I simply couldn't bear it. I telephoned the doctor, Cecilia Stephanou, whom Jackie had refused to see. Only a few days earlier, I had engineered Cecilia's visit to our villa with the help of Lotty, who introduced her as a friend – it was the only way to get Jackie examined, since he refused point blank to be looked after. This time I had no second thoughts about calling Cecilia – I thought Jackie was dying. She came round immediately, and took one look at him before calling an ambulance.

'I couldn't fit into the ambulance, so Cecilia and I followed in her car. I had one thought in my mind as we raced through the empty streets of Nicosia: "Don't you die on me now. Don't you dare die on me now." I was willing him to live, and terrified he would die. The ward Jackie was taken to was a nightmare. It was like something out of a television programme of the Boer

War – influenza was sweeping Cyprus, and the hospital was full. Patients on trolleys filled the entrance hall, groaning and weeping, and I stood in the centre and thought: I don't believe this. I couldn't comprehend that I was there, in this nightmarish scene, so soon after Jackie had triumphantly left the clean, sweet corridors of RAF Lyneham and RAF Headley Court. The hospital doctor passed a cursory look over Jackie, then roughly grabbed his shirt and hauled him up off the stretcher. Jackie screamed in pain, and I leaped on the doctor, shouting at him to let go. The man shrugged and said, "How else you think I make X-ray?"

'I turned to Cecilia. "He's not staying here a moment longer," I sobbed, tears pouring down my face. "You've got to call the British High Commissioner, and ask him for help. It's Jackie's only hope."

'Cecilia nodded, and put a call through to David Dain. He responded magnificently, and suddenly things began to happen. David contacted the RAF hospital at Akrotiri, where Jackie had spent his first night of freedom when the VC10 had had problems with its undercarriage. Fortunately Air Vice-Marshal Sandy Hunter was there, and he immediately promised all the help the RAF could offer. Cecilia judged Jackie too sick to travel there by road, since it was a two-hour journey, and the RAF dismissed the problem. A helicopter was requisitioned, and Jackie mustered a smile as he was stretchered into it from the UN helipad in the buffer zone between the Turkish and Greek sides of the island.

'He told me later he didn't remember much about the flight. "I was just bloody glad to still be alive at the other side," he said. I couldn't travel in the helicopter with him, and sat glued to the telephone at the villa. He was diagnosed as having pneumonia and when they put him on the scales, he had lost so much weight that he was back to where he started when he was first released. I was terrified he had something more serious, and wondered how much more I could take. I had had him back for only three months. I couldn't bear the thought that he might be permanently taken from me so soon.

'Jackie has always been a fighter, and his determination to survive didn't desert him now. A litre and a half of fluid was removed from his lungs, and I held my breath for the first crucial forty-eight hours of his illness. But Jackie gathered his strength and rallied, and for once I was delighted when I heard him two days later furiously berating the doctors. At six o'clock one evening, a physiotherapist breezed into the room and announced cheerily: "Right then, Mr Mann, time to do your exercises."

'"You said you were coming at four o'clock," Jackie retaliated testily.

'"I'm sorry, I had other patients to examine," the physiotherapist replied, somewhat nonplussed. "Anyway, I knew you weren't going anywhere!"

'"Well, you can bugger off," said Jackie stubbornly. "And don't bother to come back!"

'The doctors delighted in the return of his crusty bad temper, saying that they'd be far more worried if he was all sweetness and light. I thought that a fairly unlikely eventuality. Jackie kept asking me what had happened to some money we had trapped in a Beirut bank account, the British Bank of the Middle East, which Jackie had visited on the day he was kidnapped. To pacify him I told him the bank in Cyprus had said fifteen thousand pounds had been transferred to our account here.

'"It can't be fifteen thousand!" Jackie worried. "There was only eleven thousand to begin with, and the interest can't have made it more than thirteen or so. You'll have to ring the bank."

'I reiterated that that was what the Cyprus bank had told me, but there was nothing for it but to ring them again and check. When they confessed the money was still in Beirut, Jackie raged once more at what he considered to be my mistake. I gritted my teeth and said nothing; if it meant he was on the mend, I was prepared to put up with it. Stubborn and difficult he might be, but he was my husband, and I loved him.

'On the morning of Friday 7 February 1992, nearly a month after he was taken ill, Jackie was finally discharged from hospital, and returned to his home in Nicosia. As we crossed the threshold again I trembled at the thought of how close I had come to losing him. We walked through the home, Jackie pausing now and then to touch a familiar object as if he had feared never to see it again. The sun poured through the windows, and I moved on to the verandah and gazed unseeingly at the panorama spread out before me.

'I thought for a moment of our many years in Lebanon. I still loved the country I had come to think of as home, and nothing, not even Jackie's terrible ordeal, could change that. I spent some of the happiest years of my life there, and made many lovely friends whose companionship I cherished. So many had left or been killed during the civil wars which had raged across the land and devoured its beauty and peace. Yet even in the rubble, the burned out cars, the pock-marked buildings that had been raked by a so many rounds of gunfire yet still remained standing – in the midst of all this, there was a charm about Beirut which seemd to hold me to it in some way. I would walk on the filthy beach in the mornings with Tara, and later Missy, and behind me rose the mountains covered with snow, and sometimes, when the sun shone, I could have thought it was almost like a gate to heaven, if I had believed in such a place. Only a painter, an artist, could really capture that wonderful moment, which glimmered like a jewel and then was gone.

'I looked towards Jackie, unbowed by his ordeal. He stood

on the patio beside me in the early afternoon sunshine, gazing out towards the Cypriot mountains of Troodos, a distant look in his eyes. It was quiet, and we could hear nothing but the beating of our own hearts. There were no bombs, no shellfire, no fighter aeroplanes screaming overhead, no threat of kidnapping. I knew we had both been tempered by what we had been through, and it had changed us both in many ways, but we were together still, now and for ever. I asked for nothing more than to live out our remaining time together here on this beautiful island, our friends around us. Quietly I followed Jackie's eyes, as he gazed lost in thought at the glistening snow capping the mountains. I knew what he was thinking, and the years slid away as I reached for his hand, gently humming the words of our song beneath my breath.

> *Yours till the stars lose their glory,*
> *Yours till the birds fail to sing,*
> *Yours till the end of life's story,*
> *This pledge to you dear I bring;*
> *Yours to the end of a lifetime.*

'Jackie smiled, and turned to me.
   '"Let's have another beer," he said.'

Index